A CENTURY ON
THE CRAGS

Also by Alan Hankinson

The First Tigers: early history of rock climbing
in the Lake District

Changabang

Camera on the Crags

The Mountain Men

Man of Wars: William Howard Russell
of *The Times* 1820–1907

A CENTURY ON THE CRAGS

The story of rock climbing in the Lake District

ALAN HANKINSON

J. M. DENT & SONS LTD
London

First published in Great Britain 1988

© Alan Hankinson 1988

This book is set in 11pt Baskerville on 12pt body
by Butler & Tanner Ltd
Printed in Great Britain
by Butler & Tanner Ltd, Frome and London
for J. M. Dent & Sons Ltd
91 Clapham High Street, London SW4 7TA

British Library Cataloguing in Publication Data

Hankinson, Alan, *1926–*
A century on the crags: the history of
rock climbing in the Lake District.
1. Cumbria. Lake District. Rock climbing,
1880–1980
I. Title
796.5′223′094278

ISBN 0-460-04755-8

To A. J. P. Taylor
historian and teacher
friend and fell walker and 'Pillarite'

⟶ CONTENTS ⟵

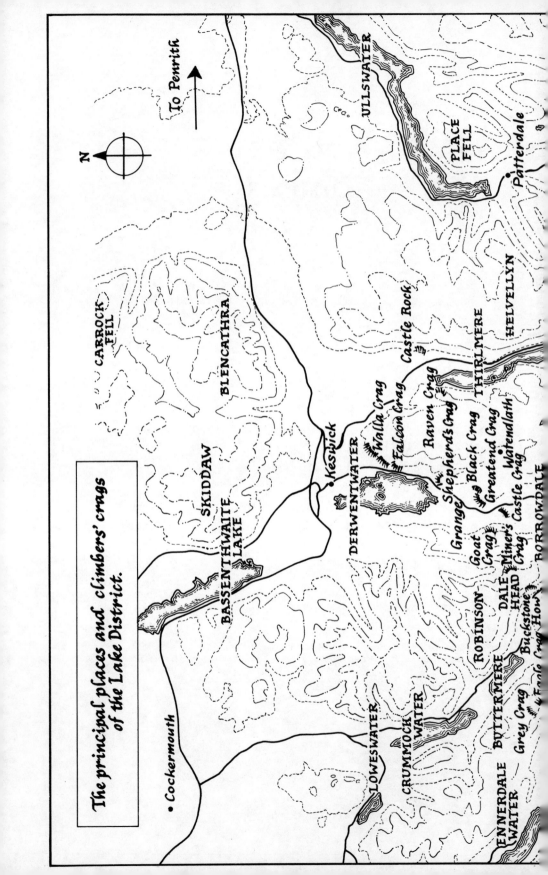

The principal places and climbers' crags of the Lake District.

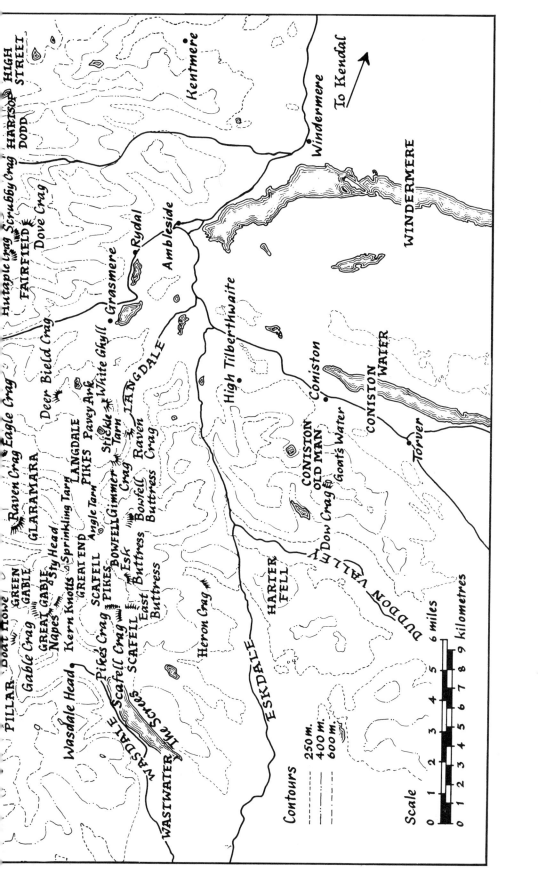

── ACKNOWLEDGEMENTS ──

MANY people have helped.

I have interviewed climbers, ancient and modern, and this book owes much to their recollections and reflections. They are: Ivan Waller; A. B. Hargreaves; Sir Jack Longland; Bobby and Muriel Files; Sid Cross and his wife 'Jammy'; Harry Griffin; Dr Darbishire and Mrs Betty Cameron, both of Coniston; Charlie Wilson of Carlisle and Jack Carswell of Silloth; Jim Birkett and his son Bill; Frank Carruthers; Allan Austin and Brian Evans; Peter Greenwood; Tony Greenbank; Chris Bonington; Tom Price of Portinscale and Sid Thompson of Maryport; Des Oliver; Jim Barber; Ian Smeaton; Ian Conway; Dave Nicol; Colin Downer; Ray McHaffie; Walt Unsworth, formerly editor of *Climber and Rambler*, and Bernard Newman, current editor of *Mountain*; Geoff Oliver; Peter Livesey: Pete Whillance and Dave Armstrong; Al Phizacklea; Rick Graham and Paul Ingham.

I am grateful to Rod Hewing of Nottingham for lending me H. V. Reade's climbing diary; and to Sid Cross and his son for letting me see the climbing diaries of H. M. Kelly. Mrs Enid Wilson of Keswick lent me her father's (George Abraham) book of press cuttings. Mrs Eleanor Winthrop Young has given much help with researches into her late husband, Geoffrey, and her late father, Cecil Slingsby. Mr Hugh Sansom, the son of George Sansom, sent me his father's photograph albums and some letters from S. W. Herford. Mr Lindsay Barker and his wife, and Dr Michael Cox of Caldbeck gave me information about Mabel Barker. Mr Jim Wilson of the Packhorse Hotel, Keswick, lent me the climbers' books from there. Mr George Bott, also of Keswick, was – as he invariably is – generous with loans from his extensive library. Mrs M. J. Parker, Librarian of the Fell and Rock Climbing Club, gave valuable information.

With the photographs, I was particularly helped by Al Phizacklea,

xi

Austin Barton, Colin Downer, Ken Wilson, Sid Cross, Chris Bonington, Brian Evans and Adrian Bailey. Two Keswick friends, Jim Scott and George Holt, gave much-needed technical assistance.

Mary Gay Pearson, again of Keswick, drew the map.

Two points of explanation are necessary. First, the directions 'left' and 'right' are used throughout as from the point of view of the climber, facing the crag. And secondly, if some of the technical descriptions seem painfully obvious to readers who are also climbers, this is because it is hoped the book will also attract non-climbing readers interested in the 'wilder shores' of human activity.

Finally, the areas of my greatest gratitude: to Trevor Jones who, although engaged on a parallel undertaking and some six months ahead of me, contrived to remain friendly and helpful; to Peter Shellard of J. M. Dent and Sons, the book's publisher and editor, who has been encouraging and patient in roughly equal proportions; to Mr and Mrs Bobby Files of the Fell and Rock Club who have given me much invaluable information and advice and who kindly read through the earlier chapters and made improving suggestions; and to Mrs Joan Wilson of Keswick who read every chapter as it was completed and offered many useful ideas and who, in the meantime, managed to put up with my (sometimes) preoccupied manner.

—→ ILLUSTRATIONS ←—

—→ INTRODUCTION •——

JUST over three miles south from Keswick, and then only two or three minutes' walk above the Borrowdale road, stands Shepherd's Crag, probably the most frequented climbers' playground in the Lake District and certainly one of the most popular in Britain.

It is an odd place to begin this history. When the sport of rock climbing was beginning, one hundred years ago, no one even knew of its existence. The first 'cragsmen', as they sometimes called themselves, practised their eccentric pastime on much bigger cliffs on the mountains around Wasdale Head. For four decades, on countless occasions, they walked or cycled up Borrowdale, heading for a day's climbing on Great Gable or Scafell, and passed within 100 yards of Shepherd's without noticing it. It is not that the crag is invisible. Much of it, it is true, is shielded from view from the road below by trees and shrubs and big boulders, but the higher reaches of the cliff can easily be seen from the road, even at the height of summer, and the whole spreading range of rock can be clearly made out from the fells on the far side of the valley.

Nevertheless, for whatever reason, it was not until 1922 that two men turned off the road at this point and scrambled up to explore. One of them, Bentley Beetham, Second Master at Barnard Castle School in County Durham, recalled the moment in an article he wrote for the *Journal* of the Fell and Rock Climbing Club in 1948:

> One wet day when walking back from Wasdale to get the train at Keswick, we happened to catch a glimpse through the foliage of a rib of rock that looked sufficiently attractive to cause us to halt to investigate it. We were mildly surprised at its quality; climbed it; and thought no more about it. The rib is what we now call Brown Slabs Arête, and the significant point about the incident is that, although this particular rib caught our eye and attracted us, we never saw the far finer expanse of rocks that lies screened by trees a little to the south.

The other man, another schoolteacher, called Claud Frankland, was

1

killed a few years later in a fall on Great Gable. But Beetham went on climbing – elsewhere. It was not until a further 24 years had passed and he had reached the age of sixty that he returned to Shepherd's, vigorously cleared away all the obstructing vegetation and débris, and set about creating climbing routes along the whole, broken face of the cliff.

When he started, in April 1946, there was only the one climb there, his own Brown Slabs Arête. Within two years there were more than twenty, all but one of them of his making. Today there are more than a hundred routes, many of them of a severity that Beetham, for all his boldness, would have thought physically impossible, or unacceptably dangerous, or both.

There are good reasons for the crag's popularity. The first is its accessibility. Modern climbers are, on the whole, lazy. They prefer to spend their time actually climbing and regard the hours spent trudging up the fell side to some remote cliff as so much wasted time. The closer their crag is to somewhere they can park the car, the better.

This is one of the ways in which attitudes to rock climbing have changed greatly. In the early and middle periods of the sport it was generally accepted that a proper day's mountaineering meant a long walk up from the valley, an afternoon's roped exploration of steep rock, a visit to the summit cairn, then the long walk down again to dinner. One of the central figures in this story, Sid Cross, takes pride in the fact that, although he climbed in the Lake District for more than fifty years, he never set boot on Shepherd's. It was, and is, a matter of principle: 'Climbing means going into the mountains, getting on to the high crags, not playing around on road-side boulders. Fancy climbing all day on Shepherd's when you could be up on Pillar or Scafell! To finish a climb on Scafell – you've got the whole world there.' Sid Cross was a good friend of Bentley Beetham's but he flatly refused, when Beetham asked him, to help with the grading of the routes on Shepherd's.

Although it is not high, the crag is complex and varied and richly vegetated. The rock has been, for the most part, 'gardened' clean of moss and slime and loose rubble. There are spacious ledges and grassy terraces where trees flourish. All the climbs at the southern end lead to a wide and welcoming Belvedere.

Shepherd's faces westwards. It dries out quickly after rain, an important consideration in the Lake District. And it commands handsome views: north across the 'shining levels' of Derwentwater to the slopes of Skiddaw and, on a clear day, the hills of Galloway in the distance; west across emerald water meadows and the darker greens of Manesty Wood to the heather and bracken fell sides of Maiden Moor and Cat Bells.

It is one of the lesser-known virtues of rock climbing that it intersperses periods of concentrated and often strenuous activity with equal periods of comparative idleness. You climb for a while; then, while your companion climbs, you rest, paying out or hauling in the rope. It affords lots of time 'to stand and stare', and for many climbers the aesthetic is an important part of their motivation. To be comfortably and safely perched on a high ledge, flushed from your recent exertions but basking now in the sunshine and quietly absorbing the view, is a vivid and delightful experience. The still-flowing adrenalin heightens the perceptions into unusual and stimulating perspective. You feel at one with a world that is bright and harmonious and whole.

The feel of the rock is another pleasure. On Shepherd's it is reassuringly rough to the touch, and variegated to the eye. The wall of Brown Slabs assumes a warm brown hue in the sunlight. Elsewhere, the rock ranges from jet black, through the greys, to a sparkling near-white. Bentley Beetham says it was because he found the crags at the southern end 'so shapely and clean-cut, so *aiguille*-like and spectacular' that he named the area Chamonix.

In a very compact space Shepherd's Crag offers a remarkably wide range of climbing, from the easiest of routes to many that are graded Exceptionally Severe. In the course of a fifteen minutes' stroll you can watch hordes of schoolchildren being introduced to the sport on climbs that are graded Difficult and Very Difficult, and, at the other extreme, young men (and sometimes women) performing almost unbelievable feats of strength and gymnastic agility and persistence on vertical or overhanging faces of rock that seem bereft of holds for hands or feet. And between the two you will see many more – of all ages, sizes, classes, sexes and styles of movement – operating in the middle reaches of the sport, on routes graded Severe or Very Severe.

It is not a place to go if you seek solitude, escape from your fellow-men and Wordsworthian communion with nature and your soul. But if you want to make a rapid survey of today's rock-climbing scene in the Lake District, there is probably no better place to start. It is a sight that, if they could see it, would fascinate the first generations of climbers, delighting some, dismaying others, astonishing them all.

For many years there were very few climbers, and most of them spent very little time on the crags. They worked, usually as professional men, in the big cities, and went to Wasdale Head for a few days at Bank Holiday times and perhaps for a week or two in the summer. They wore old tweed suits and stout country boots, heavily nailed. They carried a length of hemp rope. At the foot of the crag, they would tie the rope's end round their waists and set off. Sometimes they climbed simultaneously. But even when they moved singly and one man manipulated the rope while his companion climbed, the stationary man would not be 'belayed', anchored in some way to the cliff face so that he could not be pulled off. It was, from today's vantage-point, a suicidal proceeding. And it was only very gradually that they improved their methods. After twenty years or so, and a particularly tragic accident, they began to devise sensible belaying techniques. After the First World War many of them took to carrying a pair of cheap rubber plimsolls to wear if the rock was dry and the climbing difficult. In the 1930s some of them, very occasionally, would hammer a metal spike – a piton – into a crack and attach the rope to it, sometimes to assist the climbing, more often simply to afford the leader some protection on particularly dangerous ground. But it was not until after the end of World War Two that several elements came together – new materials and equipment, longer holidays and easier travel, the appearance of a new generation of highly talented and enthusiastic young men, the development of efficient ways of protecting the leader – to bring about the transformation of the sport.

There is no mistaking the modern climber. In his specialised and often highly colourful clothing, he is festooned, hung about like an incontinent Christmas tree, with the tools of his trade. On his feet he wears light-weight, tight-fitting rock boots, soled with high-friction rubber that gives a comforting adhesion to the rock. On some of them, more expensive, the rubber is tacky, which makes them even more comforting. They usually have a metal stiffener through the soles so that the foot can remain horizontal, without undue strain on the leg muscles, while the toe is poised on the tiniest of holds.

Some climbers wear climbing breeches, some tracksuit trousers. The fashions are generally of the casual kind and many take the opportunity to wear out old shirts and sweaters. In very fine weather a few young 'trendies' will display their expertise, and much else, in California-style body-stockings in psychedelic colours and patterns.

Around the waist everybody wears a webbing sit-harness, from which hangs a jangling armoury of gear – metal nuts of different sizes and shapes, all threaded with short wire or nylon slings, each of these clipped into the webbing harness, at the back, by a snap-link karabiner. Round his neck the climber carries a few more slings of varying lengths, each with a karabiner attached.

The karabiner requires explanation. It is a small metal ring whose purpose is to clip things together and whose special virtue is that it can be worked one-handed. One side of the ring can be pushed inwards to admit the rope, then snaps shut again on a spring when the finger pressure is removed. Karabiners, known as 'krabs', were in general use in the Alps and the Dolomites in the 1930s but were rarely seen in the Lake District until the 1950s. Today they are ubiquitous and invaluable.

One karabiner is clipped into the climbing harness, at the front, and it is through this that the climbing rope is tied, using a bowline knot – one of the few survivors from the first days. Modern climbing ropes are made of artificial fibres, developed during and after World War Two. They are stronger and lighter than the hemp ropes the pioneers used, easier to handle, more supple and also more elastic – which helps to reduce the injurious impact of a long fall. They come in various colours, and in lengths of 150 or 120 feet.

The rope that joins the climbers together is called 'the active rope'. Modern climbers on hard routes often use two, of differing colours. They also often carry, dangling from the back of the waist harness, a little pouch of chalk to keep their fingers absolutely dry – and in one pocket a piece of rag to wipe their boots clear of moisture before they set off.

They carry one other vital piece of equipment, a guide book. For forty years, when the sport was starting, men went off for a day's climbing with no more information than what they had been told by others or what they had been able to find in the hotel books. In the 1920s the Fell and Rock, the climbing club for the Lake District, began to issue specialist guide books. Updated every ten years or so, they give details of all established climbs – when they were first ascended and by whom, where they are located, the length and standard of difficulty, any particular qualities, and exactly where the route goes, pitch by pitch (a 'pitch' is a section of actual climbing, between the resting places).

Some climbers nowadays wear protective helmets but in the Lake District most do not. They are uncomfortable and slightly claustrophobic. The danger of being hit by a falling stone is remote, and rope techniques are now so efficient that there is little likelihood of a long fall.

For the first sixty years and more of the sport climbers had one fundamental rule: the leader must not fall. The results were almost certain to be serious, very possibly fatal. Indeed, the belaying methods the pioneers used, when they used any, were so ineffectual that for the first twenty years of the sport it was highly desirable that no one else on the rope should fall either.

That situation has changed completely. The second man – or anyone else protected by a 'top rope', a rope held from above – can now expect to have his fall arrested within a few feet. Even the leader, unless he is careless or very unlucky, will not fall far. The techniques are so effective that today's top climbers do not consider they are climbing properly, at or near the limits of their abilities, if they are not regularly falling off. The rope catches them and they try again. They fall off once more and try again ... and so on until they either climb the thing or retire exhausted.

The basic rules are simple. While one man climbs, his companion on the rope remains stationary on a ledge or 'stance' of some kind and manages the rope, keeping it fairly taut between them. The stationary man is belayed, firmly anchored, to the cliff face. And the leader, as he climbs, protects his progress, as far as he can, by putting in what are called 'running belays', 'runners' for short. If he comes across, as he often does, a crack in the rock face, he selects a metal nut from his armoury and slots it into the crack, making sure it lodges firmly; then he clips his climbing rope through the karabiner which is attached to the nut by a loop of wire. If he passes a spike of rock or a tree root, he will thread a sling round it and clip his rope into the attached karabiner. He does this one-handed, holding on to the rock with the other. With these securely in place, he can climb on in reasonable confidence that, if he falls off the next bit, the runners will hold and the rope, firmly held by his attentive second, will catch him.

It is one of the signs of the serious modern expert that he is prepared to spend a long time, often poised over a big drop on awkward and tenuous holds, making sure his runners are reliable. Sometimes they fix so many in that the friction drag on the rope, passing through so many karabiners, becomes a problem. This is why they use two climbing ropes, clipping one into the runners on the right-hand side, the other into those on the left, enabling both ropes to run out freely.

It is the last man's task to recover all the nuts and slings as he climbs. They are expensive – and may be needed again, higher up.

These safety techniques, perfected during the 1960s, have done more than any other single factor to revolutionise rock climbing. What was an undeniably dangerous game has become a comparatively safe one. There used to be several serious accidents each year in the Lake District. Today, although the number of climbs being made has increased enormously, there are very few. Over recent years fewer than two roped climbers have been killed, on average, each year. People still die mountaineering but nowadays it is usually in the high-altitude mountains, the Himalayas especially. When rock climbers have been killed on the British crags it is generally because they were climbing solo. More cautious climbers remember the minatory and prophetic words of *Ecclesiastes*, chapter 9, verses 9 and 10:

> Two are better than one; because they have a good reward for their labour.
> For if they fall, the one will lift up his fellow: but woe to him that is alone when he falleth; for he hath not another to help him up.

There are some people today who believe the protection techniques have, by their very effectiveness, fundamentally changed the nature of the game. They argue that the thing that distinguished the great men of the past was their boldness, the drive that made them run the rope out for 100 feet or more, up unknown and difficult rock, in the near-certain knowledge that the slightest false move would have terrible consequences. They are thinking of men like Godfrey Solly on Eagle's Nest Ridge Direct and Owen Glynne Jones on the Pinnacle Face of Scafell, both before the turn of the century; of Fred Botterill and H. M. Kelly; Colin Kirkus and Maurice Linnell on the forbidding walls of Scafell East Buttress; of Jim Birkett and Bill Peascod and many others, before and during and after the Second World War.

Most modern climbers, contemplating the making of a new route, have themselves lowered down the cliff face in complete safety to study the problems at close quarters, clear away obstructing débris, perhaps knock in a piton or two for the running belays, sometimes rehearse the sequence of moves for a particularly difficult, 'crux', section. It enables them to tackle and conquer routes that were not considered possible forty years ago. But they do it in a more calculated, less adventurous way.

Allan Austin, who created scores of quality climbs in the Langdale area in the years when the running belay method was being developed, does not read the climbing magazines now:

> I don't like them. They refer to a style of climbing which I've nothing to do with. The routes follow no natural line up the cliff. They have pre-placed runners everywhere. It's no problem if you fall off. There's no need to be crag-wise, or bold. The worry has gone out of it. Giants of the past – like Joe Brown and Don Whillans – combined enormous climbing ability with enormous guts. They were genuine hard men, mentally very tough, unflappable, and with terrific drive. The lads today have amazing ability – they're a lot more gymnastic and a lot fitter than we were – but there's no need for the guts any more.

Climbing is safer now than it used to be and also considerably slower: the business of fixing belays, and recovering them, can be time-consuming. This is one reason why rock climbing is not a spectator sport. Although it can be thrilling, for a few minutes, to watch an expert moving with fluent grace across very difficult ground, the spectacle soon palls. The action is intermittent, and there are long periods when nothing seems to be happening. It is too distant and detailed. And the vital factor is invisible, for what matters more than anything else is what is going on in the climber's mind. It is a sport that requires a sense of balance and some measure of physical fitness and strength, but what it demands, much more than these, is confidence and mental control. 'It's all in the mind' is an often-heard remark – usually from the leader, grinning down at his struggling second. As a result, great crowds do not gather at the foot of the cliffs to see climbers in action, and the television companies seem to have lost their earlier interest in 'live coverage' of climbs at holiday weekends. And as a result of that, the sport has been spared the frenetic public attention and massive injections of money that have reduced soccer and tennis, for example, to their recent depths of greed and acrimony and loutishness.

It is a participation sport, but the great majority of mankind sees no sense at all in the deliberate seeking-out of difficulty and discomfort and danger, with no prospect of material reward for all the suffering. Even keen climbers, who are – generally speaking – neither inarticulate nor noticeably reluctant to speak their minds, have trouble explaining what it is they find so compelling about it. They tend to take the line that Louis Armstrong took when he was asked what jazz was: 'If you have to ask, you'll never know.' Climbers might amend it to: 'Unless you try for yourself, you'll never know.'

Tom Patey, the Scottish climber and wit who was killed, abseiling, in 1970, wrote: '"Why do you climb?" The answer should be apparent to the veriest moron. *"Because it is the natural thing to do"*. Climbers are the only genuine primordial humanoids, heirs to a family tradition inherited from hairy arboreal ancestors.' This is the atavistic, Darwinian explanation and it has some force. Others have offered widely different explanations, ranging from the high seriousness of G. R. Speaker's 'deep craving for beauty, truth and happiness' to the self-deprecating and flippant: Colin Downer talks of his 'pursuit of tinsel glory', and Neville Drasdo is quoted as saying, 'The only reason I climb is because I can't think of anything else to do.'

The founding fathers of Lake District climbing, in the 1880s and '90s, stressed two aspects: the comradeship, the sense of *camaraderie* that springs from shared hardship and achievement; and the healthiness and freedom of it – the stretching of muscles and mind in God's fresh air, the escape from all the pressures and restrictions and preoccupations of everyday life in the city.

Other mountain areas, North Wales and the European Alps and the Yosemite Valley in California, have given rise to a lot of high-flown prose, quasi-religious or romantic or drug-induced. In the Lake District the traditional attitude has been more down-to-earth. Many of the leading Lakeland men confess that they were first attracted to the sport, as boys, by reading about the adventures of Whymper and Mummery in the Alps, O. G. Jones and George Abraham in the Lake District. Others took up climbing because, not much good at the ball games they were made to play at school, they discovered, with delight, that it was something for which they had a natural aptitude. The competitive instinct is strong. So is the 'macho' instinct, the need to assert the manly qualities, which led to the 1960s cult of 'the hard man', swilling his beer and swinging his fists and going out next morning to create a ferocious new route on the crags. Then there is the element of one-upmanship; people with ropes feel superior to mere fell walkers, infinitely superior to the hordes who never venture more than fifty yards from their cars or coaches. And, as they improved their climbing skills and ventured further afield, many found they were falling in love with the sport – the fun and the challenge of it, the smell of the air and the feel of the rock, the ever-changing light and weather, the special fitness that comes from days of climbing, the rich and varied and unique beauty of the landscape. A case in point is Jack Carswell who grew up in industrial Workington on the Cumberland coast in the 1920s, read O. G. Jones's book, and, when he became a climber himself, saw the Scafell Crag area as a kind of cathedral: 'One of the most delightful things I can think of is to be climbing on the Pinnacle Face in the late afternoon in summer, when the sun is on the rocks and it's all warm and beautiful. You needn't do any particular route. You just wander and climb about.'

Many answers are given to the question 'Why do you climb?' but there is one recurring theme; climbing makes you feel more intensely alive. Modern techniques may have diminished the actual danger, but it still feels dangerous when you are doing it and, however convincing your running belays may be, falling off still involves a moment or two of apprehension. Climbing engages and stretches the whole of you, sinews and muscles and joints, the nerve and the mind and the will. The blood and the adrenalin flow strongly. Everything seems more real and vivid as all powers are concentrated on the single problem of getting up the next bit of rock. When it is all over and the climb accomplished, the elation can take a long time to subside.

Jim Birkett, the Langdale quarryman who is as reticent in conversation as he was creative on the crags, states it very plainly: 'There's no common sense in climbing. But I loved it. You feel very good after a hard climb.' Peter Greenwood still remembers in detail the epic second ascent he made of Deer Bield Buttress with Fred Williams some forty years ago. It is a formidable route and it was a dreadful day, the rock wringing wet, the crag shrouded in mist. Almost everything that could go wrong did go wrong. 'And I've never been so elated in all my life', Greenwood says, 'as I was when we'd done that climb. Fred and I were actually dancing in the mist and rain as we went back to Langdale. We just felt so good.' Nearly two centuries ago the poet Samuel Taylor Coleridge, who was an acute self-analyst, described the effects on his spirit of moving into the high mountains: 'The farther I ascend from animated Nature, from men, and cattle, and the common birds of the woods and fields, the greater becomes in me the Intensity of the feeling of life.'

It is this that makes the sport addictive and keeps people climbing into old age. The leading figures of each generation have been comparatively young and now, as in other sports where gymnastic ability is important, they are getting younger. But rock climbing is something you can go on doing for as long as you enjoy reasonable health. As the years pass, of course, the muscles slacken, the limbs stiffen and climbers find they have to settle for less exacting routes than they could manage in their prime. But the delight does not diminish in proportion. Sidney Thompson, 'Owd Sid' as he is generally known, is in his mid-'70s but still regularly cycles from Maryport to the mountains for a day's climbing and still hopes one day to lead an ascent of the classic Central Buttress route on Scafell, which is graded Very Severe (Hard). He has climbed it more than forty times but has never led the crux section, the Great Flake.

Ivan Waller, who lives in Kendal, re-climbed his own Belle Vue Bastion in Snowdonia on the fiftieth anniversary of his first ascent. Colonel 'Rusty' Westmorland, who spent his long and active retirement in Threlkeld, climbed Pillar Rock when he was eighty – sixty-five years after he first did it. There have been, and still are, many others whose climbing lives spanned half a century or more.

There is a strong tradition of conviviality in the sport. Its first Lake District home was a licensed hotel and ever since then climbers have gathered together in the evenings, usually within reach of a drink, to exchange news and gossip, plan their next adventures or remember old ones, and to argue.

There has always been plenty to argue about. In the first days they spent hours discussing the best kind of nails for their boots and how they should be patterned, and disagreeing about whether or not new routes should be written up in the hotel book. Today, in pubs and clubs all over Britain and in the pages of the magazines, they wrangle about the role of climbing in the education process; whether competition climbing (already flourishing as a spectator sport on the continent) should be countenanced in Britain; the likely effects of commercial sponsorship on the character of the sport; and many other matters. But the greatest debate by far, the most complex and durable, is that on the ethical question: what methods are justifiable on the crags?

In the very first years, though not for long, Haskett Smith thought the rope itself – universally used by the Alpine mountaineers – was an 'illegitimate' aid on British rock. Later, when rubber-soled gym shoes came into fashion, many old-stagers complained that they made it all too easy and encouraged sloppy movement. The ethical issue grew fiercer in the 1930s when pitons began to appear in Lakeland cracks. Some denounced them as interfering with nature, changing the character of the crag. Others said the use of pitons and other 'artificial' aids enabled lesser climbers to make routes which should, by rights, be the preserve of their betters. The reply was that the new methods opened up areas that would be impossible without them.

An important distinction has to be made. These devices can be used solely to protect the climber or they can also be used to assist the climbing. If you hammer the piton in and clip your climbing rope to it and then climb past, using only the rock face for foot and hand holds, then you are using the piton purely for protection. But if you hang a sling from the piton, grab it as a hand hold, step into the sling, and then step on to the piton, you are using it as a direct aid to the climbing. Traditionally, in the Lake District, the former is regarded as permissible and the latter is not. It is an unwritten though not an unspoken rule, and it has often been broken, most notably by Paul Ross and the Keswick 'iron men' of the 1960s.

There have been many heated disputes and angry confrontations. The subject is endless and fascinating, and has given rise to subtleties and sophistries of argument that would have reflected credit on a medieval philosopher.

At one extreme there is the purist, who marches to his chosen cliff with nothing more than his boots and a rope, selects his line, tries to climb it and, if he fails, goes away and does something else. At the other extreme there is the man who carries, with all his other clanking paraphernalia, an electric drill, wired to a generator. He drills holes in the rock face, plugs them with metal bolts from which slings or short rope-ladders can be hung, and in this way, very laboriously, makes his way up a blank wall. Anything can be climbed, given sufficient stamina and patience and electricity. Reinhold Messner called it 'murdering the impossible'. The most famous, or infamous, practitioner of extreme artificial methods was the Italian Cesare Maestri, but 'bolting' as it is called is much in evidence on some British cliffs – Malham in the Yorkshire Dales, Chapel Head Scar on the southern edge of the Lake District, Hodge Close Quarry at High Tilberthwaite – and there are widespread fears that it might spread to the classic crags.

Between the two extremes there are countless complexities and gradations of conduct. Most climbers in the Lake District do not carry pitons but are happy, when they come across one in place, to use it as an anchor or a running belay. Most try to avoid grabbing hold of it or stepping on to it. But what if you feel yourself falling? Are you allowed to seize the sling that hangs from the piton? What if you are making a strenuous new route and, utterly exhausted, see a comfortable ledge only a few feet to one side? Is it cheating to traverse across and take a rest and then traverse back, refreshed, to resume the struggle? These, and countless other questions, fuel the fires of climbing controversy.

There is no prototype rock climber. They come in almost every shape and size, and many of the best of them have looked anything but athletic or heroic. But because it is an odd and unlikely way of enjoying yourself, it tends to attract odd and interesting people – individualistic, irreverent, strong-minded and outspoken, naturals and originals and characters.

When the sport began in the early 1880s Queen Victoria was on the throne and Mr Gladstone was Prime Minister. There was serious trouble in Ireland but one-quarter of the land surface of the world was coloured red on the maps, part of the British Empire, and the Royal Navy ruled the seas. Britain was the world's leading industrial and commercial nation, and the sense of national confidence must have played some part in the emergence, in these years, of the adventure sports.

The first rock climbers, who met for infrequent holidays at Wasdale Head, formed a small community of young men, predominantly English, entirely middle-class, many of them university-educated and prospering in the professions or in business. Today there are hundreds of thousands of people who spend as much of their spare time as they possibly can on the crags. They are not men only, not necessarily young, by no means exclusively middle-class. They come not just from Britain but from all parts of what is called 'the advanced world' – in the Third World the daily struggle for survival is sufficiently demanding and no one sees any sense in creating additional problems.

The Lake District is a beautiful and also a friendly place. In the story of Lakeland climbing there is nothing like the bitter conflicts which took place in the Highlands of Scotland and the Peak District when the interests of ramblers and climbers collided with those of land-owners and game-keepers. Nor has there been anything like the xenophobic hostility which sometimes greets visitors to Snowdonia. In the Lake District local men, from the mountain valleys or nearby towns, traditionally joined in the sport and often played a leading part.

The fells and the crags are free to all. Most of the climbing in Lakeland has also been 'free' in the climbers' sense, done without artificial aid. And the great majority of those who climb today on the Borrowdale volcanic rock do so for the motives that inspired their predecessors more than a century ago – for fresh air and exercise, fellowship and the sense of freedom, above all for fun.

—•1•—

Beginnings

IT WOULD be impossible to find any consensus among mountaineers as to the point at which scrambling up steep rock becomes rock climbing. The decision must be subjective. Many climbers look for the reassurance of the rope on routes where others, of greater competence or confidence or stupidity, would reject it with disdain.

But the sport of rock climbing evolved out of scrambling and the historian has to start somewhere.

There can be no doubt that routes which are today graded as rock climbs and listed in the guide books were first ascended long before the sport itself emerged – by birds' nesters or shepherds rescuing their crag-fast charges or simply by young men taking risks for fun or for bets. Their exploits were unrecorded and are now unremembered.

Even so, there is a sort of general agreement about the first recognised rock climbs made in Britain. There were two and they took place, within four years of each other, nearly two centuries ago. One was in North Wales, the other in the Lake District – which is appropriate since rivalry between the two regions, not always friendly, is a recurring theme of this story. Both were in the British tradition of discovery by inadvertence.

In 1798 two Anglican clergymen, the Rev W. Bingley and the Rev Peter Williams, climbed the East Terrace of Clogwyn du'r Arddu in Snowdonia. They were keen botanists, in pursuit not of adventure but of rare specimens. Bingley described what happened when they found themselves halfway up and on steepening ground:

> ... We rested a moment from our labour to consider what was to be done. The danger of again descending was much too great for us to think of attempting it, unless we found it absolutely impossible to proceed. On looking down, the precipice, for at least three hundred feet, seemed almost perpendicular. We were eager in our botanical pursuit, and extremely desirous to be at the top, but I believe it was the prospect downwards that determined us to brave every difficulty. It

13

happened fortunately that the steep immediately above us was the only one that presented any material danger. Mr. Williams having on a pair of strong shoes with nails in them, which would hold their footing better than mine, requested to make the first attempt, and after some difficulty he succeeded. We had along with us a small basket to contain our provisions, and hold the roots of such plants as we wished to transfer to his garden; this he carried behind him by means of a leathern belt fastened round his waist. When, therefore, he had fixed himself securely to a part of the rock, he took off his belt, and holding firmly by one end, gave the other to me: I laid hold, and, with a little aid from the stones, fairly pulled myself up by it. After this we got on pretty well, and in about an hour and a quarter from the commencement of our labour, found ourselves on the brow of this dreadful precipice, and in possession of all the plants we expected to find.

In August 1802, in the course of a nine-day walk around the fells of Lakeland, the poet and philosopher Samuel Taylor Coleridge found himself on the summit of Scafell and decided to take the short cut to the Mickledore Gap. This involves descending a series of rock steps by a route known as Broad Stand and graded 'Moderate' (the lowest category) in today's climbing guide books. The day was Wednesday, 4 August – 'this first downright summer Day', Coleridge said, 'that we have had since the beginning of May'. He was alone – 'I *must* be alone if either my Imagination or Heart are to be enriched.' He recounted his adventure, with some understandable exaggeration, in a letter to the woman he was in love with, Sara Hutchinson:

> ... the first place I came to, that was not direct Rock, I slipped down, and went on for a while with tolerable ease – but now I came (it was midway down) to a smooth perpendicular Rock about 7 feet high – this was nothing – I put my hands on the Ledge, and dropped down – in a few yards came just such another – I *dropped* that too – and yet another seemed not higher – I would not stand for a trifle so I dropped that too – but the stretching of the muscles of my hands and arms, and the jolt of the Fall on my Feet, put my whole Limbs in a *Tremble*, and I paused, and looking down, saw that I had little else to encounter but a succession of these little Precipices ... So I began to suspect that I ought not to go on, but then unfortunately tho' I could with ease drop down a smooth Rock 7 feet high, I could not *climb* it, so go on I must and on I went – the next 3 drops were not half a Foot, at least not a foot more than my own height, but every Drop increased the Palsy of my Limbs – I shook all over, Heaven knows without the least influence of Fear – and now I had only two more to drop down, to return was impossible – but of these two the first was tremendous, it was twice my own height, and the Ledge at the bottom was so exceedingly narrow, that if I dropt down upon it I must of necessity have fallen backwards and of course killed myself ...

He lay there for a while to let the trembling subside. He started to laugh at himself, then 'blessed God aloud, for the powers of Reason and the Will, which remaining no Danger can overpower us!' Then he clambered to the foot of the crag and walked down towards Eskdale. Caught by a violent storm, he crouched in 'an imperfect Shelter' and found his spirits mightily uplifted: 'O God! what thoughts were mine! O how I wished for Health and Strength that I might wander about for a

Month together, in the stormiest month of the year, among these Places, so lonely and savage and full of sounds!'

It was a remarkable feat for a man in his condition. For though he was not yet thirty years old, Coleridge was a tormented man – his marriage collapsing, his health deteriorating, already hopelessly addicted to the opium that was prescribed to allay his pains, agonisingly aware that the poetic power (which he prized above all else) had deserted him and at a time when his friend William Wordsworth was writing more powerfully and prolifically than ever.

For all his tribulations, Coleridge had the stuff of which rock climbers are made. A few weeks after the Broad Stand adventure he clawed his way, alone and in pouring rain and fiercely gusting winds, up Moss Force, a waterfall on the northern slopes of Robinson. He terrified himself but, describing it in another letter to Sara, he added: 'However, I have always found this *stretched and anxious* state of mind favourable to depth of pleasurable Impression, in the resting Places and *lownding* Coves' ('lownding' is a Cumberland dialect word meaning 'sheltering'). It is amazing how much of the spirit of rock climbing Coleridge was able to express on the basis of such limited experience. Had he stayed in Keswick and enjoyed the health and strength he longed for, the story of English rock climbing might have started much sooner than it did. But just over a year after his descent of Broad Stand he left the Lake District in search of a more benign climate, and that was the effective end of his mountaineering. Soon after, according to tradition, two local men – Thomas Tyson of Wasdale Head and John Vicars Towers of Tawhouse – went and climbed up Broad Stand.

Such meagre activity as there was in the next two decades concentrated on Pillar Rock, the impressive and craggy dome which rears up on the northern shoulder of Pillar mountain. It is the only sizeable summit in the District that cannot be gained by walking; even on its easiest routes you have to use your hands and are sometimes made aware of considerable exposure, a word which rock climbers use to denote the sense of a long drop beneath their boots.

A competition developed among the local dalesmen to be the first to stand on its top. The 1825 edition of Jonathan Otley's *Descriptive Guide to the English Lakes* described it as 'unclimbable'. Within a year of that an Ennerdale shepherd, John Atkinson, walked up the valley of the Liza and scrambled to the summit, establishing the tradition whereby predictions about the impossible in climbing are promptly confounded. On 25 July 1826 *The Cumberland Pacquet*, a weekly newspaper published in Whitehaven, informed its readers:

> On the 9th inst. Mr. John Atkinson, of Croftfoot, in Ennerdale, succeeded in attaining the summit of the rock called the Pillar Stone, and although the undertaking had been attempted by thousands before him it was always relinquished

as hopeless ... His dog, the faithful attendant of the shepherd, lay by his staff at the bottom, and, as if conscious of the danger his master was incurring by the attempt, uttered the most piteous cries during his absence. The only precaution he took for his descent was placing pieces of moss on the track by which he ascended.

A few months later three more shepherds followed Atkinson's route to the summit. There is no firm evidence as to which approach these pioneer 'Pillarites' used. It is usually assumed they climbed what is called the Old West, a rambling route that picks the easiest way gently upwards on broken ground on the west face to the lower summit, Low Man, and then – by steeper but still straightforward scrambling to High Man, the true summit. It is not listed in the climbers' guide books.

This brief flurry of activity was not immediately followed up. It was not until twenty-two years later that the next recorded ascent took place. Lieutenant Wilson of the Royal Navy climbed the Old West in 1848 and left an empty ginger beer bottle at the top, containing a piece of paper on which he wrote his name. Two years after that an experienced mountain explorer, C. A. O. Baumgartner, found a new and longer route – the Old Wall Route – and added his name to the list.

In the years that followed, the ascent of Pillar Rock became a popular expedition for adventurous young men, some of them locals, some of them brought by the new railways for holidays in the fells. A corn dealer from Penrith, George Seatree, who started his long climbing career on Pillar Rock in the 1870s, worked out the statistics:

1826–50	6 ascents
1850–66	22 ascents
1866–73	31 ascents
1874	10 ascents
1875	50 ascents

These early climbers had nothing in the way of clothing or equipment to distinguish them from fell walkers. They wore rough old tweed suits, thick socks and stout country boots, usually hob-nailed. Their information came not from detailed guide books but from what they could gather from predecessors or accounts in the newspapers. Some of them carried fell-poles, eight feet long, which must have been much more of a hindrance than a help on steep rock. None of them used a rope.

In 1861 the keeper of the lighthouse at St Bees and four of his friends made the first recorded ascent of the east face of Pillar Rock, by the route called Slab and Notch which is now used as the easy way down. It is shorter than the Old West and not quite as easy, and the first part, crossing the slab, is above a big drop. Two years later a party of Cambridge men led by J. W. E. Conybeare made what they called a 'new route' in the same area, though it was probably nothing more than a minor variation of the Slab and Notch. In 1869 a fourteen-year-old boy, Lawrence Pilkington, went up with his elder brother Charles. They came from the Lancashire family which owned several collieries and was to establish the famous glass works at St Helens. A decade or so later the brothers were to make great names for themselves in Alpine moun-taineering by dispensing with the services of local guides.

The first woman to the summit was Miss A. Barker of Gosforth in 1869. Nothing else is known of her but she must have done it wearing the heavy tweed, ankle-length skirts required by the manners of the time. The awkwardness of her clothing, which meant that she would not have been able to see exactly where she was placing her feet, made it much harder for her than it was for her escorting men-folk.

In the summer of 1873 another woman stood on the top of Pillar Rock, Miss May Westmorland of Penrith. She was accompanied by her brothers, Thomas and Edward, who six years later built the landmark cairn near the summit of Great Gable to mark what in their opinion was the finest viewpoint in Lakeland. They had had several days of vigorous fell walking in mid-July 1873, mostly in atrocious weather, and now felt strong enough to tackle Pillar Rock. When they reached the foot of the crag, it began to rain again and the clouds swirled round them. Thomas described the moment in doggerel verses later published in *The Whitehaven News*:

> Quoth Tom, "To be or not to be?
> The top of this bold rock for me".
> Quoth Ned, in calm response, "Agreed",
> And May, "I'll follow if you lead".
> With ready hands and cautious feet,
> Not rashly bold or indiscreet,
> We clung and climbed in single file,
> Right hopefully...
>
> Tradition said from time of yore
> This Pillar on its summit bore
> A bottle, which the names contained
> Of those who had its summit gained.
> Tradition had not spoken guile
> There, bottom upward in the pile,
> The fabled bottle met our view.
> With eager haste the cork we drew.
> Nine gentlemen of hardy frames
> In it had placed nine honoured names.
> A lady's name now graced the list;
> We added ours; then in the mist
> We stood erect, with May between,
> And proudly peal'd 'God Save the Queen'.

The verses, published in the summer of 1874, had a significant sequel.

They were read by an elderly Church of England clergyman, the Rev James Jackson, at his home at Sandwith on the west Cumberland coast. He had been retired for nearly twenty years and had spent the time tirelessly tramping the fells, fell-pole in hand, until – as he put it – 'I can almost say "I kna ivvry crag." ' More than once he had looked longingly at Pillar Rock but had not summoned the courage to attempt it. He could not believe it had been climbed by a woman. He wrote to the editor of *The Whitehaven News*: 'Sir, – In a recent number of your paper I read, with incredulous amazement, the rhythmical account of an alleged ascent of the Pillar by two gentlemen and a lady...' He suggested that what the Westmorlands had climbed was Pillar mountain, not the Rock.

The brothers responded promptly and forcefully. They resented the 'accusation of falsehood'. They could distinguish the mountain from the Rock and it was the latter they had climbed. May, in 'an Alpine dress', had made the ascent with 'a brother above and a brother below'. They gave the names they had found in the bottle and ended by saying that if the Rev James Jackson could not climb the Rock 'let him send his card and we will put it in for him'.

Jackson now withdrew the charge and added: 'Though I am now in my 79th year "There is life in the old dog yet" ... I have not yet abandoned the hope that on some future day, with some instruction from your two correspondents who have lately performed the feat, I may be able to put my name in the bottle.'

He was, as he claimed, a very vigorous old man. During his years as vicar of Rivington near Bolton, Lancashire, he had scaled the church steeple to replace the weathercock and commemorated the exploit with a quatrain:

> Who has not heard of Steeple Jack,
>   That lion-hearted Saxon?
> Tho' I'm not he, he was my sire,
>   For I am Steeple Jackson!

Retired to his native Cumberland, he became a prodigious fell walker – he once covered sixty miles in under twenty hours – and a scrambler about rough ground. Now he sought the advice of George Seatree, already the leading Pillar Rock expert, and planned his attempt. He wrote to Seatree: 'If under your guidance I should succeed in reaching the top of the Rock you will have an opportunity of crowning me with parsley fern or heather as "The Pedestrian Patriarch of the Pillarites" for in April 1875 I shall have entered my 80th year.'

Jackson took no unnecessary chances. His ascent of Pillar Rock on 31 May is notable, as part of a history of Lakeland climbing, partly because of his age and also because it involved the first systematic use of artificial aids. Much of the sport's more recent history and many of its fiercest arguments have centred upon the ethical question of how much, if any, extraneous assistance the climber is justified in using on any given route. Jackson was not in any way trouble by considerations of that sort.

He took a much younger man, John Hodgson, as his companion. On Seatree's recommendation they followed the Slab and Notch route and Hodgson led the way across the slab and hammered four 'spike nails' into a crack, hanging lengths of rope from each of them. With the help of these the old man followed:

> Nothing was now wanted but a good head and a good heart, and I and my *avant courier* were possessed of both. After proceeding a few yards on a narrow heather-covered ledge, Hodgson disappeared from my sight, and I awaited, in hopeful mood, the result. At last a cry significant of success struck my ear (though, by the way, my lugs are not so good as my legs), and without hesitation or fear I began to climb, and successfully joined my leader on the summit of the Pillar Rock. At that moment we were 'quite uplifted', and the Queen had no two prouder or more joyous subjects in her Realm.

The passage comes from the long account he sent to *The Whitehaven News*. There was to be no room for doubt that he had done it. He had prepared a card for the summit bottle inscribed with the words: 'The Patriarch of the Pillarites, born A.D. 1796. Ascended the Pillar Rock A.D. 1875.' He also left there 'some titbits of travel from Rome, Vesuvius, Loretto and Niagara' in another bottle, together with some Latin hexameters and a reminder that he had been the first student at St Bees theological college. Finally, as 'crowning proof of the Patriarch's verdancy', he produced yet another bottle and inscribed a card in Greek, which he translated for readers of the newspaper: 'Jacobus Stylitus, with John Hodgson, ascended the Pillar Rock on the last day of the 5th month, A.D. 1875. Written on the summit without spectacles.'

A quatrain was quickly produced:

> If this in your mind you will fix,
>   When I make the Pillar my toy.
> I was born in 1, 7, 9, 6,
>   And you'll think me a nimble old boy.

He got enormous fun from his 'mountain pranks'. He extended his fatherly blessing to subsequent conquerors of the Rock. Hearing of a sixty-year-old who had done it, he immediately conferred on him the title 'Patriarch Presumptive of the Pillarites'. He proposed climbing the Old West route, at the conclusion of which he would be greeted on the summit by May Westmorland and her brothers: 'Here on the dizzy height would be a realistic union between May and December.' He described himself variously as 'Senex Juveniles', 'that wonderful Old Boy' and 'An aged errant Knight'. He saw himself, with pre-Freudian unselfconsciousness, as a latter-day Don Quixote, part-hero, part-buffoon. He determined to climb the Rock again, this time alone.

Two weeks after his eightieth birthday he set off from the hotel at Wasdale Head at 4.20 am – he was a great believer in 'the Alpine start' – and four hours later he was on the summit once more. Once again he took the Slab and Notch route and this time, with no companion, he used even more elaborate aids:

> I was soon at the rock with the transverse nick which has to be traversed; then I scrambled to the sloping rock, which is about six yards in extent, and may be called the *pons asinorum* of the climb. Into this rock I drove a spike, on which, by the means of my staff, I raised the loop of a rope ladder with four rungs, hanging it on the spike; as an additional security, a hand-rope was also attached to the same point; and with these appliances I gained, without slip or injury, the narrow heath-covered ledge ...

For reasons unknown he did not attempt the Rock the year after. But on 1 May 1878, at the age of eighty-two, he set off once again from the hotel, alone but equipped as before. Two young men who saw him leave thought he gave the impression of much physical weakness. If the flesh was frailer, however, his spirits were undiminished. He carried in his pocket yet another verse of self-praise:

> Two elephantine properties were mine
> For I can bend to pick up pin or plack;
> And when this year the Pillar Rock I climb
> Four score and two's the howdah on my back.

By nightfall he had not returned to the hotel. Next morning the landlord, Will Ritson, organised search parties. After two days of searching, the body was found near the foot of the Great Doup, steep and broken ground only a few hundred yards from Pillar Rock. It must be assumed that the 'Patriarch' was still on his way there when he slipped and fell to his death.

On 9 May *The Whitehaven News*, which had published so many of his effusions in recent years, told the story of the inquest under the headline, 'Frightful Death on the Fells'. The same issue carried editorial comment:

> We have this week to record a very sad death, under circumstances of a most exceptional character ... To most people this inextinguishable desire to excel in feats of physical prowess, which fourscore years could not tame, is inexplicable ... why a gentleman of Mr. Jackson's years should not only be smitten with a desire to climb this beetling crag, but to repeat the feat with each returning year is, as we have said, simply incomprehensible. It has no explanation. It can only be set down to one of those eccentricities of disposition wherein, if we may give heed to our Continental neighbours, Englishmen differ radically from the rest of the human race. This yearly feat of crag climbing ... savoured of mere bravado, and was utterly unproductive of aught save danger.

In fact, Jackson's obsession with Pillar Rock had enlivened his last years and given him many days of excitement, exercise and fun. For climbers the danger is not just an unfortunate occasional side-effect of their sport but the vital ingredient. As Mick Burke, who disappeared on the summit of Everest in 1975, was fond of saying: 'If you knew that when you fell off you could sprout wings and fly safely away like a bird, there'd be no point in doing it.' Climbers have had to learn to accept, usually with pained resignation, the ill-informed and uncomprehending strictures that are heaped upon them by coroners and leader-writers and many members of the general public in the wake of every serious accident. In the decade before Jackson's death, when four men were killed descending from the first ascent of the Matterhorn, *The Times* itself had thundered: 'Why is the best blood of England to waste itself in scaling hitherto inaccessible peaks, in staining the eternal snow, and reaching the unfathomable abyss never to return? ... Is it life? Is it duty? Is it common sense?' Even Queen Victoria wondered if ways could be found to prohibit mountaineering.

They could not. During the 1850s and '60s, in what came to be known as 'the golden age of Alpine mountaineering', all the major summits of the European Alps were climbed. The Alpine Club was formed to bring together the growing band of British professional men who liked to spend long summer holidays exploring the high regions of rock, snow and ice. At first they hired local guides to do the route-finding, carry their provisions and cut steps for them. Later the more adventurous spirits took to guideless climbing, looking for harder routes, roped together and carrying long-shafted ice axes.

Most of the Alpine men regarded the British hills as, almost literally, beneath their dignity. For them, mountaineering meant long days of exploration at altitude on glaciers and snow slopes and ridges, and anything other than that was not mountaineering. But a few were broader minded. Professor John Tyndall was on Helvellyn one stormy day in 1859 and wrote in *The Saturday Review*: 'It was surely an antithesis to the heavy air of a London laboratory ... It was a day of wondrous atmospheric effects – indeed we had scarcely seen anything grander among the Alps themselves.' Charles Packe climbed Scafell Pike in 1850 and was a regular visitor to the Lake District over the next four decades. Leslie Stephen failed to find the way up Pillar Rock in 1863 and, although he was successful two years later, must have been unlucky with the weather as he said he found the Lake District 'ennervating'.

A few of the Alpinists formed the habit of going to Wasdale Head or North Wales each winter to practise their snow and ice techniques. The influential Harrow schoolmaster, John Stogden, was a regular guest at the hotel at Wasdale. An entry in the old Visitors' Book there reads:

Jan. 10 1870 Geo. H. Wollaston, H. M. Geological Survey Elterwater, A. R. Stogden St. Cath. Coll. Cambridge, J. Stogden B. A. Harrow came up Bow Fell by Grunting Gill and turned to the right to Flat Crags, up a gully 400 feet high filled with hard snow, which required a good many steps cutting. The angle of the snow rose from 35 near the bottom to nearly 70 at the top where a cornice had to be cut away. We then passed under the N. end of Bow Fell on to Esk Hause and soon to Great End. The slopes on this side of Great End down to Lingmell Gill where we had hoped for good glissades we found to be hard ice, and required a good deal of step cutting.

John Stogden was a pioneer of guideless climbing in the Alps and one of the first to draw the attention of his fellow-Alpinists to the opportunities offered by hills nearer home. A Manchester merchant, Eustace Hulton, then took to organising spring meets for Alpine Club members, sometimes in the Lake District, sometimes in North Wales. A Birmingham solicitor, C. E. Mathews, one of the founder members of the Alpine Club, had been a regular winter visitor to Snowdonia since 1854 and some time around 1870 formed what he called the 'Society of Welsh Rabbits' to explore the area when it was under snow. In early 1880 a party of some twenty Alpine Club men with a few women mountaineers gathered in Borrowdale. An account in the *Alpine Journal* said:

> On Sunday the party ... leaving the carriages at the farmhouse above Seatoller, climbed Scafell Pike by a very interesting chimney or 'couloir', which, being filled with snow and ice, gave unexpected satisfaction. There is a very remarkable natural arch in this couloir, which Mr. Cust claims to have been the first to discover, and he was therefore entrusted with the guidance of the party.

This was Arthur Cust and the gully, on Great End, still bears his name.

Most of the Lakeland rock scrambling in the 1860s and '70s was concentrated on Pillar Rock, but not exclusively so. Broad Stand on Scafell, the route descended by Coleridge, was ascended by C. A. O. Baumgartner in September 1850 and nine years later by Professor Tyndall who dismissed it as 'a pleasant bit of mountain practice and nothing more'. In 1869 two more routes in the same region were created, the North or Penrith Climb by Major Ponsonby Cundill and Mickledore Chimney by C. W. Dymond. In August the same year Mr T. L. Murray Browne of Lincoln's Inn, London, was staying at the Wastwater Hotel and wrote in the Visitors' Book:

> ... did Scafell Pike by Piers Gill and Scafell by the direct route from Mickledore also Pillar mountain and rock. The attention of mountaineers is called to a rock on Scafell on the right (looking down) of a remarkable gill which cleaves the rocks of Scafell and descends into Lingmell/Gill. It looks stiff. Piers Gill should certainly be visited.

The cleft was Deep Ghyll, the rock Scafell Pinnacle.

A later entry in the Visitors' Book read:

> Sept. 22 1872. W. M. Pendlebury, R. Pendlebury, J. Hosking, Frederick Gardiner, H. J. Priest ascended Pillar Stone today – yesterday crossed Mickledore Gap and ascended Broad Stand on Scafell.

The Pendlebury brothers, William and Richard, and Frederick Gardiner were Liverpool men of considerable means and great physical vigour. The climb they did on Pillar Rock that day was a new route, a variation on Slab and Notch, which was called the Pendlebury Traverse. It is now graded merely 'Moderate' but for a while was regarded as the hardest route on the Rock. It won the Pendleburys great and unwelcome esteem especially when the legend was put about that the climb was led 'by the famous Senior Wrangler after walking from Keswick in his smoking-room slippers'. The Senior Wrangler, the leading Cambridge mathematician of his year, was Richard, the younger of the brothers who became a Cambridge don. The elder brother, William, who was a businessman, later dismissed the smoking-room slipper story as 'bosh' and added that anyway the route had been led by Gardiner. The Pendleburys made a number of impressive Alpine routes in the later 1870s. In 1879 Gardiner accompanied the Pilkington brothers on the first guideless ascent of the Meije in the Daupiné Alps. The year after that the Pilkingtons made the first ascent of the Inaccessible Pinnacle on the Cuillin Ridge in Skye. It is a remarkable fact that three groups of brothers from industrial Lancashire – the Pendleburys of Liverpool, the Pilkingtons of Alderley Edge and, soon to make their appearance, the five Hopkinsons from Manchester – should have made such a formative impact during this period in Britain and in the Alps.

One quality they had in common was a dislike of publicity. They were serious, prosperous, middle-class English gentlemen. To them, any attempts to publicise achievements on the mountains smacked of bragging and was inimical to the best spirit of the sport. To give even the briefest account of a new route, even if it was only for the small circle who would read the hotel Visitors' Book, was to deny to others the chance of the true exploring experience. Let the crags retain their mysteries. Let each newcomer go out and discover the good things for himself. That was the attitude and it stands in diametric contrast to modern climbers who publish the news of their new routes as soon as possible.

The Pilkingtons never wrote anything in the Visitors' Book except the date, their names and the one word 'Lancashire'. Edward Hopkinson, according to his daughter's account in *Manchester Made Them*, did not even mention having taken part in the first descent of the north-east ridge of the Nesthorn in his own diary: '... he was not in the least interested in mountaineering records ... He climbed because he enjoyed climbing and because mountain scenery appealed to him. And he climbed difficult climbs because his spirit rose to danger.' Another of the Hopkinson brothers, Sir Alfred, who became an MP and Vice-Chancellor of Manchester University, wrote in the Fell and Rock Climbing Club *Journal* of 1925:

To the best of my belief I have never written a word, not even in the old Visitors' Book at Wasdale, on any climb in the Lake District. I do not know or care whether any of them is classed as easy or severe. I expect they have now all become easy, but I do not know their names. The labels – Cust's Gully, Westmorland's Climb, Botterill's Slab, to take a few examples – convey nothing to my mind. These proprietory brands, though useful, no doubt, for purposes of identification, are sometimes a little trying to those who like to find out things for themselves.

Ironically, the crags of the Lake District bear more 'labels' to the Hopkinsons than to any other family, with Hopkinson's Cairn and Hopkinson's Gully on Scafell and Hopkinson's Crack on Dow Crag. Sir Alfred cannot have been best pleased about that. Fortunately, his extreme attitude was not shared by all the brothers for the *Climbing Book* at the Wastwater Hotel included a full account of the day, 2 April 1893, when all five of them explored the face of Scafell Pinnacle and one of them, John, climbed down it from top to bottom.

Had Sir Alfred's view prevailed, the history of rock climbing would be largely unknown and the development of the sport would have followed very different lines. Climbing is like other fields of human endeavour. Each new generation operates from the point reached by its predecessors. The best recruits to the sport work their way up through the grades, studying the guide books closely and picking out the most attractive and challenging routes already climbed before they go on to open up new routes of their own at an ever-rising standard of difficulty. Most climbers are interested in the history of their sport and remember the pioneers of the past with gratitude, for the climbs they made and also for the fact that they recorded them.

The chief primary sources for the earliest days are the pages of the visitors' books and special climbing books that were kept at the mountain hotels. They kept a Visitors' Book at the Pen-y-Gwryd Hotel, the mountaineers' favourite Snowdonia resort, and when that became 'the receptacle for all sorts of nonsense scribbled by the casual passer-by' a Locked Book was provided, in 1884, for serious accounts of mountain exploits and discoveries.

At Wasdale Head there were two rival establishments – the Wastwater Hotel and, a little higher up the valley, Row Farm guest-house. The latter was teetotal; the former was not. Row Farm was run by Tom and Annie Tyson, offering comfortable bedrooms and excellent food – Annie became a legend for her ham and eggs and her gooseberry pie. Their Visitors' Book for the years 1876–86 has survived and was published in 1980. It contains the names of many of the leading figures of that key period, together with a few significant accounts of their adventures on the crags.

Wastwater Hotel was a little bigger than Row Farm and, by all accounts, a good deal more rough and ready in style. It was presided over by Will Ritson, generally known as 'the King o' Wasdale', and his wife Dinah. They built a small wing on to the farmhouse and acquired a drink licence in 1856 and opened it to visitors as The Huntsman's Inn. Ritson himself was the chief attraction, a larger than life character. He is the man who boasted that Wasdale had the 'highest mountain in England, the deepest lake, the smallest church, and the biggest liar'. He was the liar, regular winner of the annual competition for the telling of tall stories. 'The lees Aa tell', he said, 'isn't malicious; they're nobbut gert big exaggerations.'

A Visitors' Book was kept at the hotel from the early 1860s onwards and, though many of the entries are in the facetious tradition and some of the more important pages were ripped out and lost long ago, it bears clear witness to the growing interest in fell walking and rock scrambling, especially among visitors from the industrial areas of Lancashire and Yorkshire.

The Ritsons retired in 1879 and handed over to a genial but less flamboyant landlord, Dan Tyson, no relation to the Tysons of Row Farm. The hotel was further extended and its name changed to the Wastwater Hotel. It acquired its special Climbing Book, presented by Mr R. C. Gilson of Trinity College, Cambridge. On page one it says: 'This Book was started for the use of Climbers Jan. 1890 with a view of relieving the pages of the Ordinary Visitors Book and of rendering the information concerning the rocks of the District more accessible to those who are interested in it.'

For the next three decades the book was used by climbers to record their achievements. By 1919 its pages were full and another book was started. The original book was kept at the hotel, where John Ritson Whiting had succeeded Dan Tyson as landlord, and when Whiting finally retired in 1951 he took it with him. After his death five years later it disappeared.

Naturally, this was a matter of concern to the Fell and Rock Club's archivist, Mrs Muriel Files. The archives had a typed copy of the first Climbers' Book, prudently made in 1922, but this lacked the original's illustrations and photographs. The proper place, clearly, for the original – by far the most important source for the early days of the sport – is the club archives. Mrs Files's efforts to find it, however, led nowhere for many years. The mystery was only recently and providentially solved – in 1986 when the club was celebrating the centenary of Haskett Smith's ascent of Napes Needle – by the arrival of first a letter, then the original book itself from an address in Anderson, South Carolina.

It seems that after Whiting's death, his relatives gave the book to Mr R. H. Nicolson, a climber who had been a regular guest at the hotel for years. Later Mr Nicolson went to live in the United States. But he retained his membership of the Fell and Rock and, exactly forty years after he joined the club, he decided to give them the book. It is stored in the bank but available for historical research. It is invaluable, giving contemporary accounts of most of the major climbs made between January 1890 and August 1919. All the great names are there, as well as those of dozens of others who were happy to play supporting roles in the exciting new sport that was emerging.

Wasdale Head was the birthplace of British rock climbing. It could accommodate the holiday enthusiasts. It was far enough removed from the popular tourist path through the Lake District to retain the true mountain atmosphere. Most vital of all, it was within easy walking distance – two hours at the most – of three great climbing grounds, Pillar Rock, Great Gable and Scafell Crag.

The sport was born in the early 1880s. Rock routes had been climbed before then and some of them are still listed in the climbers' guide books. But the climbing was intermittent and haphazard, the result of adventurous holiday exploration by a few groups – fell walkers who enjoyed scrambling, Alpinists who wanted winter practice, young men and women from nearby towns and villages having a day out in the fresh air. By the end of the decade this was completely changed. A community of climbers had been formed, small and cheerful but serious about the sport, gathering regularly at Wasdale Head, pushing back the frontiers of what seemed possible to the human frame on steep rock, passing on information to each other by word of mouth or in the pages of the hotel books.

There can be no doubt that, if it had not happened at Wasdale Head, the sport would have emerged, elsewhere in Britain or in Europe, during these years. At the beginning of 1882 T. W. Wall and A. H. Stocker made the first attempt on the big steep face of Lliwedd near Snowdon and in 1883 they succeeded in forcing a route up the rocks to the west of the Central Gully. On the bigger and steeper cliffs of the Eastern Alps young German and Austrian climbers were making routes from 1875 onwards. In his book *Big Wall Climbing* Doug Scott recounts their achievements and makes it clear that they were similar, in background and motivation, to their British counterparts. Both groups came, for the most part, from comfortable middle-class homes in the industrial cities. They were seeking, as Scott says, 'to escape the restrictions society was imposing upon them'. Neither group was aware of the other's existence.

Clearly the time was ripe for rock climbing. The sport was a maverick by-product of the Industrial Revolution. For the first time in human history there had grown up, in the leading industrial nations, a large and prosperous urban middle class, well able to afford travel and regular holidays. Their work, sedentary and intellectual, left them an abundant surplus of physical energy. Many of them found their outlets in organised team games, but others sought their release in less regulated sports which would take them away from the smoke and bustle of the cities. It is no accident that the years which saw the arrival of rock climbing also introduced other adventure sports like pot-holing and small boat sailing.

For all this historical inevitability, though, the arrival of rock climbing as an integral and developing part of the Lake District scene owed almost as much to inadvertence as did those very first British climbs, eighty years earlier on Clogwyn du'r Arddu and Scafell.

— 2 —

The Birth
1881–1886

SOME time in the first half of 1881 a student at Trinity College, Oxford, sat in his rooms with a small group of friends, discussing where they should go for their summer vacation reading party. His name was Walter Parry Haskett Smith and he was to become renowned in the sport as 'the father of British rock climbing'. Many years later he recalled:

> None of us had ever been to the Lakes or heard the very name of Wasdale Head, but we procured the Ordnance map of Cumberland, found that there was on it a sombre region thronged with portentous shadows, found that there was an inn at a spot which seemed the centre of all this gloom, and finally engaged rooms at Dan Tyson's for a month.

Haskett Smith was twenty-two years old. The year before he had gained a Second in the Classical Moderations examination. Now he was reading for an Honours degree in *Literae Humaniores* (classical literature and philosophy). Born into a land-owning family at Goudhurst in Kent, he had been educated at Eton where he made the first of his many first ascents – on the high wall that borders one side of the famous playing fields. He was a natural athlete, slim and wiry, a good hurdler and an outstanding long-jumper. Although he had done some mountain walking in the Pyrenees and in Snowdonia, there was nothing to suggest that this visit to Wasdale Head would be anything more than the usual summer holiday of students in search of 'a healthy mind in a healthy body'.

In the event he spent two months there, the first four weeks at Row Farm, the next four at the hotel. Almost immediately he had what he called 'a great stroke of luck'. A fellow-guest at the farm was Frederick Herman Bowring, a barrister and Fellow of Trinity College, Cambridge, and a veteran explorer of the hills of England and Wales. Although he was nearly sixty, Bowring had great physical as well as mental vigour – 'a man of exceptional elasticity', as Haskett Smith phrased it – and was

28

eager to pass on his enthusiasm for adventurous fell walking to the new generation.

It was a formative encounter. The two men took to each other from the start. They had much in common. Bowring had studied classics and Haskett Smith was soon to go on and study law. There are other indications that Haskett Smith was greatly influenced by the older man in more than just the mountaineering sense, most notably in the way he came to combine a precise academic manner with a highly individual scruffiness of appearance. He never forgot his debt to Bowring in whom, he wrote, 'we soon found an exhaustive catalogue of every rock and every gully in the county. For eight hours in every day we absorbed Aristotle and Plato; for six or seven we scoured the surrounding fells and climbed furiously. In this way we soon began to develop a fine taste in gills.'

Haskett Smith was back at Row Farm for a further month's stay the next summer with three Oxford friends and his younger brother Edmund. This was the time – from mid-July to mid-August 1882 – when British rock climbing was 'born'. In those weeks, usually with his brother following him but never roped together, Haskett Smith set himself systematically to find new, harder and more exciting ways up the cliff faces.

On Great End he climbed two long, broken gullies, the Central and the South-east. In the Langdale area he climbed the North-west Gully on Gimmer Crag, the North Gully on Bowfell and the Great Gully on Pavey Ark. He explored the lower part of Deep Ghyll on Scafell. He went to the Ennerdale Face of Great Gable and 'found that it was an easy matter to coast along the face of the cliff at about two-thirds of the height of it'. On the short, southern side of Pillar Rock he made two routes from the Jordan Gap, Central Jordan and West Jordan, neither of them much more than fifty feet in vertical height but both still graded Difficult in the guide books.

He also went round to the much more forbidding northern face of the Rock and made an attempt, unsuccessful and nearly fatal, that shows how rapidly he had grown in climbing confidence. The North Climb was not conquered until nine years later and it was Haskett Smith who led the party then. On this day, while brother Edmund waited at the foot of the crag, he clambered up nearly 300 feet before being brought to a halt by the increasing steepness of the rock. He was descending but still high up when he had to slide round the outside of a big boulder, precariously balanced against the cliff wall. As he clung to it with his right hand the whole block began to topple on to him. He wrote:

> Letting go with my right hand, I rolled over on my left side, wrenched my waist-coat free of the stone, and hung over the precipice by my left hand only. If the stone did not fall quickly I was lost. It seemed to hesitate but then came slowly

over. My right hand seizing the tottering mass and weighing heavily upon it, eased for a moment the strain upon my left; then as the great stone dipped for its first plunge, my right foot swinging up onto it and kicking viciously downwards gave sufficient upward impetus to enable my right hand once more to clutch the hold above. It was a near thing; but a moment later I swung into the cleft just vacated by the stone. My arms were benumbed, my lungs empty, my mind an utter blank. I felt, rather than heard, my late enemy thundering down into the valley, and meanwhile someone near me grunting and gasping out 'autis – epeita – pedonde – kulindeto – laas – anaides'. The grunter was myself!*

The brothers attempted Piers Ghyll during that holiday, too, and this time it was Edmund's turn to run into trouble. A few years later Haskett Smith described the Cave Pitch:

Dry weather is certainly advisable for it, but by no means necessary. In 1882 the gill was on 'speat' after heavy rains, but my brother and I got up by dint of dashing through the fall into the Cave for breath and then fighting up through the rush of water. This was so heavy that while my brother was hauling himself up with the aid of my hand the pressure of the water on his head forced him to let go my hand and he was washed to the bottom again. There is a capital hold at the top but it is right under the water.

F. H. Bowring was at Row Farm in August and an entry for 11 August in the Visitors' Book there, the first above Haskett Smith's name, shows them finding a variation route on the East face of Pillar Rock:

There is a way of climbing Pillar Rock starting from the Eastern side and coming up the Ennerdale face above Low Man. Quitting the neck which joins the rock to the mountain, and on the eastern side of the rock passing the beginning of the 'easy way', descend the gully as far as you can, to where the great chimney runs straight up to the summit ... Climb this, keeping the wall on the right to about 20 feet from the perpendicular rock, then get out on the right and cross the low wall of rock ... In front of you, on the right, you will see a vertical cleft with a step in the middle. Climb this and scramble to the top as you please. Though longer than the 'easy way', it is not difficult with care and a good fair climb from end to end.

This was the first attempt, in any of the Wasdale Head Visitors' Books, to give a detailed description of a rock route for the guidance of those who might wish to try it for themselves. It was Haskett Smith's urge to inform others that created the binding basis of the group that soon began to form around him.

The Pillar entry in the Row Farm Book was immediately followed by others – one giving a full account of explorations, on 9 and 12 August, of routes up Scafell from the Eskdale end of the Mickledore Gap; the other simply noting that on the 12th he also climbed the face of the Lingmell crags.

*The quotation is from Homer's *Odyssey*, the passage where Sisyphus is seen in Hades at his eternal task of pushing a great boulder up a hill, only to lose it at the last moment. Dr E. V. Rieu, in the Penguin Classics translation, rendered it as 'the misbegotten rock came bounding down again to level ground'.

One other event of importance occurred in the summer of 1882. A farmer from Lorton, John Wilson Robinson, who had already done much fell walking and some scrambling, noted in his diary: 'June 28 with J. E. Walker via "Easy Way" in thick mist – rain came on while on the Rock – crossed Mickledore for the first time on the same day.' It was Robinson's introduction to Pillar Rock which he was to climb more than a hundred times in the next twenty-four years. His companion, Walker, was the headmaster of a Quaker school. Robinson too, now twenty-nine years old and the son of a yeoman-farmer at Whinfell Hall, was a devout Quaker. But there was nothing of the pious killjoy about him. Although he was never known to swear or smoke or drink alcohol, and these are not characteristics that normally endear a man to climbers, he became the favourite of the Wasdale Head community. One friend, George Muller, summed up the apparently unanimous view with the words: 'John smiled through life.' In the 1880s and '90s he walked and climbed with all the pioneers of the sport, many of them men of high professional and academic distinction, and he seems to have impressed them all with his natural intelligence and wit, his knowledge of the fells and their history and wildlife, his physical strength and stamina, the careful patience of his style on steep rock, his unfailing courtesy and consideration for others, the irrepressible cheerfulness of his conversation.

He was of medium height, straight, compact and sturdy. Richard Hall described him as 'a well-built figure, sandy side whiskers, extremely bald and shining head and merry blue eyes'. He habitually wore a Norfolk jacket of yellowish-brown Harris tweed, twill knickerbockers, brown stockings and nailed boots, and a hat of the deer-stalker variety with ear-protectors and a peaked 'neb' fore and aft.

There has probably never been a more complete Lake District man. It was his home, his place of work and his place of pleasure. He was a pioneer of marathon fell walking as well as of rock climbing. He enjoyed snow and ice climbing, too, and is said to have ascended Deep Ghyll at least once each winter for twenty consecutive years. His Wasdale Head friends liked to vary their climbing with trips to North Wales and the Western Highlands of Scotland and the Alps. Robinson tried it once, in 1898, when he went to the Alps and did a number of good routes, including the Matterhorn. But he was not impressed and did not leave the Lake District again.

Haskett Smith did not visit Cumberland in 1883. It was the year of his Finals and he got a Third Class degree. But he was back at Wasdale Head in the summer of 1884, staying at the hotel this time. The entry for 5 September in the hotel Visitors' Book, above the initials 'W.P.H.S', reads:

The Scafell Pillar. This rock, which for the last year or two has attracted a good deal of attention from climbers and has by some been considered to be inaccessible, bears a striking resemblance in structure and cleavage to the larger and better known Pillar in Ennerdale. It forms with its two summits one side of the fine ravine called Deep Gill which owes to it much of its amazing rock scenery. It is readily got at by turning to the right after ascending from Mickledore by any one of the usual ways – the Broad Stand, the Chimney (now becoming better known) or the Penrith Climb on Rake's Progress ... Here, as in Ennerdale, there is a 'Pisgah' from which the summit is almost within jumping distance: but in order to be duly appreciated the rock should be viewed from Deep Gill or from the second summit. It was climbed by a gentleman staying at this Inn on Wednesday last – probably a first ascent since above the foot of the rock no signs of a previous attack could be detected. Of course no ropes or other illegitimate means were resorted to.

His 'Scafell Pillar' is now known as Scafell Pinnacle. The person he modestly refers to as 'a gentleman staying at this Inn' was Haskett Smith himself. It was the first ascent and he did it alone so there would have been little point in taking a rope but his concluding remark in the above passage reflects his thinking at that time. 'In those days', he later wrote, 'we were heretical in our attitude towards the use of the rope. Not having one ourselves, we were inclined to scoff at those who had; and in the gall of bitterness we classed ropes with spikes and ladders, as a means by which bad climbers were enabled to go where none but the best climbers had any business to be.'

No rock climbers used the rope in the Lake District at this period and there were several serious accidents. On Good Friday 1883 a youth of seventeen, going to the rescue of two scramblers who had got themselves crag-fast near the Jordan Gap on Pillar, slipped on a snow slope and plunged to his death at the foot of the chasm which now immortalises him with its name, Walker's Gully. In 1884 Lawrence Pilkington had his thigh smashed by a fall of stones in Piers Ghyll. A few weeks later a medical student from Edinburgh, Michael Petty, fell a hundred feet on to the broken screes below Mickledore and was terribly lacerated about the head and face. John Robinson was nearby and managed to get him down to Burnthwaite at the head of Wasdale where he was stitched together by 'an eminent surgeon'. Two weeks later Petty was well enough to be moved again. Robinson wrote to say he would walk over and help. On the appointed morning Haskett Smith and F. H. Bowring, neither of whom knew Robinson except by reputation, went up to Sty Head to meet him. It was the start of the first great creative partnership in Lakeland rock climbing.

The three of them walked down to Burnthwaite where Haskett Smith and Robinson lifted Petty on to a handcart and pushed him down to the road, just below the inn, where he was helped into a carriage. At Bowring's suggestion they then made their way up the lower slopes of Great Gable towards the scree funnel known as Great Hell Gate.

Although they are closer to Wasdale Head than either Scafell or Pillar Rock, the crags of the Great Napes on the south-eastern shoulder of Great Gable had never been investigated by the climbers. 'In those days', Haskett Smith said, 'climbers had never really looked at the Napes. The vast slopes of cruel scree below them not only kept explorers away, but gave the impression that the whole mass was dangerously rotten.' But one day two years earlier, during his first sustained burst of exploration, Haskett Smith had looked across the valley from Piers Ghyll towards the Napes and noticed 'a slender pinnacle of rock, standing out against the background of cloud without a sign of any other rock near it and appearing to shoot up for 200 or 300 feet'. Robinson had heard tell of the pinnacle too; his father had found it and sketched it over fifty years before.

Now, while Bowring walked back to the valley, the two young men traversed along, keeping as close to the foot of the Napes crags as they could. 'It was a jolly climb', Haskett Smith reported, 'and before long we came rather suddenly into full view of the rock which we were seeking. Robinson's delight was unbounded, and he eagerly inquired whether any Swiss guide would be ready to tackle such a thing.' This was Napes Needle, nothing like so tall as Haskett Smith had expected but formidably steep on all sides, certainly too forbidding for them at that stage. So they 'threaded the Needle', scrambling up between the pinnacle and the face of the crag, and picked a way up Needle Gully. In the hotel that evening Haskett Smith mentioned 'these excellent rocks' in the Visitors' Book.

A lifelong friendship was launched that day and they returned to the same area a few days later to make the first climbers' route on Great Gable, Needle Ridge, which is today graded Very Difficult. Haskett Smith confessed, however, that they did it 'in a somewhat desultory fashion', avoiding the harder sections.

Their outstanding achievement that holiday was made on 20 September. Haskett Smith had been the first man to the top of Scafell Pinnacle a few weeks before, building a cairn there to prove the point. On that occasion he had taken the shortest, easiest route. Now he and Robinson, unroped, tackled its much longer and harder side, by way of Steep Ghyll to the top of Low Man where they built a 'good-sized cairn', then straddling the Knife-Edge Ridge and so to the top of High Man. Next day Robinson wrote a full account in the Visitors' Book at Row Farm which concluded:

> The climb up the latter part of the arête is charming, as the holds are splendid in comparison to the previous experience in the chimney below. On the top you will observe in a hole in the cairn a bottle, in which to deposit visiting cards. To descend from here into the Pisgah Gap there is no great difficulty, as the holds, if not numerous, are sound.

A few weeks earlier a London journalist, C. N. Williamson, had written in the Row Farm Book a lively account of a fortnight's climbing, with a cheerful party that included two young women, on Pillar Rock and Scafell: 'Mr. Michael Petty', he said, 'carried his guitar to the top of the Rock and entertained the company with songs. Nap and other games of cards were also played on the top of the Rock.'

On his return to London, Williamson wrote a long article 'The Climbs of the English Lake District' which was published, in two parts, in the magazine *All the Year Round*. It gave a comprehensive survey of the routes made so far and an attractive picture of the scene at Wasdale Head:

> Either at the inn, or at Mrs. Thomas Tyson's famous farm-house, climbing men linger through the summer. Some come in winter, and then the surrounding peaks offer excellent practice for Swiss mountaineering. They are enthusiastic fellows, these climbers. They ascend their favourite mountains time after time; they are unwearied at finding new ways up everywhere; and their talk, when they get together, is of nicks and notches, ladders and ledges, gullies, ghylls and chimneys, and even of cols, arêtes and couloirs. All Cumberland and Westmorland is familiar to them

It was the first time the new sport had been noticed in a national journal. Now the word was beginning to spread and it may be no accident that, within a few weeks of publication, two Yorkshiremen who were already leading explorers in the higher European ranges arrived at Row Farm to see what the Lake District had to offer. One was Geoffrey Hastings, prosperously engaged in the worsted spinning industry at Bradford; the other was William Cecil Slingsby, the heir to an old family of land-owners and textile manufacturers at Carleton in Craven.

Slingsby was thirty-five years old. As a child he had roamed the moors around his home, climbing trees and scrambling up rocks. He loved everything about the Yorkshire Dales – the birds and animals, the flowers and fresh air, the people and their dialect. He was fascinated by their history, especially by their descent from the Viking invaders who had colonised Northern England a thousand years before. He read poetry and travel books and Edward Whymper's *Scrambles in the Alps*. On his first visit to Norway he had immediately been taken by the similarities in language and character between the people there and his own home folk. He went back year after year, in the summer, learning Norwegian, learning to ski, exploring the unknown mountain regions. He was a natural climber and quickly became a superb one – good on rock, better on snow and ice, incomparable as a route-finder across unmapped and difficult terrain. In 1876 he made the first ascents of six high peaks, culminating in the dramatic Store Skagastolstind – climbing the final 500 feet of steep rock alone because his Norwegian guides thought it too dangerous. There was some initial resentment of the foreigner who had snatched their great prizes but his generous, outgoing nature prevailed and he became an almost legendary hero in his adopted land. They called him 'the father of Norwegian mountaineering'.

In 1878 he paid his first visit to Switzerland and thereafter alternated his summer holidays between Norway and the Alps, climbing with the strongest team of the period, A. F. Mummery, Professor Norman Collie and Geoffrey Hastings.

Until well into the 1880s and '90s most of their fellow-members of the Alpine Club regarded Lake District rock climbing with contempt, dismissing its enthusiasts as 'chimney sweeps' and 'rock gymnasts'. But there was nothing contemptuous in the approach of these men. Mummery paid one visit to Wasdale Head and pronounced his judgement: 'Climbing in the Caucasus was easy and safe; also it was usually easy and safe in the Alps, though sometimes difficult; but climbing as practised at Wasdale was both difficult and dangerous.'

The first visit of Slingsby and Hastings, the first of many, proved Mummery's point. One of their group wrote in the Row Farm Book: 'February 28 to March 2 1885: Spent three days amongst the peaks with ice axes and ropes and found the snow in most splendid order – were five hours climbing gullies and couloirs about the Pillar Rock.' They attempted Deep Ghyll on Scafell but were defeated by the ice-glazed rocks below the first chockstone. They determined to return.

Haskett Smith did not go to Wasdale Head that year – he went to the Pyrenees with his friend Charles Packe, looking for chamois – but the local men, John Robinson and George Seatree, made two innovations. They took a tent so they could sleep closer to the crags. They also took an 'Alpine rope'. This rope had been used in the Lake District for some time but only by Alpinists, practising their snow and ice techniques. This was the first time it was used for rock climbing, though Robinson's account makes it plain that they were merely experimenting and had no idea how to deploy it properly.

On 11 June Robinson and Seatree walked over from Buttermere and pitched the tent on the best bit of ground they could find near the Jordan Gap on Pillar. Then, with Ernest Peile of Workington who had helped to carry the loads, they started climbing. Robinson takes up the story:

> Over the 'notch' we went for our first climb and entered our names as usual. I then ran down and tried Pendlebury's Crack ... and thought it rather easy. We hung the rope down at the corner as a precaution, but it was not used. I then descended and attacked the 'Corner'. HS and I had both been a little way up on a former visit ... It is 2 chimneys and they miss each other and this makes the only real difficulty at that point. I drew myself up by hands entirely. Seatree and I then went up right Pisgah. S. went first and had a tightish struggle. Says he nearly caught at the safety rope once – he is very proud of this climb and considers it beats North Climb (on Scafell) hollow in point of strain and difficulty – from the top we went down East climb and I went into Great Chimney to look at HS's

> climb. It looked very bad and the rocks were wet – I then found I had left my
> rope on the top and went up climbing direct to slab and then over notch.

The ground they slept on 'turned out to be sadly uneven that night' so
they struck camp next morning and walked over to Wasdale Head to
camp in a field at the foot of Lingmell. They were spotted, one of them
with the rope across his shoulder, by the landlord of the inn, Dan Tyson,
who asked 'if theer was gaahn to be a hangin' job on?'

During the next few days, with Peile and F. H. Bowring and a young
tourist called Walter, they explored Piers Ghyll, Lingmell and Scafell.
Seatree led them up North Climb, which Robinson forbade Peile to
attempt as 'he had no nails in his boots'. Later, while Bowring and Peile
went up Broad Stand, the other three tackled Mickledore Chimney:

> I was standing [Robinson wrote] on the edge and shewing Seatree the holds,
> Walter standing behind him. I heard the voice of F. H. B. and a noise of falling
> stones, it seemed to come from the direction of Broad Stand – my heart stood still
> for I thought either he or Peile had fallen. The noise increased to a deafening roar
> and we realized in a moment that large masses of falling stones were coming down
> our chimney. I cried 'look out' and ducked under a crag with my face turned
> towards the edge above me over which it must come. I could not see the other
> two, they got a little higher towards the great over-hanging rock. Those were
> awful moments; Seatree says he hopes never to go thro' such again; he thought
> the great rock might give way too. The next moment a great stone about 18 inches
> square came bounding over, dancing from side to side as it came down and making
> great stars on the sides of the chimney where it struck. It was followed by a great
> fall of fragments of every size and shape across the entire chimney, more or less,
> and the air seemed darkened for a few moments. These went clattering down the
> chimney with a terrific din. I jumped up and said are you hurt? No. Mr Bowring
> are you there? 'Yes. We are alright.' Who set it off? 'Peile. He is in the chimney
> above.' 'What did he go up there for, tell him to sit where he is or he may set off
> another.' We were a good deal shaken and I fastened the rope as a safeguard for
> them to come up by.

The incident illustrates one important way in which the pioneer
climbers faced greater hazards than those who climb now. The crags,
unvisited except by wind and weather, were strewn with the detritus of
the ages – precariously poised boulders like Haskett Smith's 'misbegotten
rock' on the north side of Pillar, loose flakes and stones, steep runs of
uncertain scree, soggy mosses and slimy vegetation, the rotten roots and
stumps of long-dead shrubs – all waiting for the weight of the passing
climber to succumb finally to the force of gravity. It put a premium on
smooth, cautious movement. In the worst places, every hold had to be
tested before use. If it seemed unreliable, the ice axe was brought into
play to 'garden' the débris out of the way. It was dangerous not only for
the leader but also for those below, crouching against the rock while
the rubbish whizzed past. And it was noisy too. Lawrence Pilkington
described the first ascent of the Inaccessible Pinnacle on the Cuillin
Ridge on Skye, made with his brother in 1880, in these words:

There was a foot or more of loose rock which had been shattered by the lightning and frost of ages. This formed the edge of the pinnacle and had to be thrown down as we climbed up. The noise was appalling; the very rock of the pinnacle itself seemed to vibrate with indignation at our rude onslaught.

Many years later Haskett Smith recalled a wall on Sergeant Crag in Langstrath that was 'evenly covered with a thin layer of bright green moss which was starred all over with the beautiful little Filmy fern. It was a perfect picture, but it so thoroughly lubricated the rock that the climb was impossible till J. W. Robinson remorselessly raked it down, so that next time we attacked it the holds were not only visible, but dry.'

Modern environmentalists, particularly those who are concerned for the survival of rare plants, take great exception when they hear of such conduct. The feeling is understandable. But when life or limb are at stake, the mind may be hardened as well as concentrated. The pioneer climbers 'gardened' almost as ruthlessly as their successors do today.

At the end of their camping/climbing holiday in June 1885 Robinson and Seatree walked over to Rosthwaite for lunch with Jackson, a guide who took tourists up the mountain paths. They told him what they had been doing and heard his judgement: 'In my opinion yon Askatt Smith will break his neck upon some of yon crags before long.' This was the dalesman's general view of the new sport. In the previous decade Will Ritson had asked Seatree: 'What's makkin' ye fellas fash yer'sels seea mich aboot climmin' t'crags? Isn't t' fells big eneugh for ye?'

The year 1886 has been seen by some as the birth-year of British rock climbing because that was the year when Haskett Smith climbed Napes Needle. It was certainly a most important advance. But the fact is that climbing was already firmly established, evolving and expanding, not only around Wasdale Head but also in Snowdonia where the cliffs of Lliwedd had been climbed by two separate routes by this time.

In the Lake District the first significant event of the year was the return of Cecil Slingsby and Geoffrey Hastings for another go at Deep Ghyll on Scafell Crag. The year before they had been defeated by icy rocks. Now, on 28 March, they were helped for much of the way by hard-packed snow. They were roped together in the Alpine way and Hastings led, using Slingsby's shoulders as footholds at the first obstacle. Higher up they found the gully blocked by boulders and were forced on to the side wall:

... On the left hand of the ghyll, a small tongue of rock, very steep, juts out perhaps 40 feet down the gully and forms a small crack and this crack is the only way upward. From the mountaineer's point of view the stratification of the rocks here is all wrong. The crack ends in a chimney about 20 feet high, between the wall and a smoothly polished boss of rock. Hastings, still leading, found the crack to be difficult, but climbed it in a most masterly way. All loose stones, tufts of grass and moss had to be thrown down, and, in the absence of hand and foot hold, the knees, elbows, thighs and other parts of the body had to do the holding on,

whilst, caterpillar-like, we drew ourselves upward bit by bit. The chimney is best
climbed by leaning against the Pinnacle wall with one's back and elbows, and, at
the same time, walking with the feet fly-like up the boss opposite.

Deep Ghyll was the first of the gullies on Scafell Crag to be ascended
but the chief importance of this climb stems from the fact that Slingsby's
account of it was printed in the next edition of *The Alpine Journal*. It paid
tribute to Haskett Smith as 'a gentleman who has done much brilliant
rock climbing in Cumberland', and concluded with the words: 'Do not
let us be beaten on our own fells by outsiders, some of whom consider
ice axes and ropes to be "illegitimate". Let us not neglect the Lake
District, Wales and Scotland whilst we are conquerors abroad.'

Until this time, most of the routes made in the Lake District were in
the gullies. Haskett Smith explained: 'It is one great merit of a climb if
it clearly defines itself ... If you climb just to amuse yourself you can
wander vaguely over a face of rock; but if you want to describe your
climb to others, it saves a lot of time if you can say – "There, that's our
gully! Stick to it all the way up!"' It sounds convincing but it was a
rationalisation rather than a reason. The gullies were attacked first
because they were the most obvious lines of weakness up the cliff face.
For most of the way they take you up easy, broken, scrambler's ground.
The ledges tend to be big, the steep bits short. The enclosing walls afford
a sense, however false, of security. But the fact is that Lakeland gullies
are, for the most part, dark and cold and dripping with moisture. They
are also, from time to time, blocked by overhanging boulders that force
the climber out on to the retaining walls. It was when they moved out,
as they frequently had to do, that the pioneers discovered not only that
the holds there were dryer and more reliable but also that the climbing
was more exhilarating, with a more stimulating drop beneath their boots.

The first historians of Lake District climbing, H. M. Kelly and J. H.
Doughty, categorised the 1880s as the 'Gully and Chimney Period'. It
is only partially true. Several of Haskett Smith's routes prior to 1886 –
his climbs from the Jordan Gap on Pillar, for example, and his attempt
on the North side of the Rock – had little to do with gullies and
chimneys. And towards the end of June 1886 – the exact day has not been
established – he made a climb that had nothing to do with either.

On the last day of a short holiday at Wasdale Head he rose early, took
some friends climbing on Buckbarrow, then helped them carry their
luggage to the foot of the lake. His account of the rest of the day,
published in the *Journal* of the Fell and Rock Climbing Club in 1914, is
the best-known passage in the story of Lakeland climbing:

The long walk in the sun left me with a headache by the time I got back to the
Inn. The afternoon was cooler and it occurred to me to stroll over into the head
of Ennerdale and have a look at the cliffs on that face of Gable. These had never
been climbed at any point.

The marks of a recent stone-fall drew my attention to a part of the cliff where I found a very fine gully and climbed it, not without difficulty, being impeded by a long fell-pole. Coming out on top of the mountain I thought of the ridge beside which Robinson and I had come up two years before and made for it, intending to follow the edge down as strictly as might be. This proved to be quite feasible, though at one point my pole gave me a lot of trouble by dropping down a deep and narrow crevice. However, the ridge was so steep at that spot that some 20 feet below, on peering into the crack, I espied my stick stuck upright, and by thrusting my arm in was at length able to reach it with my finger-tips and finally to draw it out.

Continuing down into the gap and now warmed by exertion, I forgot my headache and began to examine the Needle itself. A deep crack offered a very obvious route for the first stage, but the middle portion of this crack was decidedly difficult, being at that time blocked with stones and turf, all of which has since been cleared away. Many capable climbers were afterwards turned back when trying to make the second ascent not by the sensational upper part but by this lower and (under present conditions) very simple piece.

From the top of the crack there is no trouble to reach the shoulder, whence the final stage may be studied at ease. The summit is near, being as they say in Trans-Atlantic cities 'only two blocks away', but those same blocks are set one upon the other and the stability of the top one looks very doubtful. My first care was to get two or three stones and test the flatness of the summit by seeing whether anything thrown up could be induced to lodge. If it did, that would be an indication of a moderately flat top, and would hold out hopes of the edge being found not too much rounded to afford a good grip for the fingers. Out of three missiles one consented to stay, and thereby encouraged me to start, feeling as small as a mouse climbing a milestone.

Between the upper and lower blocks, about five feet up, there is a ragged horizontal chink large enough to admit the toes, but the trouble is to raise the body without intermediate footholds. It seemed best to work up at the extreme right, where the corner projects a little, though the fact that you are hanging over a deep gap makes it rather a 'nervy' proceeding. For anyone in a standing position at the corner it is easy to shuffle the feet sideways to the other end of the chink, where it is found that the side of the top block facing outwards is decidedly less vertical. Moreover at the foot of this side there appeared to my great joy a protuberance which, being covered with a lichenous growth, looked as if it might prove slippery, but was placed in the precise spot where it would be most useful in shortening the formidable stretch up to the top edge. Gently and cautiously transferring my weight, I reached up with my right hand and at last was able to feel the edge and prove it to be, not smooth and rounded as it might have been, but a flat and satisfactory grip. My first thought on reaching the top was one of regret that my friends should have missed by a few hours such a day's climbing, three new things, and all good; my next was one of wonder whether getting down again would not prove far more awkward than getting up!

Hanging by the hands and feeling with the toes for the protuberance provided an anxious moment, but the rest went easily enough, though it must be confessed that it was an undoubted satisfaction to stand once more on solid ground below and look up at my handkerchief fluttering in the breeze.

The route, the Wasdale Crack, involves no more than fifty-five feet of ascent. But it is steep and exposed and varied – crack climbing, then an easy slab, then an awkward mantelshelf move with a formidable drop on your right, and finally a few feet on small holds on the open face of the top block. Today it is graded Very Difficult (Hard). If the bottom pitch is easier now, as Haskett Smith claims, because all the débris in the crack has been removed, the top part has been made harder by the grinding and polishing of the holds through the passing of countless thousands of boots.

It was a remarkable thing to have done, alone, at the end of a long day, in nailed boots. (The Needle had to wait three years for its second ascent, by Geoffrey Hastings.) It was arguably the most significant short climb ever made. It signalled the movement out of the gullies and chimneys and on to more challenging ground. And because of the Needle's dramatic and photogenic shape, it did more, perhaps, than any other single factor to spread the word about the new sport. Before long photographs were appearing in shop windows and in the press. There was an article about the Needle in the *Pall Mall Budget* in 1890. Lakeland climbing began to gather pace.

— 3 —

The Wasdale Head Years
1886–1899

THE COMMUNITY which now began to form at Wasdale Head and which grew and flourished there over the next decade was a unique, creative and, on the whole, a very happy one. It was small – never more than a few dozen enthusiasts – and predominantly, though not exclusively, male. They did not, as their counterparts in North Wales did, organise themselves into a formal club with rules and restrictions. Their conduct, on the crags and back at the hotel at the end of the day, was governed only by their acceptance of the codes of behaviour for British middle-class gentlemen in Victorian times.

It is clear from their writings that they thought of themselves as an élite group though they never made the claim explicitly. And they were an élite, going into places where men had never ventured before, pitting their nerves and muscles and suppleness against the uncompromising rock and the force of gravity. The overwhelming majority of their contemporaries thought they were crazy and they took delight and encouragement from that. The most detailed and evocative, if somewhat idealised, portrait of the period can be read in the chapter 'Wastdale Head at Easter' in Lehmann J. Oppenheimer's book *The Heart of Lakeland*.

The competitive spirit, which attends most worthwhile human activity, was undoubtedly present among them. But it was not allowed to approach the heights of acrimonious intensity that have marked, and marred, the sport in the latter half of the twentieth century. They climbed for fun, not fame. They recorded their achievements for the guidance of others, not for acclaim. Most of them were more than content to spend the day, not attempting new routes but introducing beginners to old favourites. They admired the courage and skill of the leading figures but they enjoyed comradeship as well and respected common sense and (with one notable exception) there was no rancour in the things they wrote or said. The one thing they would not tolerate was bragging.

Their headquarters was the Wastwater Hotel, though a few continued to prefer the quieter ambience of Row Farm. The custom was quickly established of gathering there on the national holidays, at Christmas, Easter and Whitsun. In Oppenheimer's book he imagines a stranger approaching the hotel one Eastertime:

> As he nears the hotel, hungry and tired after a night in the train and a walk of a dozen miles from the coast, he hears an unwonted hum of voices, and entering the yard he finds a group looking up at, and shouting to a man who seems stuck like a fly some ten feet up the rough wall of the barn, feeling with one hand among the open joints of the stone-work for a hold higher up.

The stranger finds the landlord, Dan Tyson, only to be told that the place is full to overflowing – 'They come up every Eastertide, a lot of 'em – a daft lot.'

At those peak times the hotel was taken over by the climbers. Several slept in the barn, one of them on the billiard table. Their boots, ropes and ice axes littered the lobby; their wet tweeds and socks steamed through the night in the kitchen. 'The odour of drying garments', George Abraham said, 'pervades the place.' In the morning they would eat an enormous cooked breakfast, then sally forth, with a stoic disregard for bad weather, to tackle the routes they had planned the previous evening. They spent long hard days on the crags, returning at dusk or later to eat an enormous dinner and tell the others what they had done. After the meal some would sit on in the dining room to plan for the morrow. Others crowded into the little smoke room, where a coal fire would be blazing, to rest and reminisce and discuss esoteric points about climbing ethics or the best pattern of nails in the boots, while one (perhaps) would be writing up the day's new route in the Climbers' Book. From time to time they would hear loud cries and shouts from the billiard room where the rowdier elements were more violently engaged. The billiard room was unheated but the windows quickly clouded up with steam. There were contests of strength such as one-arm pull-ups on to a bar; trials of gymnastic agility like 'the passage of the billiard table leg' in which the contestant started from a sitting position on the edge of the table and had to climb under the table and inside of one of the corner legs to sit on an adjoining edge, without touching the floor; and the 'billiard room traverse' which had to be done all round the room with the hands on the billiard table and the feet on the wall, ending with a muscular swing through the doorway and into the passage beyond. Later they devised a dangerous game called 'billiard fives' in which the players, usually in pairs and using their hands as bats, had to drive a billiard ball against the cushion or, even better, into one of the pockets at the opposite end.

Dan Tyson bore it all with equanimity. He took the precaution of protecting the billiard-room windows with wire netting. He also insisted that the games should cease at midnight, to restore some quiet to his hotel and enable whoever was sleeping on the billiard table to go to bed. His bar takings cannot have been great as those who drank did so, it seems, in moderation and many restricted themselves to soft drinks or water. Clothing left behind by visitors was washed and kept in a cupboard, available to all.

The men who climbed at Wasdale Head in these years came, for the most part, from the big and growing cities of England – from London, Birmingham, Manchester, Liverpool, Leeds and Bradford. Most of them were university-educated and now, still in their twenties and thirties, prosperously engaged in business or the professions, as doctors, solicitors, teachers, engineers, research scientists and the like. They were, again for the most part, married men with families. What they were seeking on these short holiday forays was escape at several levels: from the din and grime of over-crowded industrial centres; from the sometimes suffocating conventions of Victorian domestic life; from the nervous and intellectual pressures of hard work in offices, surgeries and classrooms. At Wasdale Head, for a few days two or three times each year, they could wear what they liked, get as wet and filthy as they wanted, and hoist themselves about the crags or the billiard room to their hearts' content. It was essential, at these times, that the community should be men only. The only other qualification was a delight in climbing steep rock.

They enjoyed themselves and, when they climbed, they climbed hard. It was a holiday pastime and many of them spent the whole of their summer holidays on snow and ice routes in Europe. Yet these years brought major advances in Lake District rock climbing. In 1886 the hardest route done was Napes Needle, now graded Very Difficult (Hard). By the summer of 1903 the hardest route was Botterill's Slab on Scafell, now graded Very Severe. The men of Wasdale Head were climbing at a standard unmatched anywhere else in Britain.

Their achievement is all the more remarkable in view of the rudimentary nature of their equipment and techniques. They concentrated their attention on 'the climber's boot'. It was quickly apparent that a scattering of hob nails in the soles and heels was inadequate for the job. They experimented with nails of varying shapes and sizes and metal. Some would hammer 'ring-clinkers' all round the edge and overlapping the sides, with a patterning of 'muggers' within. These were made of soft iron and the idea was that the rock would bite into the metal and hold the boot firm as the foot pressed down. Later on, some preferred an edging of 'tricounis', hard steel nails with a serrated edge, said to bite into the rock. Many worked out their own special permutations. They theorised endlessly about the best leather for the uppers and the soles, the ideal nails for different situations, precisely how they should be arranged, how they should be hammered in, how the boots should be dried and oiled.

They loved their boots and looked after them assiduously and many of them refused to give them up when rubber soles, much more adhesive to dry rock, came into use. But the nailed boots were heavy and often uncomfortable on the long walk to the foot of the crags. The metal ground away at the smaller holds, polishing them down to a smooth, glassy surface that made the routes progressively harder for those who came after. They were the cause of considerable pain to the second man when, as often happened, the leader had to clamber up his back and stand on his shoulders or even on the top of his head to bring the next hand hold within reach. There were times when the foot holds were so small and awkward that the leader had to take his boots off and climb in stockinged feet.

They soon discovered that the long fell-pole, the traditional companion of the early fell walker, was a dangerous inconvenience in rock climbing. By this time the Alpine mountaineer always carried an ice axe, some four feet long in those days, and soon many rock climbers were taking them too. They used them to 'garden' away any loose débris and also on one famous occasion, to chip a vital foot hold in the rock. But these, too, must have been more trouble than they were worth when there was no snow and ice on the ground.

The Alpine men also roped themselves together when they climbed. It made good sense on the snow slopes; if one man slipped, the others could ram their ice axes into the snow and hold tight, with every expectation that the rope would arrest his fall. This is impossible on rock. Despite this, and in defiance of Haskett Smith's initial reservations, the 'Alpine rope' was in general use on Lakelandrock in the latter part of the 1880s. Haskett Smith saw its purpose as psychological:

> Even in places where it gives the leader no security and to some extent actually impedes him, the moral effect of it is good. It wonderfully increases those feelings of united and ordered effort, of mutual dependence and mutual confidence, and finally of cheery subordination of self, which are not the least of the virtues or the joys of mountaineering.

It was generally felt that the best rope was that made by John Buckingham (later Arthur Beale) of Shaftesbury Avenue in London. It was advertised as being made of the 'Best Manilla Hemp' and 'marked by a Red Worsted Thread twisted with the Strands'. The rope was $1\frac{1}{4}$ inches in circumference, of 'gentle lay', and available in lengths of 60, 80 or 100 feet.

But hemp rope is heavy and not, by modern standards, strong and when it gets wet it becomes very awkward to manage and greatly given to kinking. And the first photographs of Lake District climbers in action, taken by the Abrahams brothers of Keswick in the 1890s, show that, however much it did for their morale, it did little or nothing for their security.

Sometimes they are seen moving simultaneously. Even when they climbed one at a time their rope technique gave little or no reassurance. The leader would set off and the second man, tied to him, would pay the rope out. When the leader reached a convenient ledge he would simply turn round, haul the slack in, and then give a tight rope as the second man ascended. He was not attached to the rock behind him. He did not even pass the rope around his body to increase the chances of holding a fall. If there was a flake of rock nearby he might feed the rope behind that for a little extra friction; this was what they meant when they used the term 'belaying pin'. If the second man were to fall when climbing, there was some chance of the leader – if he was sufficiently alert and firmly planted on his stance – holding him. But if they were halfway up a cliff and the leader fell, there was virtually nothing the second man could do except pray that he would not be pulled off when the tug came on the rope.

They were intelligent men and some of them, the engineers for example, were men of high practical skills, and they all knew the game they were playing was a dangerous one. It seems odd that they should continue climbing for so many years without devising sounder safety methods for themselves. It seems almost a miracle that they should have climbed so long, at rapidly advancing standards of difficulty, without sustaining a single fatal accident.

In some ways they did show themselves to be both cautious and ingenious. They insisted that the best climber of the party should lead when ascending and come last when descending. If a man had his eye on a possible new route he would often climb down it, protected by a rope from above, to look at the problems and clear away any loose stones or wet vegetation. Sometimes, if the leader came across a firmly blocked stone in a chimney or gully, he would untie his climbing rope and push it up behind the block, then tie on again and carry on climbing, gaining confidence from his 'running belay'. More than once this precaution saved lives.

The one rule they repeated over and over again was: The leader must not fall. In the nature of things, the rule was honoured in the breach as well as the observance. Yet for a surprising length of time their luck – and the rope – held good.

So far in telling this story it has been possible to describe virtually all the important people and the routes they accomplished. From now on, as the numbers of both climbers and climbs increase, it will be necessary to become more selective, concentrating on the leading figures and the breakthrough achievements. The history of all sports must be, very largely, the story of the outstanding, creative 'heroes'. It is unavoidable but particularly unfortunate in the case of rock climbing because it is a sport in which the leading practitioners depend, more than in any other game perhaps, on the support and encouragement and safe seconding of many others.

In September 1887 the remarkable Hopkinson brothers made their first impact on Lake District climbing. There were five of them, all eminent in their professional fields and keen mountaineers. They were: John, a brilliant Cambridge mathematician, then a Cambridge don, later a distinguished electrical engineer; Alfred, who went to Oxford and became a barrister, a Liberal MP and Vice-Chancellor of Manchester University; Charles, the best climber of them all, who worked as a consulting engineer in the family firm; Edward, another Cambridge mathematician who went into electrical engineering and designed the world's first electrically powered underground train; and Albert who studied medicine at Cambridge and became a surgeon. There were five surviving sisters, too, but none of them seems to have taken to climbing.

On their mother's side they were related to other mountaineers of note, including the Pilkington brothers who were near neighbours in the leafy suburb of Alderley Edge. Their father had started life as a mechanic in a cotton mill but he rose rapidly, designing textile machinery and new factories, and became Lord Mayor of Manchester. He brought the boys up to be serious and competitive and concerned. They read Milton, Wordsworth and Tennyson and Samuel Smiles's *Self Help* and *Lives of the Engineers*. They went to church each Sunday, read the *Manchester Guardian* and were taken to Hallé Orchestra concerts but never to the theatre. In almost every possible way they epitomised the earnest, responsible, confident, thrusting spirit of the time.

The boys were introduced early to the pleasures of mountain rambling, in the Yorkshire dales, then further afield. In 1857 their father took them up Fairfield in the Lake District. They had holidays in North Wales, exploring the Glyders and the Carnedds. Then they graduated to Skye, the Alps, the Dolomites and the Jotenheimen in Norway. It was they, in 1884, who carried their friend Lawrence Pilkington down to Wasdale Head after his accident in Piers Ghyll. It was in honour of the eldest brother that the old Professor's Chimney near the top of Deep Ghyll on Scafell crag was named.

Their climbing was careful and skilful but their attitude to it was, by modern standards, astonishingly casual. They climbed not to make new routes but for the fun of exploring. They were as happy traversing across the cliffs or climbing down them as they were climbing up. They had descended the East Face of Tryfan but their route is not known since they left no record and even the date is doubtful. It seems to have been almost a point of honour among them neither to write nor talk about their exploits. Luckily their companions were not always so secretive.

In the summer of 1887 the three youngest brothers, Charles, Edward and Albert, and their cousin W. N. Tribe, climbed down from the top of Scafell Pinnacle. More than halfway down the cliff face they came to a narrow ledge and found they could descend no further. Edward built a cairn there, Hopkinson's Cairn, that was to act as a lure and a challenge to the best climbers for more than two decades.

Three months later Charles Hopkinson led the first attempt to climb up to the cairn from Lord's Rake. A friend of the family, Hermann Woolley (a wholesale chemist in Manchester whose occupation led to talk of black-balling from the Alpine Club until the Hopkinsons rose up in fraternal wrath and threatened to resign *en masse*), was on the holiday though not on the rope and it was almost certainly he who described the climb in the Visitors' Book:

> They succeeded in climbing 150 to 200 feet but were stopped by a steep slab of rock coated with ice. From this point, however, a good traverse was made into the first gully or chimney on the left. They forced their way up this gully to the top of the chimney. At the top there was a trough of ice about 30 feet long, surmounted by steep rock glazed with ice, which brought the party to a stop. They descended the chimney again ... considered one of the finest climbs the party had ever accomplished.

The route was not conquered for nearly twenty-five years, until June 1912, when there was no ice problem. It was done then by the leading climbers of the day, S. W. Herford and G. S. Sansom, who paid tribute to Charles Hopkinson's attempt as 'one of the finest in the history of rock climbing'.

Haskett Smith had been climbing on Pillar Rock in March 1887. Sixteen months later he was back at Wasdale Head, turning his attention to the complex and virtually unexplored Dow Crag near Coniston. There had been a little previous inspection. In 1886 he had climbed E Buttress by the Left-hand Route. In 1887 Cecil Slingsby climbed the easy pinnacle that bears his name, at the other, southern end of the cliffs. In July 1888 a formidable team – Haskett Smith, Slingsby, Geoffrey Hastings, Edward Hopkinson and two others – walked over to Dow Crag and, Hastings leading, climbed the Great Gully, a 400-foot route which is mostly scrambling but which involved over 100 feet of climbing at the Difficult (Hard) standard. The day afterwards, 15 July, the same party attacked Steep Ghyll on Scafell Crag and Slingsby led them to the top of High Man. About 100 feet up he had to stand on the shoulders of two of his companions to start the ascent of what is known to this day as Slingsby's Chimney. This route, too, is still graded Difficult (Hard).

Throughout the 1880s and '90s, while the leading climbers based themselves at the Wastwater Hotel and looked for new routes, the tradition of university reading parties was maintained at Row Farm. The Dean of Trinity College, Oxford, Charles Cannan, was the prime mover in this. Each Easter he invited his brighter classics students to Wasdale Head. Some of them went on to become famous, not as climbers but for their writing. C. E. Montague became a pillar of the *Manchester Guardian* in its mandarin days and the author of several books and short stories, including the climbing classic *In Hanging Garden Gully*. A. E. W. Mason went on to be a successful novelist, one of whose less notable works was a rock-climbing melodrama which he called *A Romance of Wastdale*. Another of Cannan's protégés was Arthur Quiller-Couch, a great teacher of literature in later years, who recalled his undergraduate days in *Memories and Opinions*. They stayed, he remembered, at the Tysons' farm where they experienced

> the monotony of sweet mountain mutton and Mr. Pendlebury's pudding (known to us as 'Pendlebags'), a delicious compound of farm milk, tapioca and raisins ... Mr. Pendlebury, though but a name to us then, was a Cambridge man famous alike as mathematician and mountaineer 'in which latter capacity' we sometimes challenged his prowess ... Our feats, of course, would not for a moment compare with the dizzy achievements of today's experts in rock work. But we 'did' a few things to our own considerable satisfaction – on the Pillar, Great Gable, and at points on the dangerous face of Scafell from Mickledore – and took some pride in doing these without aid of rope; returning at times by help of precipitous glissades to dinner, another hour of reading, final talk around the hearth, then sleep to the sound of many waterfalls near and distant.

It was at the beginning of January 1890 that R. C. Gilson presented the special Climbers' Book to the Wastwater Hotel. Almost immediately J. W. Robinson entered a lengthy account of snow climbing in wild weather in the gullies of Scafell, Pillar, Great End and Great Gable. Soon after there was an entry of historical importance:

> March 29–31 had some very interesting climbs with Professor Marshall's party. The ladies of the party accomplished several ascents believed to be records viz. the ascent of Deep Gill direct over both pitches, the Pulpit Rock, and also (by Miss Koecher) the Gable Needle. Miss Koecher also ascended the Deep Gill Pillar and all the ladies went up the Pillar by slab and notch descending by the west side. It may be noted that the tin box has apparently been blown off the Gable Needle.

This was the first ascent of the Needle by a woman. It took place on 31 March and Miss D. Koecher, who came from Manchester, was accompanied by three men, one of them called Otto Julius Koecher though it is not known whether he was her father or her brother. The leader of their party, though he was not on this climb, was Arthur Milnes Marshall, Professor of Zoology at Owens College, Manchester, and a Fellow of St John's, Cambridge.

There was another significant entry in the book that summer. It described an ascent of Scafell from Lord's Rake and concluded: 'This climb along the crags should never be attempted by any but experienced climbers – it may be added that a walking stick is a useless encumbrance ...' It is signed 'J. M. Archer Thomson, Clare College, Cambridge, and Bangor N.W.' Three years later Archer Thomson, classicist and schoolteacher, was to start the systematic exploration of climbing routes in Snowdonia.

As in all such works, the Climbers' Book was subject to misuse, facetious or malicious. An undated and unsigned entry reads. 'Pages 28–34 were formerly taken up by an irreverent and wholly irrelevant skit on a distinguished climber and contributor to this book – it has been considered appropriate to obliterate both the skit and its authors' names.'

The spring of 1891 saw the arrival of the next generation – 'April 18th 1891. O. G. Jones and W. E. Sumpner went up the Gable Needle by the cleft route'. Owen Glynne Jones was to dominate Lake District climbing in the mid-1890s as Haskett Smith had done in the previous decade. This ascent of Napes Needle was the start of a typically vigorous week's holiday at Wasdale Head during which he and his friends climbed on Pillar Rock, Scafell, Pavey Ark and Great Gable. On 4 April Jones led them up Piers Ghyll and the Climbers' Book account gave a hint of things to come:

> No difficulty is experienced in this little climb till the ledge is reached from which the Ash tree springs. Above this ledge projects the overhanging rock which offers such trouble to overcome directly. O.G.J. surmounted it by stretching over to the left hand side of the gully, and making an oblique spring to the small grass patch that seems to roof in the cleft, there being a firm hold for the right hand on the projecting rock. The rest of the party came up readily with the rope.

Jones was twenty-four years old. The son of a Welsh carpenter, he was born in Paddington, London, gained a First Class Honours degree in experimental physics at London University and got a job as physics master at the City of London School. He had done a little scrambling and climbing, usually alone, on Cader Idris. In May 1888 he had climbed the Cyfrwy Ridge there with no companion and no nails in his boots. With Dr Sumpner, a teaching colleague and electrical engineer, he had paid a brief visit to the Lake District in 1890 and climbed Pillar Rock. He was strong, especially in the arms, and bold and a lively writer:

> I have a vivid recollection of walking down the Strand one wet spring afternoon in 1891, oppressed with the commonplace of our London streets and the flatness of people and things in general, and crossing over by sheer force of habit to Spooner's photograph shop. In the centre of the window, and eclipsing to my perverted vision every other object around it, was a striking enlargement from the original half-plate of Dixon's Needle. [Professor Dixon had taken a photograph the year before to commemorate Miss Koecher's ascent.] I heard a by-stander at my elbow draw his friend's attention to the figures in the picture with the remark, 'Scott! What fools!' But that evening a copy of the Needle hung in my room; in a fortnight Easter had come round and I found myself on the top of the pinnacle.

In his book *Rock Climbing in the English Lake District* Jones gave this version
of the climb:

> Dr S. and I travelled down to Drigg one night. We breakfasted there early and
> walked the 12 miles to Wastdale, halting only for a plunge into cold Wastwater.
> After the manner of our kind we inquired at once for the Climbing Book, to learn
> the latest news from the Fells ... In the afternoon we worked our way up to the
> Napes. Being the more enthusiastic, I found the Needle first, and was breathless
> on the top of the crack when Dr S. arrived. He threw a rope up from the small
> platform and came after me. The crack up the face seemed difficult that first time;
> most people find it so ... From here the route for ten feet is directly up the right
> edge. The holds are not numerous, but good enough when the rocks are dry, and
> we found ourselves on a platform or shoulder that serves as an excellent take-off
> for the last struggle. The terrors of the crack often scare off people from the final
> piece. They almost did our little party. I found my watch-chain broken – some
> links still remain in the heart of the Needle – and my watch badly dented ... I
> took off my boots, for they had no nails, and, standing on the shoulders of Dr S.,
> stepped on to the right end of the ledge on which the top block rests. This corner
> is difficult to climb alone and exceedingly daring work, for the climber drags his
> body on to it over a sheer drop of a hundred feet, and feels no certainty of safety
> till he is up ... The disposition of one's centre of gravity must be carefully
> considered, and there is a sense of alternate peril and safety in inspiration and
> expiration. Once on the ledge the game was evidently in our hands, and traversing
> along to the left I found a rounded boss of rock 18 inches higher that offered good
> hold for both feet. Then the left was brought well up to a little ledge nearly an inch
> wide, the right hand gripped the right edge of the boulder, and on straightening out
> the top edge could be grasped. An arm pull was helped by sundry roughnesses for
> the toes and I sprawled half across the top triumphantly. In a couple of minutes
> Dr S. was by my side ... We descended without serious difficulty.

There is a mystery about this climb which will probably never be
resolved. Jones's account is completely at variance with that given by
the distinguished mountaineer and eminent scientist, Professor Norman
Collie:

> We had just climbed the Napes Needle and come down again. Two men who had
> been watching us then started up it. They got to the ledge underneath the top,
> but could get no further so I climbed up to help them. One of them got into the
> crack but could not find sufficient handhold around the corner and wanted to
> know if there was no other way up. Finally he got on my shoulders, and I pushed
> him up till he got a handhold on the top; he then scrambled up. I went down and
> began climbing the ridge behind the Needle, but I had to come down again and
> once more climb up the Needle for the last man could not get off the top; I got
> him off safely, and the man was Jones.

Norman Collie was thirty-two and already embarked on a career that
was to make him Professor of Organic Chemistry at University College,
London, and active in the discovery of the chemical element Neon and
the development of X-ray photography. He learned to love mountain
walking in his native Cairngorms and found rock climbing by chance
on a fishing holiday on Skye. Walking below the Cuillin in 1886 he had

seen two men, A. H. Stocker and A. G. Parker, making a new route up the face of Knight's Peak on Sgurr nan Gillean:

> Hundreds of feet above me, on what appeared to me to be rocks as steep as the walls of a house, they moved slowly backwards and forwards, but always getting higher, till they finally reached the summit. I knew nothing about climbing, and it seemed to me perfectly marvellous that human beings should be able to do such things.

He bought a rope immediately and became a dedicated mountaineer, particularly in his beloved Skye but also in Glencoe and on Ben Nevis, in the Alps and Norway, the Canadian Rockies, Lofoten, the Himalayas – and the Lake District.

Collie was tall and slim and strong. He had a quiet, intellectual manner, wore tweed suits and smoked a meerschaum pipe. When Cecil Slingsby took him to climb in Norway the locals were convinced he was Sherlock Holmes. He was a bachelor and something of a loner, a collector of *objets d'art* and a connoisseur of food and wine. Although he had an almost mystical attitude towards climbing, it is impossible to believe that his account of Jones's struggles on the Needle could be blamed on a lapse of memory. It seems more likely that it sprang from an urge to set the record straight and also from a sense of distaste at the new spirit Jones was bringing to the sport – brasher and louder, more swashbuckling.

Haskett Smith shared something of Collie's feeling. Many years later he wrote:

> Strangely different opinions have been held of Owen Glynne Jones and yet there is an element of truth and of falsehood in them all. He has been lauded not only as a climber but also as a good designer of climbs. He has been condemned as unsportsmanlike, conceited and self-centred ... Self-centred he undoubtedly was, but what was mistaken for conceit was his scientific determination to speak only of what he knew. He had studied his own physical powers as a chauffeur studies his car and for that reason he talked a good deal about himself.

But Jones's creative impact on Lake District climbing was not fully felt until the latter half of the 1890s and in the meantime the older generation notched up a series of notable achievements. The Climbers' Book records:

> The Pillar Low Man was climbed on Monday, July 27th, 1891, by a party of three consisting of Messrs. C. Slingsby, G. Hastings and W. P. Haskett Smith. The party left Seatoller at 10.40 and after crossing behind Fleetwith and descending Ennerdale some distance began the actual ascent of the Rock at 2 p.m.. After four hours of somewhat stiff climbing they reached the summit of the rock by way of the Low Man. The route is slightly complicated and would not be easily found by a stranger. Two men might do it but there ought to be three.

Haskett Smith led, which was as it should be since this was the route, the North Climb, that had nearly killed him nine years before. But he only completed the route by avoiding its chief difficulty, the bulging

Nose more than 300 feet up the cliff. From the ledge at the foot of the Nose he climbed down into Savage Gully and found easier ground leading to the top. He called it 'stooping to conquer'. The next problem was to find a more satisfactorily direct solution and this was done, in two different ways, within the next two years.

In October 1891 Cecil Slingsby took J. W. Robinson to introduce him to the new route. They followed Haskett Smith's line but two men who had come with them stayed on the ledge below the Nose and studied the rock above them. They were both experienced Alpine climbers. One was Godfrey Solly, a quiet and rather solemn solicitor from Merseyside who was later to become a Mayor and Freeman of Birkenhead. The other was Ellis Carr, a talented artist and musician who worked as a partner in his family's biscuit-making firm in Kendal. Nearly twenty years later Solly recalled:

> I got my hands onto a hold on what is now called the buttress, and thought it would go, but I was unroped and did not venture ... Ellis Carr from the other end noticed the crack that is now used in the Hand Traverse climb ... Carr then asked whether the traverse crack continued to the top of the wall, and, hearing that it did, he climbed up to it, and went along it. I followed and remember that I found it very difficult to get to the crack, having no one below to give me a shoulder up.

The Hand Traverse is now graded Severe (Hard).

Six months later, in April 1893, two other men who had Alpine experience but were recent recruits to rock climbing, S. B. Winser and Dr Joseph Collier, pioneered the route over the Nose itself. Dr Collier was a Manchester surgeon, an all-round athlete, lithe and tall with long arms and legs. Winser held him on a tight rope as he felt round the Nose until he found a hold for his left hand substantial enough to give him confidence to swing his left leg round and on to a concealed hold.

The outstanding climb of the period had been made one year earlier on the Napes face of Great Gable. On 16 April 1892 Godfrey Solly led Eagle's Nest Ridge Direct, the first route ever made which is now in the Very Severe category. Today's guide book describes it as 'A bold lead on good holds, with little protection'. When Solly led his three companions up it there was very little protection indeed and virtually none at all for the leader. This is how Solly described it:

> I went first and found it difficult enough to get to the little platform. When there I sat down to recover my breath with my back to the ridge and a leg dangling on each side. The party below made some uncomplimentary remark as to what I looked like perched up there, and I suggested that I was more like an eagle on its nest. That is, I fear, the very unromantic but truthful origin of the name. Those who have visited the spot know that no bird would ever build a nest on so wind-swept a ledge. Standing up, I found that the first steps of the next pitch were very difficult, and that the rock rather pushed one out. The others got out of the rope, and Slingsby, climbing up as far as possible, stood on a little step just below, with

his hands on the platform. I put one foot on his shoulder and as I climbed up, making room for him, he raised himself and finally stood on the platform, helping me as far as possible. I went on and climbed the second step. Then when I came to the third I did not like it. Retreat was even less inviting, and consultation with the others impracticable. After looking round, something of a hold for each hand and foot was discovered, and I went on, with the knowledge that even if one hand or foot slipped, all would be over. Just above this the difficult part ended.

The holds are small and sometimes sloping and the sense of exposure over a big drop is considerable. Colonel 'Rusty' Westmorland, who led it many times, used to say: 'I always think of Eagle's Nest Direct as a great test of one's serenity – if you keep calm you'll do it but if you start to panic you'll fall off.' Solly and his party were awed by what they had done:

> Talking over the climb afterwards, we felt unwilling to let it become known as a route to be followed upon our responsibility. Where one climber can go, another can follow, but we agreed that the margin of safety was so narrow that we did not wish anyone to follow in ignorance of the difficulties. We therefore left our advice on record that no one should climb it unless he had previously reconnoitred it with a rope from above.

The next day, 17 April, Solly climbed the much easier Eagle's Nest West Chimney, Slingsby led a large party up the Arrowhead Ridge on Gable, and Norman Collie discovered the Rowan Tree Gully route on Buckbarrow which is graded Severe (Mild).

The pace was quickening and the end of 1892 saw the conquest of Moss Ghyll, the hardest of the gullies on Scafell Crag. All previous attempts had been defeated at the point, 250 feet up, where the gully is blocked by a massive boulder. During the Christmas holiday Collie, Hastings and Robinson made a determined assault. First they inspected the crag above the blocked boulder to assure themselves that there was a climbable route there. Then, on Boxing Day, they launched their attack. They were soon in the cave below the boulder. Collie described what happened next in an article later published in the Scottish Mountaineering Club *Journal*:

> Over our heads the great rock roof stretched some distance over the ghyll. Our only chance was to traverse straight out along the side of the ghyll, till one was no longer over-shadowed by the roof above, and then, if possible, climb up the face of rock and traverse back again above the obstacle into the ghyll once more. This was easier to plan than to carry out; absolutely no hand-hold, and only one little projecting ledge jutting out about a quarter of an inch and about two inches long to stand on, and six or eight feet of the rock wall to be traversed. I was asked to try it. Accordingly, with great deliberation, I stretched out my foot and placed the edge of my toe on the ledge. Just as I was going to put my weight onto it, off slipped my toe, and if Hastings had not quickly jerked me back, I should instantly have been dangling on the end of the rope. But we were determined not to be beaten. Hastings' ice-axe was next brought into requisition, and what followed I have no doubt will be severely criticised by more orthodox mountaineers than

ourselves. As it was my suggestion I must take the blame. *Peccavi! I hacked a step in the rock* – and it was very hard work. But I should not advise anyone to try and do the same thing with an ordinary axe. Hastings' axe is an extraordinary one, and was none the worse for the experiment. I then stepped across the *mauvais pas*, clambered up the rock till I had reached a spot where a capital hitch could be got over a jutting piece of rock, and the rest of the party followed. We then climbed out of the ghyll on the left, up some interesting slabs of rock.

There is no record of anyone censuring the professor for his work with the ice axe and there have been many thousands since who have been happy to use 'the Collie step'.

Next day the same party made the first ascent of the Great Gully on the Wastwater Screes. Three days later Dr Joseph Collier led a party of five up Moss Ghyll, using the step and finding an alternative exit to the summit.

One of the most productive days in the rock-climbing story, certainly of the Scafell Crag story, came on 2 April 1893, when Charles Hopkinson and W. N. Tribe made the route that bears their names. Dr Collier led the route that bears his name and is graded Severe (Hard). He then led, from the rear, protecting the other two on the rope, the first descent of Moss Ghyll. Then he returned to the summit to join the assembled Hopkinsons and others in a mass reconnaissance of the face of the Pinnacle. The entry in the Climbers' Book says:

> April 2/93. J. Hopkinson, A. Hopkinson, A. Hopkinson, E. Hopkinson, S. Winser, J. Collier and A. M. Marshall climbed from the top of Deep Ghyll Pinnacle down the face of the rock to the cairn built by Dr. E. Hopkinson in 1887. Below the Low Man the rocks are very steep and considerable care is necessary; there are however no serious difficulties. About 20 feet above the cairn the party were joined by C. Hopkinson and W. Tribe who had climbed up the rock from Deep Ghyll. From the ledge in which the cairn is built J. Hopkinson descended, with the aid of the rope, to the broken rocks at the foot of the precipice, about 100 feet below the cairn, and traversed thence into Deep Ghyll. The rest of the party ascended without difficulty to the top of the Pinnacle by the route taken in the descent.

At the end of the month, on 29 April, Dr Collier led the first complete ascent of Piers Ghyll which was unusually dry.

Now the climbers were beginning to explore further afield. In September John Robinson and a friend from Lorton climbed up Raven Crag Gully on Glaramara; O. G. Jones led the two Lorton men up a couple of chimneys on High Stile, Buttermere; Jones and Robinson conquered the Gash Rock boulder in Langstrath, then made the first ascent of Sergeant Crag Gully. That Christmas there was a full house at the hotel and in the Climbers' Book Robinson drew attention to a promising outcrop on Great Gable:

> A short but interesting climb very suitable for an 'off day' may be found in the face of Kern Knotts, the knot of rocks between Sty Head and the Great Napes ...

It consists of two narrow vertical chimneys, the second being of exceptional severity.

On 26 December Jones led Robinson and W. H. Fowler up this route, Kern Knotts Chimney.

On the last day of the year there was a terrible accident. Professor Milnes Marshall had been climbing around Scafell Pinnacle with friends. While they set off up Deep Ghyll, he scrambled up the easy ground on the other side of Lord's Rake to photograph them. No one knows how it happened but he began to slide down the snow slope, plunged over a cliff and was killed.

The pages of the Climbers' Book for 1894 contain several entries by the most abrasive and outrageous of the early climbers, Aleister Crowley. The mention of his name, more than forty years after his death, can still rouse strong feelings. Crowley was the son of a rich man, a brewer, who was also a devoted member of the Plymouth Brethren. At the age of fourteen he rebelled against the rigidities of his father's faith and dedicated himself to the service of the Devil and the discomfiture of the pious and materialistic hypocrites and humbugs that he saw all around. He did this through black magic, experiments with drugs and sex, and by doing exactly as he pleased in such a whole-hearted way that, by the 1920s, he was a favourite target for the popular newspapers, reviled as 'the wickedest man in the world'. As an adolescent, growing up in Eastbourne in the early 1890s, he spent his time chasing 'flappers' on the front, playing chess or climbing the chalk cliffs of Beachy Head. Training on uncertain chalk gave him a style which he described in these words: 'One does not climb the cliffs. One hardly even crawls. Trickles or oozes would perhaps be the ideal verbs.'

But he was a good climber and an ingenious one. In 1893 he made a variation start to the Napes Needle climb. The next year, going up Kern Knotts Chimney, he carried a large stone and wedged it in to give him a foot hold. Making a direct route up Scafell from the crest of Mickledore, he wedged in an ice axe to afford a foot hold and wore rope-soled shoes 'which stick on mossy or smooth rock'. Years later, writing his *Confessions*, he said:

> I must admit that my methods were sometimes calculated to annoy; but I had no patience with the idiotic vanity of mediocrities. I took the Climbers' Record to be a serious compilation and never wrote in it without the fullest sense of responsibility. So when I found a solemn *Te Deum* being chanted on account of the fifth ascent of the Pillar Rock by a 'lady' I took my dog to the top and recorded 'first ascent by a St. Bernard bitch'.

He had a high regard for some of the Wasdale Head men – J. W. Robinson, Norman Collie, Geoffrey Hastings – but none at all for Owen Glynne Jones. They only climbed together once, in April 1895. That was enough for Crowley:

It was on Great Gable; the rocks were plastered with ice and a bitter wind was blowing. In such conditions one cannot rely on one's fingers. Our party proposed to descend the Oblique Chimney on the Ennerdale face. Robinson led the way down. The second man was a Pole named Lewkowitch, who was generally known as 'oils, fats and waxes' because of his expert knowledge of them and the personal illustration of their properties which he afforded. He had no experience of climbing, and weighed about 16 stone. It was up to me, as third man on the rope, to let him down slowly. I had, of course, to descend little by little, the rope being too short to allow me to lower him from the top. I soon found myself in the most difficult part of the chimney, very ill placed to manipulate a dangling ox. I looked up to Jones, the last man, to hold my rope so that I could give full attention to Lewkowitch, and saw to my horror that he was maintaining his equilibrium by a sort of savage war dance! He was hampered by a photographic apparatus which was strapped to his back. Robinson had urged him to lower it separately. As not Einstein nor the Blessed Virgin Mary was there to suspend the law of gravitation, I have no idea how we got to the bottom undamaged; but when we did, I promptly took off the rope and walked home, utterly disgusted with the vanity which had endangered the party.

Jones was undoubtedly a risk-taker. He had many falls and many escapes, some of them lucky, others due to clever threading of the rope behind blocked stones. He was at his best, people said, when the going was toughest – the rock growing steeper and the holds more sparse, when it was raining or snowing or getting dark. He was short-sighted: Haskett Smith said of one of his more testing routes, 'Of course, he never would have done it if he could have seen it.' He had courage and determination and depended chiefly not on neat footwork but on the strength of his arms and fingers. During term-time, when his work kept him in London, he exercised regularly with Indian clubs and climbed public buildings. In the billiard room at Wasdale Head he was the champion gymnast. If Haskett Smith was 'the father of rock climbing', Jones was the first of the climbing fanatics.

By this time he had formed the habit of spending the long summer holidays in the Alps. He climbed there with impressive vigour and stamina but he made no new routes and always hired local guides. This seems strange in the light of his achievements in only three years on the crags of Snowdonia and, particularly, the Lake District.

In 1894 Haskett Smith had brought out a small book, *Climbing in the British Isles: England.* It was the first book ever published on the subject. Illustrated by Ellis Carr's neat and accurate line drawings, it was factual, exhaustive and academic in style with flashes of the man's dry wit: Beachy Head, for example, he describes as 'a very fine bold chalk cliff, the first ascent of which is made about once in every two years, if we may believe all that we see in the papers'. But there is little in it to suggest why people climbed, or to indicate the spirit and special character of the new sport.

Owen Glynne Jones was planning a very different sort of book. He kept meticulous diaries of his climbing. Now he was thinking of working them up into a lively account of the state of the sport in the Lake District. It was primarily for this reason, perhaps, that he went to Keswick at Easter 1896 and made friends with George and Ashley Abraham, the sons of a professional photographer. Jones had met Ashley the previous Christmas at Wasdale Head so he knew that the brothers, 'the Keswick brothers' as they came to be called, were keen though inexperienced climbers. He also knew they were trained to work in the family business and he was almost certainly thinking in terms of photographic illustrations for his proposed book. George Abraham wrote later:

> My first meeting with Owen Glynne Jones was during the Easter holidays of 1896. Without any foreword he called on us in Keswick in the early hours of a beautiful April morning after a long journey from town. In two hours' time mutual keenness had promoted friendship, parental misgivings had been overcome, and we were off to Wastdale.

Jones was twenty-eight, George twenty-five and Ashley nineteen. They walked up Borrowdale and on to Sty Head where they met J. W. Robinson. They went round the corner to look at Kern Knotts. According to George's account, a dramatic confrontation ensued:

> Robinson held strong views about the unwisdom of making the ascent of Kern Knotts Crack. It was then unclimbed, and he urged that its conquest would lead to unjustifiable attempts by other less skilful climbers, and disaster would result. Jones disagreed. I remember Robinson's last 'Parthian shot' as he turned towards Borrowdale. 'Well, Jones', he said, smiling, 'if you climb that crack, I'll never speak to you again.'

In fact Jones had already reconnoitred the top part of the climb with the protection of a top rope. But he did not attempt it on this occasion. The three new-found friends walked on to the foot of the Napes crags and, within two hours, with Jones leading, climbed Eagle's Nest Direct, Napes Needle and the Arrowhead Ridge. George wrote:

> Yet that first day with Owen Glynne Jones meant much more than wrestling with those glorious crags, every muscle and sense alive to instant action as to method of rope and rock-work. Our real selves stood revealed, and a friendship was formed which proved in after years to be the most valuable possession in life.

On 20 April they made their first new route together, Scafell Pinnacle by Jones's Route from Deep Ghyll, now graded Severe (Mild). It was the first new route to be photographed in the making. When he came to write his book, Jones described the incident in detail:

> I could hear another climbing party finishing an ascent of the Pinnacle by the ordinary route, their voices echoing down the ghyll and cheering me with a sense of neighbourliness. My companions were holding an animated discussion below on the subject of photography. The light was excellent, and our positions most artistic. The cameras were left in the cave at the foot of the ghyll. Ashley was afraid I meant to go up without him; but his professional instinct got the better

of his desire to climb, and, shouting out to us to stay where we were for five minutes, he ran round to the high-level traverse on the other side of the ghyll, and down the Lord's Rake to the cavern. George had the tripod screw and could not hand it to his brother; so, asking me to hold him firmly with the rope, he practised throwing stones across the gully to the traverse. Then, tying the screw to a stone, he managed to project this over successfully. We composed our limbs to a photographic quiescence. Ashley had a splendid wide-angle lens, which, from his elevated position on the traverse opposite, could take in 400 feet of the cliff, showing the entire route to the summit. It was his turn to take the lead. 'Mr Jones! I can't see you, your clothes are so dark.' I apologized. 'Will you step out a foot or two from that hole?' I was in a cheerful mood and ready to oblige a friend, but the platform was scarcely two feet square, and to aquiesce was to step out a few hundred feet into Deep Ghyll. For this I had not made adequate preparation and told him so. 'Well, will you take off your coat?' That I could do with pleasure, and for a while his instructions were levelled at George. He was in an awkward place and was much cramped in ensuring safety, but Ashley was dissatisfied and insisted on his lifting the left leg. This gave him no foot-hold to speak of, but in the cause of photography he had been trained to manage without such ordinary aids ... The ghyll had become rather gloomy and we had a lengthy exposure. I was glad to slip on my jacket again and draw in the rope for George's ascent.

Ashley now tied on the rope and the climb resumed. Near the top they had to use combined operations:

> The other two men came up with a little assistance from the rope, and we cleared away the loose stones from our platform. It shelved badly downwards and offered no guarantee of safety in case I fell from the next vertical bit. But George sturdily rammed his brother close against the wall and intimated that the two would accept the responsibility of fielding me if necessary. I mounted their shoulders and reached up at arm's length to a sharp and firm edge of rock. A preliminary grind of my boot into a shoulder-blade and then a clear swing out on the arms, a desperate pull-up with knees and toes vainly seeking support, and at last the upper shelf was mounted...

Two days later, on the first fierce pitch of Collier's Climb on Scafell, Jones used the top of Ashley's head as a foot hold and higher up protected his progress with elaborate rope work:

> Casting around for some means of anchoring on my own rope, I saw that in the crack to my right a bunch of small stones were firmly jammed, and that daylight could be seen behind them ... The others were as yet unroped. Calling to them to let go the rope, I drew up the free end by my teeth and my 'unemployed' hand, and let it fall straight down the hole to them. If a fall occurred now in trying the next few feet I could only tumble three or four yards

There were some early climbers who felt that the only honourable way to make a new route was to walk to the foot of the cliff, look for a likely line and try it: if you failed, you could go elsewhere and try something else. Jones was not of this persuasion. When he set his heart on a route he was prepared to try again and again, using all the aids at his command. The story of Kern Knotts Crack is the best example.

It is only seventy feet high but it is almost vertical. Its current grading is Very Severe (Mild). The hardest part, the crux, occurs about thirty feet up where the crack widens out at what is called 'the sentry box'. Jones had already proved that the crack above this point could be climbed. On 23 April 1896 – the Abraham brothers had had to go back to work – he took two companions from the hotel and had another go. An unsigned note in the Climbers' Book says:

> ... The first ledge was reached from the face with the aid of a shoulder. For the last part of the ascent a rope was lowered from the great block at the top of the chimney. This was employed as a safeguard, but not used in any other way to help the climber. The ascent was a marvellous exhibition of strength and will.

One year later Jones returned and, with H. C. Bowen seconding, climbed the Crack without a top rope. This is now regarded as the true first ascent.

Wasdale Head was the undoubted vanguard of the sport at this time but the word was spreading and other craggy parts of Britain were becoming involved. Sometimes it was the work of local men – Archer Thomson in Snowdonia, J. W. Puttrell on Peak District gritstone, A. W. Andrews exploring the granite sea cliffs of Cornwall in his tennis shoes. Sometimes it was due to missionary work by the Lake District pioneers. In 1894 Professor Collie, Dr Collier, Geoffrey Hastings and Godfrey Solly made a creative expedition to Glencoe and Ben Nevis. At Easter 1897 Jones introduced the Abraham brothers to his native mountains. They stayed at Dolgelly and he took them up the Cyfrwy Ridge on Cader Idris and the Great Gully on Craig Cau. Then they transferred to the hotel at Pen-y-Gwryd, the headquarters of the Snowdonia men. Jones had to leave but the brothers stayed on to snatch one of the region's 'plum' routes, Slanting Gully on Lliwedd. Then, with Oscar Eckenstein, they made a careful but unsuccessful reconnaissance of the top pitch of the Devil's Kitchen. This was to cause trouble ten years later. Many of the North Wales men did not like to see their choice routes picked off by interlopers. Neither did they care for the rougher, more rumbustious approach of Jones and the Abrahams.

In 1897 Jones's book *Rock-Climbing in the English Lake District* was published. It was illustrated by thirty full-page photographs taken by the Abraham brothers, mostly by Ashley, and detailed diagrams of the chief crags, marking the climbers' routes. It is a big, handsome and informative book, crammed with information but also vividly personal, alive with the character of 'the Only Genuine Jones' as he called himself. In the 'Introduction', writing of the rock climber's motivations, he said:

> It satisfies many needs; the love of the beautiful in nature; the desire to exert oneself physically, which with strong men is a passionate craving that must find satisfaction somehow or other; the joy of conquest without any woe to the conquered; the prospect of continual increase in one's skill, and the hope that this

skill may partially neutralize the failing in strength that may come with advancing age or ill health.

The book gives many variations of the same theme. Here he is, for example, high above the Abraham brothers on Collier's Climb:

> I flung some loose stones far out into space, and could only just hear a faint clatter as they touched the scree. Now was the time to appreciate the joy of climbing, in perfect health, with perfect weather, and in a difficult place without danger, and I secretly laughed as I called to the others that the outlook was terribly bad and that our enterprise must be given up. But they also laughed, and told me to go higher and change my mind, for they knew by the tone that my temper was unruffled. A few feet more and I drew up to the platform.

And here he describes the climber's method when the going gets hard:

> Think of a foothold: double it. Put your whole weight on to it as you straighten out. Take away the hold you thought of, and you will find yourself wondering how you got there. In some such vague way are the very bad bits climbed, and while gasping for breath at the top the climber usually feels that it was the worst place he has ever been in.

In the 'Introduction' he gave a list of some sixty routes – he called them 'courses' – and divided them into four categories: Easy was for beginners and included Broad Stand, Cust's Gully and the Slab and Notch on Pillar; his Moderate routes included Deep Ghyll on Scafell and the Arrowhead Ridge on Gable; among his Difficult 'courses' he numbered Napes Needle and Collier's Climb; and there were nine routes in his final category, Exceptionally Severe, including Scafell Pinnacle from Deep Ghyll, Kern Knotts Crack and Eagle's Nest Direct. Jones was the first man to try to impose some order on the routes climbed, and subsequent generations must be grateful for that and particularly for the fact that he used an adjectival system. Other climbing areas have adopted numerical systems to indicate grades of difficulty, which might make for greater precision but are certainly harder for the uninitiated to grasp. The modern Lake District climbers' guide books use nearly twenty categories but they are still based on Jones's adjectives.

In his book Jones said: 'A line must be drawn somewhere to separate the possible from the impossible, and some try to draw it by their own experience.' That could stand for his epitaph.

Perhaps his most creative holiday of all was at Easter 1898. On 10 April he created Jones's Route on Dow Crag. Twelve days later he made two new routes on Scafell – Jones and Collier's Climb and Pisgah Buttress. But his most remarkable feat was his ascent, on 19 April, of Scafell Pinnacle by Jones's Route Direct from Lord's Rake. It is now graded Severe. It had been tried once before, by Charles Hopkinson who had been turned back by ice when 150 feet up.

The rock condition was much better when Jones and G. T. Walker started their assault but it was already late in the afternoon:

> In spite of the late hour I could not refrain from a trial trip ... At the point where
> the earlier party found the direct ascent barred by smooth ice on the wall, we had
> a council of war. It resulted in my throwing down my boots to Walker, and then
> crawling up 50 feet of, perhaps, the steepest and smoothest slabs to which I have
> ever entrusted myself. This brought me to a tiny corner where I essayed to haul
> in the rope attached to my companion. But he also had to remove his boots ...

Darkness fell with sixty feet of steep climbing still above them, including
the delicate 'Mantelshelf' move:

> Standing on Walker's shoulders I screwed myself out at the right-hand top corner
> of our waiting-room and started along a traverse across the right face of the nose.
> The toes of the feet were in a horizontal crack, the heels had no support, and the
> hands no grip. It was only by pressing the body close to the wall, which was
> fortunately a few degrees away from the perpendicular, and by sliding the feet
> along almost inch by inch, that the operation could be effected. It was with no
> small sense of relief that the end was reached in a few yards, and a narrow vertical
> fissure entered that gave easy access to the top of the nose. Then we put on our
> boots again and hurried.

The climb has been widely regarded as something of a breakthrough.
The Lakeland climbers were out of the gullies and chimneys with a
vengeance and moving, ever more boldly, on to the steep, airy faces of
the rock. Such places often feel more dangerous than the gullies because
the drop beneath the boots is more apparent, but they are, for that
reason, more exhilarating and the rock is not only drier but usually more
reliable.

Jones found this a few days later when he went to repeat his climb of
C Gully on the Screes. On the final pitch a lump of shattered rock broke
away under his weight and he was saved by the rope. George Abraham
gave a characteristically melodramatic account:

> 'Promise me you'll never climb C Gully on the Screes! It's a deadly place!' Such
> were the words spoken one Easter evening at Wasdale Head by my late friend,
> O. G. Jones. We had come back from a strenuous day on the Pillar Rock to find
> the famous enthusiast looking paler than the snows on the Pillar's peak. He was
> bruised and battered and had his arms in bandages; it was at last evident that the
> mountains had asserted their supremacy.

New names were now beginning to appear in the Climbers' Book.
W. R. Reade and W. P. McCulloch, young men from Blundellsands in
Lancashire who are better remembered for their Snowdonia climbing,
recorded the first ascent of the West Jordan Gully on Pillar Rock;
and the second ascent was made a month later by two brothers from
Windermere, R. W. and H. C. Broadrick, both of them fine athletes and
schoolteachers.

As usual Jones spent his summer holiday in the Alps but he was back
at Wasdale Head at Christmas with a new objective in mind, Walker's
Gully on Pillar Rock. It had been attempted many times and several
parties had reached the foot of the last short but ferocious pitch, only to

be defeated there. Jones was determined to do it but, for many days, the
weather was relentlessly discouraging, pouring rain in the valley, snow
and ice higher up. It was not until mid-day on 7 January 1899 that
Jones, George Abraham and A. E. Field, a classics teacher from Bedford,
were able to begin the climb. Despite icy rocks and ice-cold water pouring
down the gully bed, they made fast progress. Jones takes up the story:

> At last we came to the final obstacle, the limit of previous exploration. We had
> arrived at a little platform deep in the mountain, and three enormous boulders,
> one on top of the other, overhanging more and more near the top, had to be
> circumvented. There was no way behind them; the only possibility was to work
> up one side wall and climb past them. I flung off my boots and Norfolk jacket,
> expecting to give the second man a bad time standing on his shoulders in the take-
> off, and attempted to climb up a narrow fissure in the left wall. Unhappily it
> proved to be useless, and we were all supremely uncomfortable when it was
> discovered that I should have to descend again.
>
> Next the right wall was tried and I blessed the previous three months' mono-
> tonous training with heavy dumb-bells. The strain on the arms was excessive.
> Fortunately, there was no running water there, or the cold would have been
> unendurable. At the worst corner, by hanging on with the right hand, and with
> the left looping part of my rope through the recess at the side of the boulder, a
> good grip was improvised. Of natural holds there were none on that smooth, icy
> wall and the loop was a perfect boon. Even a perfect boon is hard to utilize when
> hands and toes are benumbed and all one's muscles are racked with prolonged
> tension. But the loop served its purpose, and after a few more struggles in the
> crack a ledge was reached from which it was evidently an easy scramble to the
> head of the gully.

The route is now graded Severe (Hard) but the climbers' guide book
warns that the 'last pitch may be found Very Severe by a short man'.
Jones was a short man.

At Easter he was back in North Wales. The Lake District book was
selling well and he planned a similar one for Snowdonia. The Abraham
brothers were also there together with Puttrell and F. W. Hill, a teaching
colleague of Jones's. Based on Ogwen, they discovered the Milestone
Buttress and climbed on the Idwal Slabs and Tryfan and Glyder Fawr.
Jones led two new routes near the Devil's Kitchen, Hanging Garden
Gully and the Devil's Staircase. He and the Abrahams were excitedly
planning a trip to Kanchenjunga, the world's third highest mountain,
at Christmas. But Jones was in the Alps that summer and on 28 August
his leading guide slipped near the top of the West Ridge of the *Dent
Blanche* and Jones and two other guides were pulled off by the rope. All
four men were killed.

Only a year before the eldest of the Hopkinson brothers, John, had
fallen while climbing the *Petit Dent de Veisivi*. Three of his children, a son
and two daughters, were roped to him. They were all killed.

4

Mixed Fortunes

1899–1914

THERE were more than one hundred fatal accidents in the Alps in the two years 1898 and 1899 and they brought a spate of press criticism, much of it ill-informed. But *The Echo*, reporting the death of Jones and his guides, commented with some prescience: 'The practice of roping together, supposed to be necessary for safety, is also obviously a source of extreme danger.'

Jones was thirty-two, at the height of his powers and still full of climbing enthusiasm. Had he lived, he would have gone on to do many more remarkable things. His death was a particularly hard blow to the Abraham brothers who loved him and described him as 'our indomitable leader'. But it did not stop them climbing. George had already led new routes and he now became a regular lead climber, with a new style. Where Jones had relied principally on the strength of his hands and arms, George Abraham used his hands to keep his body in balance and made his legs, as far as possible, do the hard lifting work. He was bandy – the family said 'he couldn't stop a pig in a blind alley' – and this made him a distinctive figure on the crags. He was also the most patient of men, prepared to stand a long time on small holds, working out the precise sequence of moves required to surmount the problem ahead. Punctilious about the nailing of his boots, he became an expert in placing the edge nails into the tiniest wrinkles in the rock surface and moving up with confidence on the hold. It was called 'balance climbing'. It was slower than Jones's method but also quieter and more elegant and much safer. George Abraham climbed for more than fifty years and there is no record of his ever falling.

In May 1900 the brothers went to the Western Highlands, carrying the news of the relief of Mafeking to Glencoe. They were accompanied by two men who had learned their climbing on Pennine gritstone, J. W. Puttrell who worked as a manager at Mappin and Webbs, the Sheffield silversmiths, and Professor E. A. Baker. The chief objective of the holiday was the Crowberry Ridge on Buachille Etive Mòr which some Scottish experts had pronounced impossible. They had to wait for good weather but when it came they did the climb, George Abraham leading, without great difficulty.

Back home, the brothers concentrated their attention on the Pillar Rock area. In October 1900 George led a large party up the Great Doup Buttress. Seven months later he created a much more interesting route, the New West on Pillar Rock itself.

They had tried it a few months earlier but had been driven off by hail and sleet. Now, on 26 May 1901, the weather was fine and the rock dry. George led with Ashley Abraham second, then Dr J. H. Wigner, then Claude Barton. About 140 feet up George was confronted with an exposed leftwards traverse:

> Though grassy, it was fairly continuous for several feet; but just before it reached the bottom of a long, steep chimney there was a gap about a yard wide. Footholds and hand-holds were at the time 'conspicuously absent', the latter being masked by vegetation, so one had to move along the ledge in a sitting position, with both feet dangling like useless ornaments over an absolutely sheer drop. However, the position was at least safe for those of a steady head until the break in the ledge was reached, and here the leader spent a long time in meditation before crossing this really awkward passage. There were two small hand-holds where the rock had broken away, but no foot-holds were available until the farther side of the gap could be touched by the left foot. To launch boldly out from the ledge, with such slender support for the hands only, needed both care and coolness, and everybody felt relieved when the leader swung himself safely across into the foot of the chimney ... A large fallen rock had become jammed in the foot of the vertical chimney, and this proved a good starting point for what is probably the most interesting part of the climb. Before proceeding the rope was belayed round this jammed stone; it would evidently prove an ideal safeguard in case of a slip. The leader found the second climber's shoulder of much assistance, and even his head was used as a step to bring hand-holds within reach. We wriggled slowly one by one up this narrow chimney for some 40 feet before a resting place could be found, and our direct passage was stopped by some enormous overhanging slabs.

George solved this problem by another exposed traverse, rightwards this time, to easier ground leading to the summit of High Man.

It was the first route created on the west face of the Rock since the day, seventy-five years before, when John Atkinson followed the Old West to become the first man on the summit. The four climbers hurried down, by an easier way, to the foot of their new climb. 'We lay on the rocks', George wrote, 'tasting all the joys of glorious conquest. Gazing up at those gigantic crags, which had not yielded without many anxious and exciting moments, we felt we had gained a new friend whom to know was to love.'

In the Climbers' Book at the Wastwater Hotel Dr Wigner wrote a detailed description and concluded:

> We can strongly recommend this route not only on account of the excellent and enjoyable climbing it affords but for the very fine situation through which it passes. We found it distinctly more interesting and probably decidedly more difficult than either route of the Ennerdale face. The rocks are almost uniformly excellent and we think this climb should become very popular.

It did. It became a 'classic' and remains popular to this day, not for any severity – it is only graded Difficult (Hard) – but for its variety, its sustained interest and the spectacular situations it affords. Geoffrey Winthrop Young wrote of the route's 'intricate sequence of traverses and verticals, each one presenting itself as a happy surprise when all progress seemed stopped'. The New West remained a great favourite of the Abraham brothers and was the last climb they did together, in 1936, still loyally wearing nailed boots.

A striking feature of the rock-climbing story in the Lake District, especially in the early days, was the high incidence of teams of brothers. The Haskett Smith brothers began it all in the early 1880s and were quickly joined by the massed Lancastrians, the Hopkinsons and Pilkingtons and Pendleburys. The tradition was upheld in the next decade by the Abrahams. By the turn of the century the fraternal outbreak had reached almost epidemic proportions.

The Barton brothers from Cambridge were creatively active on Overbeck, which is on the southern slopes of Yewbarrow, and on Dow Crag. In August 1901, with Claude Barton leading, they conquered the last great gully on Pillar Rock that remained unclimbed. Savage Gully had been thoroughly prospected by then but some of is harder pitches had only been done with the protection of the top rope. Now the route, still graded Very Severe (Mild), was done properly. A note in the Climbers' Book on 27 August said:

> ... It was not found necessary for the leader to run out more than 60 feet of rope at any part of the climb as the grassy ledges were found to be quite adequate to accommodate the second man who could have given assistance to the leader if called upon to do so ... the difficult traverse over the slabs, which starts from the foot of an overhanging chimney leading direct to the 'Strid', was made in stockinged feet and would be extremely risky in any other way ... The climb took about 2½ hours and is disappointing owing to the reliance that has so often to be placed on grassy tufts which are occasionally none too firm to stand on.

Other brotherly ropes of the period included P. S. and P. A. Thompson of Newcastle-upon-Tyne who did the route that bears their name on Scafell Crag in June 1900, and G. F. and A. J. Woodhouse who produced no fewer than five new routes on Dow Crag in August 1904 and two more a year later. Most impressive of all were the tall, athletic Broadrick brothers of Windermere who also concentrated their attention on Dow

Crag. In four years they climbed several new routes there including three that are still graded Severe (Hard): Broadrick's Route on B Buttress in 1899, the North Gully the year after and Broadrick's Crack in 1902.

Other new faces were beginning to appear at Wasdale Head.

In 1901 the genial landlord Dan Tyson left to run a pub in Eskdale and the Wastwater Hotel was taken over by J. Ritson Whiting. Anxious to retain close links with the climbing community, Whiting promptly hired the services of 'a first-class Dauphiné guide and climber'. This was Josef Gaspard who remained in regular attendance at the hotel, except for a few weeks each summer when he returned to the Alps, until the outbreak of the First World War. His charges were advertised as 'moderate' and his rock climbing was moderate, too. He was the first professional in Lake District rock climbing and, though he did not climb the hardest routes and made no new ones, he gave beginners a safe and entirely reliable introduction. It was his job each evening, while the climbers relaxed and variously enjoyed themselves, to scrape their boots clean and rub them with dubbin or sperm oil and bang in new nails when necessary.

One young man who was introduced to the sport in these years, though not by Gaspard, was Horace Westmorland. In 1901, when he was fifteen years old, his father – one of the Penrith brothers who had celebrated their sister's ascent of Pillar Rock in doggerel verse – took him up the Slab and Notch route, without bothering to use a rope. It was the start of a love affair with mountain adventure that was to last for seventy-five years.

Before long the young Westmorland – who came to be universally known by the nickname 'Rusty' – was climbing regularly. He was a natural athlete, small, compact and wiry, neat in movement, with good co-ordination and balance. The Abraham brothers took him on an Alpine holiday. He got a job on a survey team in the Canadian Rockies and did much exploring there. As a career officer in the Canadian army he was able to carry on climbing and also to become an outstanding skier and horseman. When he left the army in 1945 he returned to live in Threlkeld and set up the Lake District's first fully-organised mountain rescue team.

No one had a longer connection with the development of Lake District climbing. In Westmorland's earliest days he met Haskett Smith, J. W. Robinson and Geoffrey Hastings on the fells. It was through Godfrey Solly that he got his job in Canada. And he was still climbing when these men were distant memories. In 1951 he marked the fiftieth anniversary of his first ascent of Pillar Rock by leading a party up the North Climb, going over the Nose. Five years later, at the age of seventy, he led Eagle's Nest Ridge Direct. Five years after that he led the New West. And on his eighty-fifth birthday he made his final ascent of Pillar Rock, by the Old West route.

'What a brief span life is', he once wrote, 'when it is lightened by the joy of climbing.' But though the joy stayed with him into old age, he did not approve of the way the sport was changing in his later years:

> They're taking the adventure out of it. They're making it perfectly safe, as far as they can. They tell me they even boast about how many times they've fallen off. Well, I don't think that's very clever, do you? ... And all this brazen ironmongery, people going along clanking, hammering everything in, even taking electric drills (in America) and expanding bolts. They're not climbers, they're dockyard fitters. If you can't climb it just with the assistance of an ice axe and rope and boots, things that make no permanent mark on the mountain, then leave it alone. Leave the poor mountain alone.

Many of the pioneer rock climbers kept detailed diaries of their holiday adventures and achievements. The Barton brothers did and so did John Wilson Robinson, and their manuscript books are in the archives of the Fell and Rock Climbing Club. Owen Glynne Jones did, too, but his disappeared long ago. Another meticulous diarist was Herbert Vincent Reade, the squire of Ipsden in Oxfordshire and a distinguished civil servant who rose to be head of the Intelligence Department of H. M. Customs in London. One of his slim books, specially bound in black leather, survives to give an intriguing portrait of Wasdale Head at the turn of the century.

It opens with Reade's arrival at the Wastwater Hotel on 21 December 1899 to find only two other climbers in residence. Next day they were defeated by hard ice in the Central Gully on Great End. The day after, in Deep Ghyll, the leader fell and was held by the rope: '... part of the jerk was taken by the jammed stone', Reade noted. 'I had the rest.' On Christmas Day George Abraham led them up the South-east Gully on Great End and Reade commented that he 'was not very good on the snow and has no idea of cutting a step in ice, but his knowledge of the climb was needed at the pitches'. There were very few at the hotel but Reade was out climbing each day. The week's holiday cost him £6 17s 8d.

He was back at Wasdale Head the following Christmas, climbing on Scafell and Gable and Pillar Rock with the Abraham brothers, J. W. Puttrell and others.

The early summer of 1903 was blessed with an unusually long spell of fine weather and in June Reade spent a vigorous fortnight at Wasdale Head, his ninth visit there. He returned again in late September, by which time the weather had broken and the rocks were wet. He failed 'after three desperate efforts' to get above the niche on Kern Knotts Crack and was impressed by the way George Abraham 'threaded the rope behind a stone' in one of the gullies on Pike's Crag.

He spent Easter 1904 in Snowdonia, his second visit there, and wrote: 'Lliwedd looked imposing, and the whole group is finer than anything

I have seen in Cumberland, especially in its present snowy condition...
the climbing seems to me very inferior to that at Wasdale Head, both in
interest and difficulty. And the colouring of the hill scenery is not so fine.
But Snowdon is a much finer mountain than any in Cumberland.'

Some of the Wasdale Head men were beginning to say that the crags
of Scafell, Great Gable and Pillar Rock were virtually 'climbed out',
that all the possible routes had been done and the areas left untouched
were impossible. As almost invariably happens in the climbing story,
this was soon to be proved ludicrously pessimistic. Even so, many of
those who wanted to create new routes were finding new crags to do it
on.

Claude Benson found some short steep pitches on Castle Head on the
outskirts of Keswick and with Alex Goodall and F. Philipson, in the
summer of 1903, struggled up the rubble-strewn and vegetated gully on
Black Crag in Troutdale, Borrowdale. Goodall wrote:

> The presence of loose stones and wet grass made the scaling of it somewhat
> risky. In fact, when half-way up, I could not stir without dislodging something.
> Consequently Benson, who was below, had quite a lively and anxious time of it.
> As a matter of course, hard stones descending resulted in equally hard words
> ascending.

The most thorough explorations of the period, however, were those
undertaken in the Buttermere valley by a group of Manchester men,
members of the Rucksack Club. The leading figures were T. Craig who
had an extraordinarily long reach, Dr Sheldon, Tom Shaw and Lehmann
Oppenheimer, a lively writer and a talented artist, outstanding as a
designer of mosaics. Oppenheimer loved Buttermere for 'its beauty of
wood and water' and also for the quiet comforts of the Fish Hotel. In
his book *The Heart of Lakeland* he devoted a whole chapter to the siege
they laid to Stack Ghyll on Haystacks, a route which is graded Severe
and which was finally conquered, in slimy conditions, on New Year's
Eve 1900. Shaw led and solved the initial problem by climbing the wall
to the right, then traversing into the gully. The chimneys above gave
little trouble but then they came to the last pitch which was barred by
a big blocked boulder:

> Shaw tried back-and-foot work, but the cave was too wide. The walls were too
> clean cut for climbing on so he stood on Craig's shoulders, while I held the rope
> from the back of the cave. In this position he searched for some time for a handhold,
> and at last gave a spring, scraped up the top of the cave wall with his edge-nails
> and struggled out under the corner of the boulder. Craig scorned my shoulders
> and succeeded with great difficulty in backing up. I was not tall enough for this
> and had to accept the aid of the rope. 'Pull, Thomas lad', I heard Craig say, and
> before I knew what was happening I was off my feet and appeared round the
> corner of the boulder amidst roars of laughter.

In August 1903 Oppenheimer and Dr Sheldon made the first routes on Eagle Crag in Birkness Combe which Oppenheimer called 'the finest rock in the Buttermere valley'. One of these routes, Birkness Chimney, is still graded Severe (Hard). Oppenheimer's accounts make it clear that they approached their work with thoughtful care, reconnoitring the hard pitches on a top rope and going to great trouble to make sure the second man would, if necessary, be able to hold the leader's fall. At one point the second man rammed his ice axe up behind a blocked boulder so that the leader could reach the tip and use it as a hand hold.

The same group discovered another promising crag, Bowfell Buttress on the eastern flank of Bowfell mountain. The cliff had been spotted a few years earlier by Craig and Shaw. At Whitsun 1902 they were staying at Fell Foot in Little Langdale and on 24 May a party of five, with 160 feet of rope between them, went to see if the buttress could be climbed. Shaw led and Craig and Oppenheimer were on the rope. An entry in the Climbers' Book gives a detailed description of the route and makes it clear that the Manchester men, unlike many of their contemporaries, were using sensible belaying techniques:

> From the shelf at the top of the crack 90 feet up bare rough rocks lead to a grassy corner. There, there is a very convenient large block to which the second man should belay himself as the leader advances to the left, along a very exposed upward traverse with little handhold into a small rock corner. The best plan here is to climb to the right away from the corner and then to the left over the top of it, on to a grassy path sloping away to the left, beside a fine belaying pin . . .

It took them four and a half hours but, a few days later, Craig and Oppenheimer went back and did it in only two hours. Bowfell Buttress is a long climb by Lake District standards, 350 feet, and though it is only graded Difficult (Hard) the modern guide books warn that it soon becomes much harder in poor weather. Like the New West on Pillar Rock, it has established itself as a popular classic climb.

Across the Mickleden valley, on Gimmer Crag, another group of young men, from the Kendal area, were busy in these years. They included E. Rigby, who usually led, Andrew Sisson Thomson and Darwin Leighton. Among their routes were Gimmer Chimney and A Route and Rigby also led up the famous Amen Corner. Thomson wrote:

> As a matter of fact, only the leader actually climbed it; the others all came off and were hauled up ignominiously. The pitch is certainly not more than 15 feet in height, but presents difficulties quite unique. It is simply a right-angled corner with a narrow crack in the right-hand wall; but, and it is here that the 'shoe pinches', both walls overhang. It was ultimately climbed by gripping the edge of the crack with both hands, and *walking* up the left wall, the body being almost in a horizontal position. The strain on the arms is terrific . . .

The technique Thomson describes came to be known as 'layback'. Rubber-soled boots make it easier for the modern climber but the Corner still defeats many each year. Fortunately, they do not have to fall far and it is on to a grassy ledge.

The first of the leading pioneers of gritstone climbing in the Pennines, J. W. Puttrell, was already a familiar figure on the Lakeland crags. Now, in the fine weather of early summer 1903, another gritstone-trained man arrived at Wasdale Head to dispel all fears that the cliffs there were 'climbed out'.

Fred Botterill had grown up in Leeds and done much scrambling on the local outcrops. He was the first of a long, distinguished line of climbers, extending to the present day, whose experience of the rough but rounded holds of gritstone enabled them to make breakthrough routes on the volcanic rock of the Lake District. The advantages of such training were explaind by Clark and Pyatt in their book *Mountaineering in Britain*:

> In the first place, the gritstone rock had a roughness of texture and a lack of in-cut holds which encouraged the development of balance climbing rather than the push-and-pull methods which had previously been universal ... Secondly, the gritstone crags were low, averaging some 50 feet or so, and thereby allowing explorations to be made while safe-guarded by a top-rope from above; a method, usually impracticable on the greater cliffs, which gave greater scope for experiments and for the discovery of just where the border-line lay between the possible and the impossible.

Botterill had already had a few days' hard climbing with his friends, H. Williamson and J. E. Grant, when they walked up to Scafell Crag on the morning of 3 June to investigate the steep slabs to the left of Central Buttress. He tied one end of an 80-foot rope round his waist and inspected the crack where what is now known as Botterill's Slab meets the face of the buttress. He wore heavily nailed boots and carried an ice axe to clear away the masses of earth and grass. He got about fifteen feet up the crack but could get no further. So he climbed down again and moved twelve feet to his left to try the open face of the slab itself. The account that follows was published in the *Yorkshire Ramblers' Club Journal* later that year:

> Clearing away the moss from little cracks here and there I managed to climb slowly upwards for about 60 feet. The holds then dwindled down to little more than finger-end cracks. I looked about me and saw, some 12 feet higher, a little nest about a foot square covered with dried grass. Eight feet higher still was another nest and a traverse leading back to where the crack opened into a respectable chimney. If I could only reach hold of that first nest what remained would be comparatively easy. It seemed to be a more difficult thing than I had ever done but I was anxious to tackle it. Not wishing to part with the axe I seized it between my teeth and with my fingers in the best available cracks I advanced. I cannot tell with certainty how many holds there were; but I distinctly remember that when within two feet of the nest I had a good hold with my right hand on the face, and so ventured with my left to tear away the dried grass on the nest. However, the grass removed from the ledge, a nice little resting place was exposed –

painfully small, but level and quite safe. I scrambled on to it, but on account of the weight of the rope behind me, it was only with great care and some difficulty that I was able to turn round. At last I could sit down on the nest and look around me.

The view was glorious. I could see Scafell Pike and a party round the cairn. Far below was another group intent on watching our movements, a lady being amongst the party. I once read in a book on etiquette that a gentleman in whatever situation of life should never forget his manners towards the other sex, so I raised my hat, though I wonder if the author had ever dreamed of a situation like mine. I now discovered that our 80 feet of rope had quite run out and that my companions had already attached an additional 60 feet. Further, I began to wonder what had become of my axe, and concluded I must unthinkingly have placed it somewhere lower down. There it was, stuck in a little crack about five feet below me. Not knowing what was yet to come I felt I must recover it, so I lowered myself until I could reach it with my foot. I succeeded in balancing it on my boot, but in bringing it up it slipped and clattering on the rocks for a few feet took a final leap and stuck point downwards in the Rake's Progress. Standing up again I recommenced the ascent and climbed on to the second nest *à cheval*, from where, after a brief rest, I bgan to traverse back to the crack. This was sensational but perfectly safe. As usual I started with the wrong foot, and after taking two steps was obliged to go back. The next time I started with the left foot, then came the right, again the left, and lastly a long stride with the right, brought me into the chimney. The performance was what might have been called a *pas de quatre*. Complimentary sounds came from my companions below, but without stopping to acknowledge these I pulled myself up ten feet higher on to a good grass-covered ledge to the right of the crack, smaller but very similar to the Tennis Court Ledge of Moss Ghyll.

'How is it now?' my companions inquired. 'Excellent,' I replied, 'a good belaying pin and just room for three. Do you feel like following?' Without answering me the second man commenced the traverse to the chimney edge whilst I carefully belayed the rope. Up he came in splendid style and without stopping, taking only a quarter of the time it had taken me. He then untied and we threw down the 140 feet of rope to our third, who soon joined us. We hailed a climbing friend who was watching from the Progress and invited him to join us, but he very generously refused and said he would hover near lest we might not be able to advance further and so require the aid of a rope from above. We next christened our berth 'Coffin Ledge', built a cairn on it and left our names on a card.

Starting off again a long stride with the left foot took the leader back into the crack, and a stiff climb of 20 to 30 feet landed us all into an extraordinary chimney, which though only wide enough to comfortably admit the body sideways ran right into the crag for about 15 feet. Like the crack below it leaned to the left at an angle of 70 degrees or so. About 25 feet up, chock-stones and debris formed a roof, and suspended in the middle some six feet below it, were three more chock-stones. When the second man had joined me he exclaimed with astonishment; 'What a place. How can we get out?' 'Wait a bit,' I answered, although I could not then see a way. However, I went as far as I could into the crack and with restricted use of back and knee climbed upwards until the level of the suspended chock-stones was reached; from there a narrow ledge rendered these easily accessible. They were securely wedged and safe to stand upon. The ledge continued along out of the crack until the most outward chock-stone of the roof was within reach. This I seized with both hands, and a steady pull upwards landed me into the Puttrell Chimney of Keswick Brothers' Climb.

The modern guide books describe it as an 'amazing lead'. The Slab is relentlessly steep and the holds are small. Botterill had led the rope out for 120 feet before he found a ledge big enough to stop and bring up his companions. He had put in no protection. He and his friends had no doubt about the quality of their achievement. In the next two days, for purposes of comparison, they climbed Eagle's Nest Ridge Direct on Gable and Savage Gully on Pillar Rock, both of them graded Very Severe (Mild). They reckoned their route was harder than either and the gradings confirm their judgement. Botterill's Slab was the first route ever climbed to be graded Very Severe. Rock climbing was not only out of the gullies now but moving off the ridges and on to the open, airy slabs and walls. O. G. Jones had shown the way with his ascent of Scafell Pinnacle in 1898, Fred Botterill pushed it another big, bold step forward.

In twenty-one years of increasingly severe climbing not one roped climber had been killed in the Lake District. Within four months of Botterill's climb, however, that record was tragically shattered.

On Monday 21 September 1903 four young men made their way to the foot of Scafell Pinnacle, hoping to be the first to find a route from Lord's Rake to the cairn that Edward Hopkinson had built 165 feet up on the Pinnacle face sixteen years before. Their leader was Richard Broadrick, one of the three Windermere brothers and now a teacher at Fettes School in Edinburgh. The others – all climbers of some experience – were A. E. W. Garrett from Devonshire, Stanley Ridsdale of Kew Gardens, London, and Henry Jupp of Croydon. It was a wild, blustery day and the rock was wet in patches. The four men, all in their twenties, did one or two of the established routes on Scafell Crag in the morning, then returned to the foot of the cliff to lunch with another party, led by W. E. Webb. The *Manchester Guardian* report, telegraphed by a correspondent, takes up the story:

> After luncheon each party separated to make climbs at different points separated by about 200 yards. The ascent which the ill-fated party endeavoured to make was that of the Scawfell Pinnacle from Lord's Rake. This is recognized by climbers as the most difficult piece of ground on Scawfell ... The climb is what is known as a 'face climb'. It is in every way a very perilous task and was made all the greater on Monday by the strong gusts of wind which were prevalent on that day all up and down the valley. Mr Webb and his companions relinquished their task owing to the slippery state of the ground and the high wind and set out to return to the hotel. While retracing their steps they were horrified to find lying at the foot of the Pinnacle their four friends, from whom they had been but a short time separated. Mr Ridsdale alone was alive, but he was utterly unable to give any account of the accident. He was only able feebly to point towards his three friends as a direction to Mr Webb and his companions to attend to them first.

In fact, Ridsdale was able to give some account of what had happened before he died a few hours later: 'We were going up, Broadrick was first, Garrett second, myself third, and Jupp last. Then Broadrick and Garrett changed places. Broadrick said he was tired. Garrett slipped.' Other evidence – the scratches of nails on the rock – suggested that they were less than fifty feet below the Cairn when the accident occurred. Exactly how it happened will never be known. It may have been a sudden, violent gust of wind. It may have been a simple slip. One thing is clear; none of them was belayed, secured to the crag, or all four lives might have been saved.

Broadrick's body was taken home to Windermere for burial; the other three lie alongside each other in the little churchyard at Wasdale Head. In the rock at the foot of the pinnacle someone incised the date and the initials of those killed. For more than half a century this was to remain the worst accident in British climbing – until December 1954 when five climbers were killed on Ben Nevis.

The pioneer climbers knew their sport was dangerous. Many had had near misses themselves; roped climbers had been killed in Snowdonia; most of them had lost friends in the Alps. Even so, the Scafell accident came as a terrible shock. For several years the pace of advance in the Lake District faltered and the climbers turned their minds to the establishment of more adequate safety methods with the rope.

The new routes made over the next four years or so can be dealt with quickly. The Woodhouse brothers made seven on Dow Crag, at or around the Very Difficult standard, in 1904 and 1905. On 8 June 1906 Fred Botterill led the North-west Climb on Pillar Rock, graded Very Severe (Mild). With him were his brother Arthur (the first man to stand on his head on the top of Napes Needle), Lehmann Oppenheimer and Dr J. H. Taylor. The route had been closely inspected beforehand and they made full use of all available 'belaying pins'. In August 1907 A. G. Woodhead led the climb on Scafell Pinnacle that is still known by his name, building cairns on the ledges to indicate his route.

The chief event of these years, however, was not the making of any new routes but the creation, at last, of a club.

The men of the British middle class of the late Victorian and early Edwardian periods felt a powerful urge to come together in clubs. In the wake of the Alpine Club, several had been formed for mountaineers: the Cairngorm Club; the Scottish Mountaineering Club, created in 1889 to promote winter walking in the Highlands; soon after that, the Yorkshire Ramblers' Club emerged, interested in pot-holing as well as walking and scrambling in the dales: in 1897–8 the Climbers' Club evolved from C. E. Mathews's Society of Welsh Rabbits to bring together, in a more organised form, the men who climbed in Snowdonia; then came the Kyndwr Club (1900) for climbers and cavers of the Peak District; the Rucksack Club (1902) for the many Manchester enthusiasts; and the Wayfarers' Club (1906) for those in the Liverpool area. Many of the

Lake District pioneers were members of one or more of these associations. From time to time they discussed the possibility of a Lake District club – J. W. Robinson was talking about it, apparently, in the early 1880s. But, for whatever reason, nothing was done until 1906.

Towards the end of summer that year two Ulverston men, Edward Scantlebury and Alan Craig, talked further about the idea. At their instigation, a meeting was held in November in the Smoke Room of the Sun Hotel, Coniston, attended by climbers from Barrow-in-Furness and Kendal, at which it was agreed to send a prospectus for the club they proposed to all possibly interested parties. The response decided them to go ahead and form the Fell and Rock Climbing Club of the English Lake District.

At the beginning of 1907 Ashley Abraham accepted the office of Honorary President. John Robinson and George Seatree were to be Honorary Vice-Presidents. Other prominent pioneers were made Honorary Members, including Haskett Smith, Cecil Slingsby, Norman Collie and George Abraham. On 30 March the club's first General Meeting was held, very properly, at the Wastwater Hotel. By that time more than 100 members had enrolled. Rules were agreed and officers appointed: Scantlebury was to be the Secretary; Craig the Treasurer; G. F. Woodhouse and Scantlebury would edit the *Journal*.

Their stated aim was 'To encourage and foster under the safest and most helpful conditions the exhilarating exercise and sport of Fell Rambling and Rock Climbing in the Lake District'. To that end they proposed to hold regular weekend 'meets'; to establish club centres at Wasdale, Coniston, Langdale, Rosthwaite and Buttermere, where guide books, maps and ropes would be available and where Climbing Books would be kept for the recording of notable achievements and the making of suggestions; to establish a library and also a collection of photographs; and to publish an annual *Journal*.

The first *Journal* came out in early November, by which time the membership stood at 170. From this moment the annual *Journal* became, as it remains to this day, the prime source for any history of climbing in Lakeland. With very few exceptions, a *Journal* has been brought out every year since 1907. Generally speaking, standards have gradually improved – in presentation, in the breadth of mountaineering coverage, in the quality of photographs and in the quality of the writing. The modern writers tend to be more forcefully outspoken when dealing with controversial issues and the modern editors have been more ruthless in their rejections. They do not nowadays accept weakly romantic verses or the kind of feeble flights of fancy that occasionally marred the earlier issues. Yet from the start the publication established itself as a 'journal of record'. The 1907 edition, which sold for two shillings, described the formation of the club; reprinted in full C. N. Williamson's 1884 article in *All the Year Round*; carried a long article by Andrew Thomson about the climbing routes on Gimmer Crag and shorter pieces by Fred Botterill and A. G. Woodhead about their recent achievements; and included a reminiscence by John Wilson Robinson called *A Novice in the Snow*.

Sadly, the issue was dominated by Robinson for he had died in August 1907 after three months of suffering from what was referred to as 'an internal ailment'. He had been greatly loved and had introduced many to rock climbing by his lectures and articles and his unfailing willingness to lead beginners. Only the year before he had made his hundredth ascent of Pillar Rock. He was buried at the Friends' Meeting House at Pardshaw near Cockermouth in the quiet little cemetery that looks across the fields to the Buttermere fells. Almost certainly he would have been the next President of the club. A committee was formed, under the chairmanship of Haskett Smith, to devise a suitable memorial and the next year the Robinson Cairn was built at the end of his High Level path to Pillar Rock, with a bronze memorial tablet.

Although it was a latecomer to their ranks, the Fell and Rock was ahead of all the other clubs in one important respect. From the first it seems to have been taken for granted that women should be admitted to membership. The first list of members, issued in March 1907, numbered 104 and four of them were women, wives or daughters of members. By October that year there were eight women members.

There were few women climbers but, despite the fact that they were still hobbled by long heavy skirts, some of them were good. Miss Sophie Nicholls, who did most of her climbing in North Wales, became the first woman to lead Kern Knotts Crack in April 1899. In 1907, during a ten-day holiday at Wasdale, George Seatree's daughters, Annie and Evelyn, climbed more than fifteen routes, including Eagle's Nest Ridge Direct.

The Fell and Rock charged women a lower annual subscription than men – 3s 6d instead of 7s 6d – possibly because they were not expected to attend the annual dinner. Certainly, no women did attend the early dinners. But the minutes of the committee meeting on 20 November 1909 included this statement: 'The question of ladies being invited to the Annual Dinner was then discussed and it was decided that *They must be asked*.' They were and the next year, when the club held its fourth annual dinner at Coniston, there were fourteen women in the company. Godfrey Solly proposed the toast to 'The Ladies' and Mrs Ashley Abraham responded. It was widely welcomed as 'a unique feature in climbing annals – the presence of ladies at the Annual Dinner of a British Mountaineering Club'.

It remained a unique feature for many years. It was not until long after the end of the Second World War and also after years of fierce argument that the Alpine Club and the Climbers' Club admitted women to their ranks. Many other clubs – the Scottish Mountaineering and the

Yorkshire Ramblers', the Rucksack and the Wayfarers' – still do not.
In the Fell and Rock, however, the women members have increased,
gradually, both in numbers and in influence. In 1920 three women were
elected to the committee. Since 1927 the post of Librarian has been held
by four women in succession. Miss L. Kellett was Secretary from 1948
to 1958. In 1986 the club acquired a woman President, Hilary Moffat.
By that time well over a quarter of the club's 800 members were women.

The early issues of the *Journal* make it clear that the emphasis was
very much on safety. An editorial in the first volume said:

> Rock-climbing, though admittedly one of the most fascinating of pastimes, is
> fraught with very grave danger unless proper precautions are taken. So long as
> climbers will neglect these precautions and take unnecessary risks, persisting in
> their attempts to advance when they feel that it is beyond their power to do so,
> then, so long will there be such accidents.

The second issue (1908) included an article by C. H. Oliverson on the
proper usage of the rope. Photographs illustrated the tying of the two
recommended knots – the 'End Man's Knot' which was the bowline and
the 'Middle Man's Knot', a noose with two slip knots. He defines a belay
as 'anything upon which the rope can be hung in order to sustain a
weight'. The text and the photographs make it clear that they still
considered themselves belayed when the active rope was merely passed
around some convenient spike of rock. He does, however, insist that the
leader, when he reaches a ledge, should always anchor himself to the
rock before bringing up the second man. But the pictures show that the
leader did not pass the rope round his waist or over his shoulder but
merely held it in his hands. And some of his advice reads strangely now:
'Play the rope as though you were trying to tire out a whale with a piece
of string ... If a companion should slip do not jerk the rope suddenly,
gradually pull it in, even if quickly.'

In 1909, when there had been another fatal accident in Lakeland, a
stern resolution was submitted to the General Meeting. It listed twenty
'Exceptionally Severe Climbs' and recommended:

> That this Club strongly condemns any member who leads or attempts to lead up
> any of the exceptionally severe climbs given in the list below, without having
> previously climbed the difficult part of such course on the rope held from above,
> or behind a first-class cragsman who has previously led up such course.

During these years, for the first time, the momentum of the sport's
advance was being maintained in North Wales rather than in the Lake
District. Archer Thomson had led the first generation of rock exploration
there and now the charismatic figure of Geoffrey Winthrop Young, with
his parties at Pen-y-Pass, was carrying the tradition on and introducing
a brilliant group of young men, mostly from the ancient universities, to
the crags.

Although the two mountain regions are not far apart and many of the pioneers climbed regularly in both places, there was a marked difference in spirit between them. The Lake District men were practical and down-to-earth in their attitude to the sport. The North Wales men took, on the whole, a more romantic and mystical line. The Lake District men used phrases like 'a pretty little rock problem' and 'a veritable rock gymnasium': 'We had a rare little fight', one of them wrote, 'and voted it a piece of solid good business.' Geoffrey Young, on the other hand, said of Archer Thomson: 'He regarded his relations with the hills, and with what they yielded him of success, as a romantic trust.' Young took the same line and so did his disciples. Hugh Rose Pope described the climber in these words: 'He is alone with the hills, and stands like one initiated into a strange and beautiful mystery.' George Mallory said: 'A day well spent in the Alps is like some great symphony ... The spirit goes on a journey, just as does the body.'

In the Lake District, almost from the start, rock climbing had evolved as a partnership between local men such as Robinson and the Abrahams and their holiday visitors from the big cities. In Snowdonia, for a long time, it was exclusively for the visitors and some of them took a high line not only about their climbing but also about themselves. At the first annual dinner of the Climbers' Club, held in London, their President, C. E. Mathews, without any ironic intention, said of climbing: 'It is a sport that for some mysterious cause appeals mainly to the cultivated intellect. 'Arry or 'Arriet would never climb a hill.' And the second issue of the Climbers' Club *Journal*, published in 1899, included an anonymous article which complained that the sport was much further advanced in the Lake District and which then said:

> The frequenters of Pen-y-Gwryd have a strange aversion to putting their experiences into writing. Many of them resolutely decline to make even the shortest entry in the special book provided at the inn for the purpose; and although persistent inquiries will sometimes result in a verbal description being given, all efforts to obtain a detailed account are usually futile.

The Abraham brothers had run head-first into this obstructive secretiveness in the early years of the century. After the death of O. G. Jones they took up his task of producing a book, similar to his Lake District one, about *Rock Climbing in North Wales*. They acquired Jones's notes and spent many holidays in Snowdonia, climbing new routes and taking photographs. They were not made to feel welcome. In their introduction to the book, published in 1906, they said:

> We have always found it most difficult to obtain accurate information regarding the newer climbs. The authorities, with a few notable exceptions, were very reticent, and gave us but little practical encouragement. Often we have started out for a gully on the strength of an assurance that it was a well-known climb,

and almost as frequently have we encountered difficulties beyond what were anticipated. In many cases these gullies had not even been visited.

Many of the North Wales men resented the Abraham brothers' habit of snatching their choice routes, such as Monolith Crack on Cribin and Hawk's Nest Buttress on Glyder Fach. They also disliked their noisy, extrovert manner. But their strongest disapproval probably sprang from the fact that the Abrahams were known to be planning a book. The Snowdonia devotees feared that their special, spiritual relationship with the hills would be destroyed by the hordes of sensation-seekers, of insufficiently cultivated intellect, who would be attracted to the sanctum by vulgar publicity.

Among those who felt this most strongly was Oscar Eckenstein. He was a formidable figure, a pioneer of balance climbing and an inventive technician, in rope-craft and with crampons. He was one of the very few who could get along with Aleister Crowley. They climbed together in Mexico and the Himalayas. Crowley almost idolised him. He wrote of Eckenstein's 'almost fanatical objection to publicity'. It was this characteristic that led to heated scenes in the Climbers' Club when the Abrahams' book came out.

At the club's Annual General Meeting in 1907 Eckenstein introduced a resolution, the terms of which were not given in the club *Journal* but which led Ashley Abraham to express 'regret on the part of his brother and himself that what they had published had caused offence to Mr Eckenstein'.

In fact, the references to Eckenstein in the book are consistently flattering. The only passage that could have upset him was George Abraham's account of their attempt on the Devil's Kitchen in 1897 in which it is made clear that, because of the wetness of the rock, first Eckenstein and then George himself failed to climb the cracks below the final traverse. That was all. When Ashley apologised the resolution was withdrawn and the storm blew over. It had been, at best, a silly storm in a tiny tea-cup. But it revealed more than just the extent of Eckenstein's sensitivity. It sprang from real fears about the predictable effects on the sport of increasing publicity and encroaching professionalism.

Only a few years before, Oscar Wilde had written his famous line 'Yet each man kills the thing he loves', and there are scores of places – the Chamonix valley, the Cornish coast, countless Mediterranean fishing villages that are now concrete holiday jungles – to show the statement's truth in regard to tourism as well as to personal relationships. The early mountaineers went to the Alps and Norway and North Wales not just for physical exercise and adventure but because they afforded a completely different environment – dramatic landscapes, the testing challenges of an alien wilderness, the opportunity for communion and self-discovery in solitude. Many of them feared that all this would be destroyed – as, indeed, it has been in some areas – by the combined impact of widespread publicity and cheap transport.

But the current of history was running against them and the Abraham brothers went with the current. No one did more than they, in the first quarter of this century, to spread the word about climbing – through their photographs and postcards, Ashley's lantern lectures and George's many books. And they remained unrepentant. In one of his later books George wrote:

> The modern popularity of British rock climbing owes its inception either directly or indirectly to the life-work of Owen Glynne Jones. His favourite theory was that all men should climb, and they would be the better for it. This was in contradistinction to the somewhat dog-in-the-manger idea which then prevailed, that the joys of the mountain were only for men of liberal education and of the higher walks of life.

As George suggests, there was an element of snobbery in the quarrel too. The Abraham brothers were in trade. Their main income came from a retail shop in Keswick and now they were beginning to augment it with pictures and books about climbing. The spectre of professionalism loomed. Their critics felt that it went against the spirit of their noble holiday pastime to turn it to profit-making. It is shocking, perhaps, but not surprising that George had to wait till he was over eighty before he was admitted to membership of the Alpine Club. Ashley died before the offer came.

In the Lake District the creation of the Fell and Rock brought no outburst of new routes. In 1907 Oliverson, a Kendal man, created his Variation on Gimmer Crag, and Harry Lyon, another Kendal man, led his Lyon's Crawl which is still graded Severe (Mild) and one of the most popular routes on the cliff. In April 1908 Haskett Smith, at the age of forty-nine, made his last new route – Haskett Gully on the crags that enclose Mirklin Cove to the west of Pillar Rock. It was a climb in the old style, a long slimy gully with a few steep pitches, and Haskett Smith did it in his old style, chatting all the way up, chiefly – according to Oppenheimer – about the finer points of linguistics. George Mallory was at Wasdale Head that September and, with his Cambridge friend Geoffrey Keynes (brother of the great economist, Maynard), made two routes on Gable Crag.

In 1909 Fred Botterill gave himself a very long holiday. He acquired a gypsy caravan, called 'The Bertol', and transported it, by rail to Drigg and then by two-horse power, to Wasdale Head. Before the end of March he had settled there for nine months of country life and climbing. He described it, idyllically, in *The Log of Bertol*:

> March 28 ... Another day is spent in the Wood, ascending by one tree and descending by another – an old-fashiond feat. Another is trying a new buttress on the Napes. The weather is clearing and we are having one of life's greatest joys –

> meals in the open. We sit out in our pyjamas and eat our breakfast in the grateful
> warmth of the sun. How beautiful Gable looks – and the lake shimmering in the
> heat – Yewbarrow with a hundred hues...

He climbed the new route on Gable, Abbey Buttress, on 7 April with
his friend Jack de Vere Hazard (who later took part in the 1924 Everest
expedition). In May they saw the Brocken Spectre on Lingmell. In June
he found a new exit from Moss Ghyll, thirty feet to the right of Collier's,
and traversed round Napes Needle near but 'without touching' the top.
In July he wrote:

> The weeks become months and the summer slips away. People ask us if we do not
> tire of the mountains and if the holidays do not pall. We smile as we think of our
> active existence and tell them that as yet we have only touched the fringe of our
> life in the mountains, for we are in a busy world and live busy lives ...

Perhaps it was all too good to last. On 27 September Botterill went
up to the Napes crags with Thomas James Rennison, an experienced
climber who was keen to do Eagle's Nest Ridge Direct. Botterill led the
first pitch, then Rennison climbed up to him and, after a few moments'
rest, went on. The account in the Fell and Rock *Journal* said:

> It is necessary at first to climb slightly, perhaps three feet, to the left before going
> upwards. R. had gone to the left and advanced upwards about ten feet. His arms
> were both outstretched, his knees and toes occupying two parallel cracks. His feet
> would be within eight feet of B.'s head. He had not spoken since commencing,
> perhaps three minutes. He had not moved a limb for twenty seconds when ... he
> slipped ... all points of contact coming away simultaneously. He made no effort
> to save himself – uttered no cry – never turned his head – exactly like a man with
> palpitation.

Botterill had the rope 'belayed' over a nob of rock just above him. He
crouched to take the jerk and held tight. There was no time to take in
the slack and when the pull came the rope broke with a snap. Rennison
was killed outright. Botterill never climbed seriously again and it was a
great loss to the sport for he was, by all accounts, not only a cheerful
companion but the most stylish of movers, smooth and certain, rarely
hesitating, quick but never hurried.

The nature of the accident led to doubts about the method of 'belaying'
simply by passing the leader's rope over a notch of rock and hoping it
would reduce the length of a fall. The hemp ropes were not, by modern
standards, strong and the notches could be sharp. If the leader fell any
distance before the strain came, it was more than likely that the rope
would break.

Some new crags were being found. In October 1910 'Rusty' Westmorland led two of his cousins up the long broken ridge at the left end
of the face of Dove Crag near Ullswater. In May 1912 Harry Lyon
climbed Gillercombe Buttress. The eccentric Millican Dalton was exploring the climbs and caves of Doves' Nest on Glaramara which he described

as 'an excellent substitute for a pothole'. In May 1914 two Keswick men, Ralph Mayson, a professional photographer, and F. Mallinson climbed Troutdale Pinnacle on Borrowdale's Black Crag, another pre-First World War route that still retains its popularity.

But the great achievements of this period took place on the greatest of the original climbing grounds, Scafell Crag.

The leading figures were Siegfried Wedgwood Herford and George Samuel Sansom. In two short years of holiday climbing at Wasdale Head they carried the sport dramatically forward and re-established the Lake District's leadership.

Herford was born at Aberystwyth in 1891. His mother was German, which presumably explains his first Christian name, and his father was a Professor of English Literature at Manchester University. When he was eighteen Herford went to Manchester to study engineering, passing his Finals with First Class Honours in 1912. From then until the outbreak of the First World War he worked in aeronautical research at the Royal Aircraft Factory in Farnborough. He had been introduced to climbing in the Alps in 1907 and thereafter spent all his holidays in the mountains, the Dolomites, the Cuillin, the Lake District and North Wales. When he was a student in Manchester he regularly climbed on the nearby gritstone with Stanley Jeffcoat, tall and strongly-built, and John Laycock who wrote the first guide to Peak District climbing.

All accounts agree that Herford had a charming personality, sensitive and modest, 'a man of knightly qualities'. They also agree that on steep rock he was a climber of great thoughtfulness and steadiness and also of great daring. Geoffrey Young, writing about his parties at Pen-y-Pass, said:

> Herford, shapely, powerful, with a wind-blown fair mane and blue thoughtful eyes, scientific in his interests, a poet at heart, coming and going at our meetings with the spontaneousness of the wind, so near to the light and wonder of the hills in spirit that his feats upon their cliffs seemed only natural.

George Sansom was nearly three years older than Herford. Born in London, he was educated at Wellington College and University College, London, where he studied zoology. He had wide scientific skills – an eminent zoologist, he was also a pioneer of colour and stereo photography. In 1930 he was made a Fellow of his old college. Unlike Herford, he was almost exclusively a Lake District man in his climbing. 'In 1907', he wrote, 'at the age of nineteen, I first visited the Lake District and was charmed with the lovely scenery.' From then on he went to the Lakes whenever possible. Many years later, in 1974, he wrote:

> I had an intense love for Wasdale and the fells around it. The delightful view of it from the Napes Ridges often appeared to me during the long war years and I longed to see it again. As the poet expressed it: 'There are no hills like the Wasdale hills, when Spring comes up the dale'. My great love for Wasdale prevented me

from wishing to visit other regions, although my friends enthused about Skye, Scotland and Wales. I did climb in Wales for a few days but strangely enough I cannot recall a single day's climbing there that I really enjoyed. For some reason, which I do not understand, the Wasdale mountains were friendly whilst the Welsh ones seemed hostile.

He kept a diary of his early climbing years. In 1981, shortly after his death, one of his sons found it, lost behind a shelf of scientific books, and it was handsomely published. It gives a vivid picture of the delight that Sansom found on his Lakeland holidays and also of what it was like to climb on the crags around Wasdale Head immediately before the First World War.

In August 1908, staying with his mother in Keswick, he naturally gravitated to the Abrahams' photography shop where he told George he was longing to climb. He was promptly introduced to the youngest of the Abraham brothers, John, who whisked him off to Wasdale Head for a week's vigorous climbing on Great End, Great Gable, Scafell and Pillar Rock. George Sansom was hooked. He was back at the Wastwater Hotel for the New Year and back again in August 1909, climbing with Fred Botterill and Hazard and walking over to Seathwaite for 'tea at Mr. Dalton's camp in the pinewoods'. This was Millican Dalton, already adopting the outdoor life that was to make him so unmistakable and remarkable a Lakeland figure over the next four decades.

John Abraham was his usual companion and they climbed all the established routes, except the very hardest, in all weathers. They were often out for twelve hours at a time, returning by lantern light to play billiard fives. They liked to refresh themselves with a dip in the rivers and tarns, sometimes breaking the surface ice to get into the water. When the climbing was hard they took their boots off and climbed in stockinged feet. On 6 April 1910, John Abraham's twenty-first birthday, they went up to the Napes crags and Sansom led Arrowhead Ridge Direct, finding it 'very sensational'. They then went to the summit of Great Gable by a gully on the Westmorland crags. Then they descended Eagle's Nest Ridge. Sansom's diary takes up the story:

> We rested and ascended the Arête of the Needle from the platform and descended the western crack. We then ascended the Needle Ridge. From the top of the initial slab, I traversed to the left and ascended the Arête from that point. It is harder than the usual route but cleaner and much more enjoyable. We then descended Hell Gate and returned to Wasdale. As there were no others in the hotel, we dined in the Smoke Room and afterwards smoked till bed-time. Thus ended the best day's rock climbing I have ever had.

Sansom never lost his love of the Lake District and its climbing. Harry Griffin, who climbed with him in the early 1930s, recalled:

> George Sansom, at that time, was approaching middle-age – a shortish, slight, sun-burned man who smoked what looked like a home-made cherry-wood pipe

and seemed to eat a lot of barley sugar. In my naiveté I assumed this was to make his fingers stick more easily on sloping holds for George Basterfield had told me he used grapefruit for the same reason. Sansom was the neatest and quickest climber I have ever seen – his descent of Napes Needle looked more like a skilfully controlled slide – and he seemed to be able to avoid anything approaching strenuous exertion by his dexterous footwork. On the other hand his ascent to the crags was generally deliberately slow – to save energy, he would say ... To a raw youngster, half his age, he was always extremely kind, patient and generous and his examples of effortless climbing made everything seem easy.

It was John Laycock who introduced Herford and Sansom to each other early in 1912, launching a brief partnership that was to prove one of the most creative in the story of Lakeland climbing. Sansom was the ideas man, pointing out possible lines; Herford usually led. For all the boldness of their routes, they were impressively careful in their methods and thorough in their preparations.

Within days of meeting, in 1912, they made their first new route and wrote in the hotel Climbers' Book:

> *Kern Knotts. West Buttress.* What is believed to be a new climb was made on the steep buttress about 30 feet to the right of Kern Knotts West Chimney. 25 feet above, a magnificent belay is reached by a stiff pull up a knife edge of rock. An almost vertical V-shaped scoop is then entered and quitted with difficulty on the left a few feet higher up. Exposed ledges then lead to the platform at the top of the difficult pitch in the West chimney ... G. S. Sansom. S. W. Herford.

They went on to climb Eagle's Nest Ridge Direct and Abbey Ridge and considered their new route harder than either. Immediately beneath the above paragraph, Sansom added a footnote: 'Owing to the absence of much standing room at the belay on the above climb, it would seem advisable for the second man to lead up the first pitch, and thus allow the leader to continue directly upwards into the scoop.' Five days later they made a more impressive route, though the entry in the Climbers' Book was very brief: '*Scafell Pinnacle via Hopkinson's Cairn.* This climb was made today in stockinged feet. The 30 feet below the cairn was previously inspected with a rope from above. S. W. Herford.' This was the route the four young climbers had been attempting in September 1903 when they fell to their deaths. It is graded Severe and known, cumbrously, as Direct from Lord's Rake to Hopkinson's Cairn. The steep slab near the top is still called Herford's Slab.

They were back at Wasdale Head that summer. On 19 June Herford and Sansom made the first ascent of Scafell Pinnacle by Hopkinson's Gully. On 26 August Herford and W. B. Brunskill, a keen climber and a good photographer, found two variation routes on Napes Needle and then climbed down Eagle's Nest Ridge.

Many of the early climbers enjoyed climbing down as much as climbing up and believed that it improved their skill. It is one of the ways in which the early days were very different from the present, for nowadays you rarely see anyone deliberately descending a hard route – they abseil down or hurry round by some easy way to the bottom.

Climbing down is sometimes easier and sometimes harder than climbing up, depending on the nature of the route, but it is certainly different. It generally requires less muscular effort but makes greater demands on control and balance and nerve. You are more continuously aware of the drop below your feet; it is harder to see and assess the foot holds; care is needed to ensure that the force of gravity does not take over. Siegfried Herford, like many of his contemporaries and some of his immediate successors, did much descending and wrote a thoughtful article about it, 'The Doctrine of Descent', for the Fell and Rock Club *Journal*. It must have been a great reassurance, when making bold new routes, to know that he could, if necessary, safely reverse his steps.

The day after their descent of Eagle's Nest Ridge, Herford and Brunskill climbed Botterill's Slab. Although it was more than nine years since Fred Botterill had discovered the route, this was only its second ascent.

In September 1912 Herford and Sansom joined forces again, together with Brunskill, who liked to climb in bare feet, and H. B. Gibson who had done a lot of climbing with Sansom. Sansom had been studying the whole face of Scafell Crag and wrote to Herford early in the month to say he thought that a long and interesting route could be made across the face from right to left, from the top of the first pitch of Professor's Chimney to the top section of Collier's Climb.

Herford enjoyed traversing. He had already girdled Castle Naze in the Peak District and taken part, with Winthrop Young and George Mallory, in the impressive double-girdle of Lliwedd in Snowdonia, when they found their ways across the cliff from east to west, then climbed back again at a higher level. Herford wrote:

> This mode of progression is not without its special advantages. One has the novel feeling of working in a new dimension, and of seeing the rocks from a different point of view. Then there is ample scope for route-finding, and the climber has perforce to acquire the neglected art, essential to the explorer, of descending difficult rocks, and of using a doubled-rope down impossible places. Again, every member of the party has often an equal share of the responsibility, while the delights of leading are divided between the first and last man.

On 12 September the four men tramped up Brown Tongue 'with high hopes of completing the expedition that day', but they set off rather late and soon found they had underestimated the route-finding difficulties. Their usual order, though the route was so complex this sometimes changed, was Herford, then Sansom, then Brunskill taking photographs, then Gibson who used the double-rope for some of the steeper descents. At the crux of the climb, the traverse of the Central Buttress, they tried to force a horizontal route about 100 feet above Rake's Progress. Herford wrote:

The ledge on which we now stood is in many ways unique, and is certainly one of the most remarkable places in Cumberland. Above it, the wall of the Central Buttress rises sheer for several hundred feet, almost hopelessly smooth and steep, while there is a sufficiently precipitous drop down to Rake's Progress to make one move circumspectly. At the further end of the ledge Botterill's Slab shows its full height, and looks appallingly difficult. The part of the ledge where we now stood was comfortably broad – six feet or so – and we called it 'The Oval'. We now attempted to follow it to its extreme end, hoping thus to reach the foot of Botterill's Slab. I therefore moved along carefully to the left, for some distance without serious difficulty, but soon the width began to decrease until, at a point 25 feet short of the Slab, and 60 or 70 feet beyond the Oval, I felt that my balance was getting rather too delicate, and turned tail.

It was beginning to get dark as well, so they retreated. The next day it was raining so it was not until 14 September that they returned to complete their work. They made an early start – 8 am – but then wasted a lot of time prospecting for a way across Central Buttress at a much higher level. When they found the rock forcing them towards the summit slopes, they returned to the Oval ledge. There they discovered a traversing ledge, lower than the one Herford had tried two days before, and this led them to the foot of Botterill's Slab. Their route then took them halfway up the Slab, a descent to the Keswick Brothers' Climb and finally, by way of Collier's Climb, to the conclusion of their girdle traverse. Herford's judgement was that 'a party familiar with the route could finish it in from six to seven hours. There are about 1,600 feet of actual climbing, the standard of which is throughout remarkably high.'

Of course, the new route was promptly described in the Climbers' Book. Sixty years later Sansom recalled a small incident that is revealing about the spirit of the group:

> H. B. Gibson was writing up the account of it in the Wasdale book and he rightly put Herford's name first. Herford protested and said, 'Sansom planned the whole thing, he ought to come first'. I supported Gibson. At that time I would not have tried to lead Botterill's Slab. I was perhaps better at planning new routes but Herford was the bolder climber. He was essentially a very safe leader and I never felt any anxiety when he was climbing.

They were now concentrating their attention on an even more ambitious project, finding a route up the face of the Central Buttress, known to generations of climbers as C.B. They had started thinking about it almost as soon as they started climbing together. They had noticed the great flake of rock which leans out, overhanging at the top, from the face about one-third of the way up. They decided this was 'quite hopeless as a means of ascent' and investigated the grooves near Moss Ghyll. They found these too difficult. Sansom 'returned to Wasdale with the opinion that the Central Buttress would not go'.

In June 1913 they took a closer look at the Great Flake. Sansom wrote:

> The crack proper started some 30 feet above our grass ledge, the Oval, and

obviously could be reached without great difficulty. I ascended about 25 feet and found myself below a large bulge but the sight of the crack above was too much for me and Herford took my place and climbed to the foot of the crack. He also decided that to attempt to force it without knowledge as to what lay above would be unjustifiable.

Sansom had to leave soon after on a zoological expedition to Brazil, but Herford sent him a long letter, dated 16 July 1913, describing the climbing he had been doing with Jeffcoat and, in great detail, their thorough exploration of the upper part of the Central Buttress face. With a top rope Herford traversed across the top of the Great Flake and then climbed down it to the Oval:

> As you will understand, it is a very sensational place, as the greater part of one's body is hanging out over the flake. I now looked over into the crack and it certainly looked very bad; after Jeff had tied on an additional length of rope, I let myself down. There are no holds whatever inside the crack, and that jammed block near the top (which is quite firm, by the way) though forming quite a fair hold, forces one out unpleasantly.

In September Herford wrote again:

> You seem to be staying at Rio longer than you anticipated! To answer your questions about the C.B., I fancy the Flake Crack will turn out quite the severest thing you or I have ever tackled, but I am satisfied as to its feasibility.

They were reunited at Wasdale Head in April 1914, Herford and Sansom, Gibson and a new man, C. F. Holland. The weather was perfect. Holland later said it was 'the finest April I ever remember'.

On 19 April they approached the Great Flake from two directions, Herford and Gibson traversing out to it from above while the other two climbed up to the Oval. Firmly belayed, Gibson threw down a rope. Sansom tied himself on to the end, took his boots off and attacked the flake. He had a terrible struggle:

> My arms gave out long before the top was reached and a very considerable amount of pulling from Gibson was required before I joined him. Herford then tried the ascent on a rope and just succeeded in getting up without assistance. We thereupon decided to attempt the ascent in the orthodox manner ...

They had noticed that it was possible to thread the rope behind the blocked stone, wedged between the flake and the main wall. Sansom soaked the end of his rope in wet moss to make it stiff, passed it behind the boulder, tied on the end and descended to the Oval. Herford then tied on to the threaded rope and made two attempts to climb the flake. Both were repulsed. They were tired – Holland had been on the Oval for seven hours – and resolved to try again tomorrow.

They decided that combined tactics would be necessary so next morning when they gained the Oval one man went up to the chockstone and fixed a loop of rope around it. Two climbing ropes were passed through the loop. Herford tied on to one of them, Sansom the other. Herford then led off with Sansom climbing behind him:

> I followed Herford closely up the crack and hung on to the loop whilst he used my shoulders as footholds. Directly he vacated them, I climbed three feet higher and hung by my hands from the top of the chockstone whilst he again employed me as footholds which were most sorely needed at this point, for the crack is practically holdless and overhangs about 20 degrees. A minute or two of severe struggling and he reached the top to the great joy of all members of the party.

Protected by Herford's top rope, they all fought their way up the flake: 'We were well satisfied with the day's work but not with the climb, in as much as it left 150 feet of the Central Buttress still unclimbed.' Two days later, 22 April, 'greatly regretting Gibson's absence from the party', they returned to complete the job. Sansom led the delicate traverse up to the V-ledge; Herford led the rest of the way to the summit.

It had been a long siege and a complicated conquest but Central Buttress had been climbed. It demanded a new grade, Very Severe (Hard). The modern guide books describe it as 'a magnificent climb of unrelenting difficulty', and say it marks 'Probably the biggest single breakthrough in standard in the history of Lakeland climbing'. For twenty years or so it remained the hardest climb in the Lake District. Their account in the Climbers' Book ends with the words: 'This climb is extraordinarily exposed and steep and the climbing, though severe, very enjoyable.' It was the last entry made in the book for more than five years.

5

The Kelly Years
1914–1928

IN 1911 four young men, who had become friends at Eton and were now university students, set off to climb Walker's Gully on Pillar Rock. Their leader was by far the best climber among them, Hugh Rose Pope, reading classics at Oxford. The others were Nigel Madan, another Oxford classicist; Trevenen Huxley (brother of the famous biologist Julian and the even more famous novelist Aldous), who was reading mathematics and classics at Balliol; and one Cambridge man, Claude Elliott, who was studying history.

More than sixty years later, when he had retired to his house in Buttermere after a career that had made him Headmaster and then Provost of Eton, Sir Claude Elliott recalled the climb. It was a wild day and the rock was wet and finally Pope, exhausted by the long effort and drenched by the waterfall descending the gully, admitted defeat. They retreated and Elliott took the responsibility of being the last man, abseiling down where he could. As he swung down on the rope, a falling rock severed it and he fell, severely damaging a knee. 'That fall', he said, 'probably saved my life.' Within a few years nearly all his friends were dead. Pope was killed climbing in the Pyrenees, and Trevenen Huxley committed suicide in the summer of 1914. When the First World War began, Elliott's knee made him unfit for active service, and in that war more of his friends and contemporaries – Nigel Madan among them – died in the Flanders mud.

The war memorial on the summit of Great Gable gives the names of the twenty members of the Fell and Rock Climbing Club who were killed in the war. The list includes Lawrence Slingsby, who won the Military Cross as a Lieutenant in the King's Own Yorkshire Light Infantry and whose death in action in August 1917 broke his father Cecil's heart; F. S. Jeffcoat, another infantry subaltern who had been killed in April that year in an attack on the German trenches; Lehmann

88

Oppenheimer, the much-loved pioneer of Buttermere climbing, who had volunteered at the age of forty-seven 'to wipe out the ignominy of inheriting a German name', fought with distinction as a machine-gun officer in the Artists' Rifles, and died in hospital in November 1916 as the result of a poison gas attack; and Siegfried Herford, killed by an exploding rifle-grenade in January 1916. Herford had enlisted in the Sportsmen's Battalion of the Royal Fusiliers and, for some unknown reason, had not been commissioned. C. E. Montague, who was in the same battalion, wrote to his brother from the trenches near Béthune:

> I was grieved to hear last night that my oldest friend in my battalion was killed on Jan. 28. He was the only son of Harold Herford, our professor of English Literature at Manchester University. The son and I climbed together for years and he became in the end the finest rock climber in England. When I enlisted he came back from France, where he had been driving a motor ambulance at the front, and enlisted with us too. I can't feel sorry that he did, even now, but it is bad that such a magnificent fellow should be one of our first to go down. He was a sort of Norse giant, hugely tall and strong, blond, with tranquil blue eyes in which one could not imagine any expression of fear or despair as possible.

Montague's description is heightened, literally as well as metaphorically, for Herford was no more than six feet tall and not of gigantic build, but it indicates the powerful impact of Herford's personality. In one respect Montague understated the case. Herford had been the finest rock climber not just in England but in Britain.

Many other climbers, not members of the Fell and Rock, were killed in the war, and others were wounded. Geoffrey Winthrop Young, working with the Friends' Ambulance Unit, won the *Légion d'Honneur* in France and then Italian medals for valour before his left leg was shattered by an Austrian shell. C. F. Holland was awarded the Military Cross in France and was later severely wounded in the arm, though he returned to active climbing after the war and survived to work as an instructor at Frank Smythe's Commando Mountain Training School near Braemar in the Second World War.

Other losses came about more obliquely. John Laycock was so distressed at the deaths of so many climbing companions, Herford and Jeffcoat especially, that he left Britain when the war ended and devoted himself, with distinction, to the administrative service in Singapore. Fred Botterill, rejected on medical grounds by the Royal Flying Corps, worked in a munitions factory and died in 1920 of TNT poisoning.

The Fell and Rock Club continued to hold regular meets in the various valleys during the war and brought out its *Journal* annually. But, with most of the young men otherwise engaged, there was little creative activity on the crags. The only new routes of note were made on Dow Crag by D. G. Murray. He was a Flight-Lieutenant with the Royal Navy and, on sick leave in 1916, he prospected the crack that bears his name.

He returned on 24 April 1918 to complete the climb, graded Severe (Hard), though there must be some doubt about it as a pure ascent as he was protected on the long and delicate third pitch by a top rope composed of two 80-foot lengths tied together. The next day he led Murray's Route on B Buttress.

If little was happening on the crags, great things were hatching elsewhere. At Christmas 1914 a Manchester man paid a brief visit to the Lake District. He had done some climbing already, in North Wales and on the gritstone outcrops near his home in Levenshulme, but on this trip he confined himself to vigorous fell walking, mostly in pouring rain. Soon he was obsessed with climbing, spending every weekend on his local crags and going further afield, to Snowdonia and Skye, whenever possible. In August 1915, after completing the girdle traverse of Castle Naze, he noted in his climbing diary: 'It is much more difficult climbing in nailed boots than rubbers especially where holds are small and also necessitate high reach up of the foot.' By 1916 he was making new routes on gritstone. In September that year he spent ten days at Wasdale Head and climbed most of the classic routes on Scafell, Great Gable and Pillar Rock. From this moment on, the Lake District was his favourite place, Pillar Rock his favourite playground. His name was Harry Mills Kelly and he was to be the most formative influence on Lake District climbing for the next ten years and more.

H.M., as he was generally known, was an 'original', a strong and complex and, in some ways, a baffling personality. Those who met him in the 1920s and '30s retain vivid impressions. Ivan Waller says he was terrified of him: 'He seemed like a sergeant-major to me. Actually he wasn't like that but he did give the impression of being a terrific disciplinarian.' Harry Griffin also remembers him as a rather frightening figure with a brusque commanding manner. A. B. Hargreaves found him difficult: 'I didn't dislike him but I didn't really get on with him and a lot of others had the same experience. He and I somehow didn't hit it off. There was no antagonism – we were just different. He said to me once: "You have a very direct manner." Well, so had he.' Perhaps these two were too alike – both strong-minded Lancashire men, four-square and forthright and not much given to compromise – and perhaps Kelly did not like to see his own qualities reflected back at him from a younger man.

Certainly, there was another side to Kelly. He had many close climbing friends and he kept them for many years. He was a good and loyal club man – with the Rucksack and the Fell and Rock. His writings show a laconic wit and he had, by all accounts, a lively sense of fun and – with children – unlimited patience and gentleness. He was widely cultured, well read, ready to drive many miles for a Hallé concert and in later life a keen amateur artist. He loved cricket and, as a member of Lancashire CCC, was a regular spectator at Old Trafford.

Despite an age-gap of almost thirty years, Sid Cross got to know Kelly well and climbed with him in the 1930s: 'To be with Kelly meant descending a climb as well as ascending. A joy to watch, moving with neatness and balance, he would not hesitate to stand on the smallest of stances and acccept the most imaginary of belays. However serious our climbing, they were jolly occasions: he loved singing and to talk of music or cricket could mean his forgetting his luckless leader's rope.' And William Heaton Cooper, the artist who was recruited by Kelly to do the drawings for the new set of climbing guides in the 1930s, found him '... the least terrifying of giants, obviously full of enthusiasm yet very tentative – almost shy – about suggesting to an artist how he should draw'. Heaton Cooper recalls walking along the High Level Route to Pillar Rock one day, with Kelly and C. F. Holland and G. R. Speaker, when 'all three Olympian gods, without a word, swerved suddenly off to the right to a point below the track and stood in a semicircle looking down upon a spring that bubbled out from among the rocks and mosses and a variety of rare and lovely saxifrages. Wordlessly they returned again to the track having fulfilled their ancient and mysterious rite.'

For many years Kelly stayed at the farmhouse at Middle Row in Wasdale when he was visiting the Lake District. E. ('Ernie') Wood-Johnson, nearly sixty years later, recalled his first encounter with Kelly, when he went in for dinner on his first evening: 'At the far end sat H. M. Kelly, who was lord of all he surveyed at Middle Row. He was a very powerfully built man, about average height or perhaps a little less. He had a russet-red face adorned with a dark, upturned moustache, which made him look like a brigand out of *Carmen* – especially in hot weather when he wore a red handkerchief on his head. For some years he had done no paid work and lived for climbing, music and literature, in that order, I think.'

Kelly was a very private man, secretive about his personal life, and this has left intriguing mysteries.

Why, for example, did he play no part in the First World War? He was thirty when it started and, as far as is known, more than usually fit and strong. Perhaps there was some physical disability that did not affect his climbing but disqualified him from fighting – both the Abraham brothers were rejected on medical grounds, George for varicose veins, Ashley because he had had tuberculosis. This seems a likelier explanation than the alternative – that he was a conscientious objector. Kelly held firm views on many subjects and was not afraid to state them. He was a Socialist and an agnostic and no respecter of authority. But in the First World War pacifists who could claim no religious basis for their refusal to fight were sent to prison. Kelly was not. He spent the duration of the war living in Manchester and scrambling and climbing as much as he could.

Another, even greater mystery is what, if anything, he did for a living. No one seems to know. Some thought he might be a schoolteacher but the only evidence for that was his magisterial manner. Others suspected banking – Kelly was a good account-keeper, 'a great totter-up' as Sid Cross puts it. The Crosses knew him better than most but they say he never talked about his job, if he had one. They had an idea that perhaps he ran a small business, like a dairy, a milk round. When he died in 1980 at the age of 96 there were many obituaries – in *The Times* and the *Guardian* as well as in club journals – but none of them mentions work. Perhaps he had independent means. He could afford to run a car in the 1920s and had several holidays in the Alps and Norway and one trip to Russia. Even so, the pattern of his life as revealed in the climbing diaries – gritstone climbing every weekend – suggests that some responsibility kept him in Manchester on weekdays. We shall probably never know what it was.

He was a married man but there were no children and his wife, Emily, who was universally known as 'Pat', was almost as keen on climbing as he was and almost as good. She went with him on most of his weekends on the outcrops and many of his longer trips to the higher cliffs. When they climbed together he would lead but they often dispensed with the rope and soloed, climbing up and down, traversing, constantly exploring.

Kelly kept a meticulous diary of all his expeditions, from August Bank Holiday 1913 when he made his first climb, the North Ridge of Tryfan, to 4 July 1957 when Sid Cross led him along the Holly Tree Traverse on Raven Crag in Langdale. The diary is contained in two stout quarto-sized notebooks, each of them indexed. In his small, legible handwriting he gives the dates, his companions, the routes climbed, the conditions, sometimes the timings. When a new route was made he would write a spare, pitch-by-pitch description, very much in the manner he was to introduce in his guide books. If something unusual happened – they were avalanched out of Central Gully on Great End at Christmas 1916 – he would give a fuller account. But for the most part the diary is drily factual, giving only rare glimpses of the man's feelings.

It is clear, though, that Kelly loved everything about climbing – the fresh air and strenuous exercise, the planning and preparation of new routes, the stretching of nerve and muscle, companionship and conquest, the changing beauty of mountain landscape: 'The colouring of the hills was beautiful', he wrote in the Lake District on Boxing Day 1917. 'At times the reds were simply startling. Outlines of hills sank into heliotrope mist. Innumerable greens mixed up with browns and patches of snow here and there.'

As a rock climber he had all the vital qualities and one quality in unparalleled abundance, his appetite for the sport. His climbing diary is scrupulously, almost pedantically accurate. If it were not for that, some of the days he recounts would be hard to believe. On Sunday, 28 April 1918, he went to Laddow rocks in the Peak District and began climbing at 9.15 am. By 11.30 he had soloed up and then down twenty-five routes. He rested for half an hour, then led George Bower up and down six more climbs before taking an hour's break for lunch. The weather was fine but there was a very cold north wind blowing strongly. Resuming at 2.45 pm, Kelly soloed up and down seventeen more routes before knocking off for the day at about 5.30. He reckoned he had climbed a total of 4,310 feet.

Kelly climbed down almost as much as he climbed up and enjoyed it just as much. 'What a wonderful fillip the art of descending has given to rock climbing', he wrote. 'Even the old climbs have become new because of this.'

He has sometimes been praised as the man who introduced 'rubbers', cheap plimsolls, to rock climbing. He was certainly very quick to appreciate the greater adhesion they gave on dry rock, but he was not the first. At the beginning of the century A. W. Andrews was climbing Lliwedd 'in tennis shoes, the soles being as thin as possible to help the feel of the rock'. C. F. Holland, who had worn nailed boots on the first ascent of Central Buttress in 1914, discovered the value of rubber soles when climbing, on leave from Flanders, during the war. But it was undoubtedly Kelly's conversion to rubbers, together with the quality of the new routes he was soon making in them, that persuaded most climbers in the post-war period that this was where the future lay.

It did not persuade them all. Some of the old guard, the Abraham brothers among them, continued to climb exclusively in nailed boots; some new men, most notably Jim Birkett, were tackling ferociously difficult routes in nails more than thirty years after the end of the First World War. The pros and cons were debated endlessly. Some said rubbers were 'unfair to the rock', making adhesion too easy; others thought they encouraged sloppy climbing; many argued that, though rubbers had their uses, beginners should always wear nailed boots so that they learned the precise placing of the feet and the art of moving smoothly up without altering the angle of nail to rock. In the Fell and Rock *Journal* of 1924 J. H. Doughty countered this last point by saying that what beginners needed, above all, was confidence and balance, and these were not gained by making things artificially difficult: 'We do not set the young batsman to practise on a bad wicket, nor make the young bowler use a wet ball, because they must ultimately learn to cope with these unfavourable circumstances.' The next year R. S. T. Chorley fought back by arguing that you did not inculcate good habits by making things too easy: 'In fact, getting up easy rocks in rubbers is not climbing at all, and is as valueless from the point of view of learning our craft, as is playing French cricket with a tennis ball and racket to the would-be county cricketer.' But the advantages of rubbers, when the rock was dry, were clear and most of the new route-makers were soon using them most of the time. The grip they gave on the tiniest wrinkles or the merest bulges in the rock was immensely reassuring. If the rock was wet and the smooth-soled plimsolls proved too slippery you could always pull a pair of socks over them or revert to the nailed boots you wore to walk to the crag. Rubbers were much lighter than boots and much cheaper, too – you could get them in Woolworths, usually one size too small to give a tight fit, for about one shilling (5p) a pair. Today nobody climbs in nailed boots, except on the rare occasions when the film cameras want to show how men climbed in antediluvian days.

Emboldened by rubbers and also by the now-general employment of sensible belaying methods, the post-war generation brought about a rapid resurgence which immediately re-established the Lake District's leadership in the sport. For a long time nothing was climbed that was harder than Herford's pre-war Central Buttress, but within a very short space of time many new routes were made that fell only marginally short of that standard. It was the work of several men, many of them newcomers to the scene, but one man was predominant.

H. M. Kelly spent three weeks in the Lake District in the summer of 1919 and in that brief period he subjected the classic climbing-grounds – Scafell Crag, the Napes face of Great Gable and Pillar Rock – to the most searching exploration they had ever known.

In early June he and his wife had a week at Burnthwaite farm in Wasdale. On their first full day there, together with George Bower and R. E. W. Pritchard, they climbed up Botterill's Slab, then down the Keswick Brothers' Climb. Then Kelly led the Girdle Traverse Reverse, solving on the way the problem of 'the Bad Corner' leading to the foot of Jones's Arête. Next day they all went to Great Gable where they climbed Ling Chimney and then made what was probably the first descent of Eagle's Nest Ridge Direct, Kelly climbing last. They traversed round to Kern Knotts and Kelly attempted the Innominate Crack, which the great Herford himself had declared to be unjustifiable without the protection of a rope from above. Kelly said in his diary: 'Gave up after 15 feet. Gale of wind nearly blew me off.' Bad weather made serious climbing impossible for the next few days but on Friday the 13th they returned to Gable and Kelly led a new route, Tophet Bastion. One of the party – there were five altogether – described the route in the Climbing Book at the Wastwater Hotel, the first entry since the Central Buttress triumph in April 1914.

On the final day of the holiday they returned to Scafell Crag and Kelly noted in his diary:

> June 14. *Central Buttress, Scafell.* H. B. Gibson, Prior, Crawford and Self. Made an attempt on this. Did new start and reached Oval O.K. Gibson ascended Flake Crack to just below chockstone for thread, came back however. Self did same afterwards. No enthusiasm in party for threading rope so gave attempt up.

He was to return to C.B. but never to climb it. They spent the rest of the day exploring the Pinnacle Face and repeating the Girdle Traverse.

Kelly was back at Burnthwaite a few weeks later for a fortnight's holiday and this time his production was phenomenal. His companions were C. F. Holland, an experienced and expert deviser of new lines; C. G. Crawford, the unquenchable optimist; and a young Cambridge geologist, Noel Odell, who was to become famous five years later for his work on Mount Everest. On their first day, Sunday 27 July, they did no fewer than nine routes on Pillar Rock, up some and down others, devising variations here and there and often climbing unroped for greater speed. One of their descents was of the North Climb and Kelly, in his usual last-man position, climbed down over the Nose.

In the days that followed they spent many hours casting about on Scafell Crag and doing all the established routes (except C.B.). Kelly had a look one day at Moss Ghyll Grooves but retreated after getting up about fifty feet. Holland and Crawford both led new routes in the Steep Ghyll region.

Kelly conducted a determined investigation of the Kern Knotts area of Gable. On 5 August he made the first ascent of Kern Knotts Buttress, Very Severe (Hard). Two days later he created two more routes, the Central Climb and the Flake Climb, both of them graded Very Severe (Mild). His second on these climbs was R. E. W. Pritchard, so, on the final day of the holiday, he took Bower and Holland up to Kern Knotts to introduce them to his three discoveries. One of the later guide books said Kelly had converted Kern Knotts into 'a boulder problem'.

It was impressive but the great achievements of the holiday were made on the west face of Pillar Rock. It was nearly a century since the shepherd John Atkinson had first climbed the Rock by that side but since then only two more routes had been made, the Abraham brothers' New West in 1901 and Hugh Rose Pope's South-west Climb in 1911. Now, within a few days, the number of routes on the west face was more than doubled.

On 27 July Kelly had improved Pope's route by finding a harder and more direct finish. Two days later Holland led the Rib and Slab Climb which follows a superb line, graded Severe, to the left of the New West, and Kelly led his delightful, though not very difficult, West Wall Climb. On the same day they climbed down Walker's Gully and this may well have been its first descent.

On 9 August Kelly and Holland returned to Pillar for a remarkable day's climbing. To loosen up they climbed Savage Gully and descended the Old West. Then, with Kelly leading, they created the long climb that would be known for many years as Route 1. After that, they descended the Rib and Slab – a first descent – then prospected another possible line to the left of Route 1. But there was a problem. Holland's rubbers were collapsing – half the sole of each of them had separated from the upper – and his boots had been left at the foot of Savage Gully. More than fifty years later Kelly wrote:

> Naturally this caused us much concern but Holland, optimistic as ever, thought bare or stockinged feet would overcome the difficulty but after a few tentative efforts in this manner decided to go back to rubbers gleefully remarking he thought he had found a solution – this was that, when stepping up to a foothold he would jerk his knee upwards, causing the dangling flap of the shoe to do likewise and then quickly slap his foot down onto the hold.

The method worked until they were some 200 feet up the cliff. The route they had planned took Kelly up a greasy crack at the back of a chimney and he quickly realised that Holland would find it virtually impossible. So he traversed out to the right and found a little ledge where he could anchor himself.

> Holland was now out of my sight and after assuring him that I was reasonably comfortable and ready for him to join me he started to do so but after ascending a few feet of the chimney the flip-flap footholds apparently petered out and with a cry of 'I'm off' I found him, after a swing of several feet, added to by those of the shoulder belay gradually bringing his fall to a halt, grinning, but breathlessly peering up at me some distance below. It was from then on that calamity, not without its comic side, overtook us. I should mention here that it was customary for Holland to smoke a pipe whilst climbing and this day was no exception to his rule. What happened next was that as I was swinging the rope over a bulge, in order to have more direct contact with my partner, I knocked the pipe out of his mouth, distinctly and mournfully it tinkled its way down the crag until it reached the screes. Furthermore, after joining me and when I was bringing him up the remaining 30 feet or so to the top of the crag and our climb, I mis-manipulated the rope again and in doing so disturbed a small stone which after impact drew blood from Holland's forehead and nose.

According to Kelly's account, Holland submitted him to a barrage of articulate abuse, then lapsed into a brooding silence which persisted while they descended the Slab and Notch, collected their boots and rucksacks and made their way back to Wasdale:

> ... as we neared Burnthwaite Farm, our headquarters, he shattered the silence by exclaiming, 'Kelly, if you want names for those climbs we've done today, I've got a couple!' Relieved at this relaxation of the tension between us I gladly responded by asking what they were and got the significant reply – 'SODOM AND GOMORRAH!

Those are the names by which the routes, both Very Severe, are known today but for many years they were felt to be too strong for general circulation. It was not until the 1968 edition of the Pillar guide book came out, nearly half a century later, that Routes 1 and 2 were officially accorded the names that Holland had given them on the day of their discovery.

Although Kelly was the chief figure, he was by no means the only important one. It is surprising, in view of the heavy wartime casualties, how many lead climbers emerged in the Lake District the moment the war was over.

The first to make his mark was George Bower, a short, stocky York-shireman who had learned on gritstone and developed his skills on the bigger cliffs of Lakeland when he was sent to work at Vickers, the ship-builders at Barrow-in-Furness, during the war. His job was designing mines and torpedoes. He was a mathematician and engineer and liked to bring the scientific approach to bear on climbing techniques. He experimented with footwear, knots, methods of belaying: 'It is no use', he wrote, 'the second passing the leader's rope round a rock belay, for, should the leader "come off"', on steep, open rocks, the rope will assuredly break. The correct method, it cannot be too strongly urged, is for the second to belay himself to the rocks with his own end of the leader's rope and to pass the latter over his shoulder, controlling it with his two hands. The shock of the leader's fall is than taken up gradually ...' Bower was the first to advocate the use of much thinner and lighter 'line' for the leader's rope, instead of the customary thick hemp. On a long run-out the weight of the thicker rope acted as a drag. The 'line' was strong enough to hold the second man, so long as he was being given a tight rope from above, and would enable the leader to fix anchor belays on notches of rock that were too small to accommodate the rope.

Bower was quiet-mannered and utterly reliable. Ivan Waller says: 'He was one of the most solid bundles of toughness I have ever known. His head was round like a football with close-cropped hair and bright twinkling eyes and a smile bursting with humour, with an array of shining gold teeth.' At the end of May 1919 Bower launched the year's spate of achievements when he led D Route on Gimmer Crag which is short, only 100 feet, but full of interest. A later Langdale guide book said of him: 'His ascents of "D" on Gimmer and Crescent Slabs on Pavey Ark advanced Langdale climbing by almost one full stage in severity.' In 1920 he led Bower's Climb on Esk Buttress, which is Severe (Hard), and the year after, on 9 April, he led the first ascent of the Innominate Crack on Kern Knotts which is graded Very Severe and, although only sixty feet, is both steep and delicate. It was a formidable undertaking in the days before running belays.

Bower's second on Innominate Crack was another new man, a school-teacher from the North-east called Bentley Beetham. In 1922, together with another teacher called C. D. Frankland who had learned to climb on his local gritstone crags at Almscliff and Ilkley, Beetham discovered Shepherd's Crag in Borrowdale and made one route on it.

As a rock climber, Frankland was in Kelly's class. It was he, with Beetham in support, who, on 20 August 1921, made the second ascent of Central Buttress. By coincidence Kelly and Bower walked up to Scafell Crag on the same day with the same objective in mind. Kelly's diary says: 'Found Frankland and Beetham already on the job.' So they went elsewhere and left the first-comers to it. Beetham's account, in the Fell and Rock *Journal*, makes it clear that they used methods similar to those employed by Herford and Sansom on the Great Flake. They threaded a rope round the chockstone. Frankland then spent more than half an hour struggling, in vain, to climb the overhanging crack above. They retreated to the foot of Deep Ghyll for lunch and a rest, then returned to the Oval where Beetham proposed that he should go up to the jammed stone and secure himself there so that he could assist Frankland's ascent:

> With the ropes already 'in situ' this was an easy matter, and in ten minutes the required lump of flesh was dangling like a pendant, free but perfectly secure, immediately beneath the jammed stone. All my limbs were then quite free to form steps wherever wanted, and Frankland came quickly up on the other rope. First he stood on my left thigh, held horizontally, and braced into a firm strut by both arms, then upon the shoulders, next upon the head, a final step or rather stay being afforded by the upturned palms of both hands. The corner of the horizontal edge of the flake could now just be reached and by a strong arm pull he was up in a moment . . . Above the Flake we found Bower and Kelly, who were prospecting downwards; they joined us, and we finished the remainder of the climb together.

Four years later Frankland, whose favourite saying was 'The difficulties are only mental', led C.B. again to become the first man to do it twice. His companion this time was a remarkable young woman, Mabel Barker, the first woman to climb the route. Frankland secured himself to the chockstone to give her a hand as she clambered over him, and then squirmed up, half inside the flake, to grasp the top edge.

These two climbed together a lot. In August 1926 they traversed the Cuillin Ridge in Skye, she being the first woman to do so. In July the following year he was leading her up Chantrey Buttress on Gable, an easy route by his standards, when a spike he was grasping with both hands came away suddenly. He toppled backwards and fell. Miss Barker succeeded in holding the rope and arresting his fall but in the course of it he had smashed his head on the rock and he died soon after, to be buried in the churchyard at Wasdale Head.

Mabel Barker was a spirited woman. She went on climbing for many more years, made many new friends, and introduced scores of children – she ran a school at Caldbeck – to fell walking and rock climbing. But she never married, and those who knew her best said she was never quite the same after Frankland's death.

While Frankland and Kelly operated mostly on the central crags, another innovative group was hard at work to the south. In September 1919 a Barrow man, J. I. Roper, led a breakthrough climb on Dow Crag, the Great Central. George Bower was his second and Roper wrote:

> The get-away from the 'Bandstand' can be facilitated by the second man holding the leader's foot on a tiny knob of rock, until a very unsatisfactory finger hold is grasped and passed quickly, as the vertical character of the rock gives the body and feet no effective purchase ... Rubber shoes must be used.

The Great Central Route is graded Very Severe and ten months after making it Roper led a shorter but harder route, Black Wall. The climb is only 110 feet but the wall is very steep, overhanging at one point. Roper's second on this occasion, George Basterfield, said it was virtually impossible to offer the leader any effective protection.

The Barrow men formed themselves into a small, informal and very vigorous group. They went climbing every weekend, usually on Dow Crag. They called themselves 'the Yewdale Vagabonds' because they stayed regularly at Rosemary Cottage in Low Yewdale. Many of them were fervent Socialists – 'Joe' Roper was a member of the Barrow Independent Labour Party, studied economics at Ruskin College, Oxford, and later dedicated himself to his job with the Workers' Educational Association. Their central figure for many years was George Basterfield.

He is another of those men who seems to have been liked by everyone – a big, generous, warm-hearted man, who loved to tell stories in the Cumberland dialect and sing his own songs. No musician, he could only pick out the tune on the piano with one finger, but he wrote many songs and some of them were published. The words of one of them go:

> A cragsman am I, and I crave for the gladness
> That beats in my heart when I breast the green hills,
> And view on the skyline the scene of my madness,
> The crag on the height, where my happiness spills.
> Ruck, rags and rope are the signs of the calling,
> Skies may be silver, or skies may be grey,
> O'er moorland and mountain my footsteps are falling,
> And no one to question my vagabond way.

Basterfield was a grocer by trade and active in public life, a JP and twice the Mayor of Barrow. His daughter married George Bower. He was a great club man, joining the Fell and Rock in 1915 and becoming its President in 1930–31. He climbed occasionally in the Alps but the mountains on his doorstep were the ones he loved. He knew them well and he knew a lot about them, especially about their wildlife. There was nothing he liked better than introducing enthusiastic young men to the delights of fell walking and climbing.

As a climber he was strong and steady. The only serious accident he had was not his fault. He was paying out the rope for his leader, A. B. Reynolds, on Tower Buttress, Ben Nevis, when Reynolds fell off and shot past him.

He managed to hold him and called down: 'Are you all right?'

'Yes. I landed like a fairy.'

'O.K. Come on up.'

Then Basterfield looked at his hands: 'Christ Almighty! I've lost me thumb!' As the rope came down it had wrapped itself round his thumb and when the strain came it nipped the top off.

But his appetite for climbing was unaffected. He retired early so he could spend more of his time in the hills. He liked company but he often climbed alone. It was said that he could do intermediate Gully on Dow Crag, which is 170 feet and graded Severe (Hard), in $7\frac{1}{2}$ minutes. Well into his sixties he was soloing Napes Needle.

One of Basterfield's Barrow protégés was a strange, introverted man, H. S. ('Bert') Gross. He was employed as a draughtsman at Vickers. Although it was said that his health had been seriously undermined by life in the trenches during the war, he was, for a brief period, a formidable climber. At Easter 1922, together with Basterfield and Bower, he began a prolonged and detailed examination of Dow Crag, working out the best route for a girdle traverse. In the course of these investigations, Bert Gross spotted three unclimbed lines on the three great southerly buttresses and duly climbed them; Eliminate C in July that year, Eliminate B in October and the classic Eliminate A in June 1923. All three are graded Very Severe and Basterfield was with him on all their first ascents. Initially Bower had been the driving force in the search for a girdling route across the buttresses but later it was Gross, with Basterfield again as his second, who pioneered and then, in October 1922, completed the route. The climb is about 1,000 feet long and varied. It involves some abseiling and is graded Very Severe, with some moves that are delicate, awkward and very exposed. In 1924 Gross sailed from England for New Zealand to take up a new life as a sculptor. Although he returned after a few years he did little more creative climbing and his last years were a catalogue of disaster. He had a bad motor cycle accident. He took up gliding and a crash left him with chronic double-vision. He married but his wife died after two years. He became a recluse and, on the first anniversary of her death, he committed suicide.

Although the best work of this period was on Dow, there was also considerable activity on Gimmer Crag. In 1920 and 1921 George Bower, usually seconded by Dr A. W. Wakefield of Kendal who was a formidable fell-runner, made several new routes there. In 1923 H. B. Lyon of Kendal, who had climbed in the Langdale area before the war and then served in the Indian Army, had a productive summer holiday. Sixteen years before he had looked at the steep chimney on White Ghyll Crag. Now he was delighted to find it had not been done, so, after considerable reconnaissance, he did it. White Ghyll Chimney was the first climb ever made on that profuse and popular crag and, although it is only graded Severe, it is still regarded as a classic route. The next day he went to Gimmer Crag and created another classic, Bracket and Slab. Many years later a great fan of the route, Tom Price, wrote:

> It has the wonder ingredient, it is a Severe that everybody can do. But it has much more than that. It has a peculiarly Lake District quality of originality and charm. In good conditions, it flatters the climber, and persuades him he is on form. It does much to sustain the fallacy that rocks were made to be climbed on.

There can be no doubt that the advent of rubbers and the careful use of the rope had done much to make these advances possible. But some of the best climbers were sometimes inattentive on easier ground. This is illustrated by a story told by Raymond Greene in his book *Moments of Being*. Greene was a distinguished member of a most distinguished family – his younger brothers included Graham the novelist and Sir Hugh Carlton Greene who became Director-General of the BBC. Raymond was a boy at Berkhamsted School, where their father was headmaster, when Ashley Abraham came to lecture about rock climbing. The boy had already done much fell walking and was now inspired to take up rock climbing. In 1920, having reached the top of Pillar Rock with his sister Molly and C. F. Holland, he decided to descend by way of the New West – he himself leading, Molly in the middle and Holland in the key position at the back:

> We came to a place where we climbed down a vertical chimney, and struck out horizontally on a traverse before descending vertically again. I took up my stance at the end of the traverse, but, being inexperienced, did not belay myself and merely took in the rope as Molly climbed across to me. I assumed that Holland would be, as he should have been, protecting her with the rope above. Suddenly she fell, and, instead of being supported by Holland, she plunged downwards. The rope ran through my hands until, about 50 feet below, she struck a grass ledge, and was momentarily halted before bouncing off again. At this moment I twisted her rope round my forearm and stopped her. The rope between her and Holland had almost run out and he, against all the rules, was himself climbing down the chimney. Had I not stopped her when I did, he would have been pulled off. I could not have held them both and all three of us would have been killed.

Holland, for all his long experience, had a reputation for being over-confident and careless at times.

There were some remarkable, almost incredible incidents in this period. On 21 June 1921 a holiday visitor from London called Mr Crump, walking to Wasdale Head from Coniston, lost his way in mist and wandered into Piers Ghyll where he fell and injured his leg. Search parties went out day after day but failed to find him. Not for twenty days after his accident was he discovered. Piers Ghyll was rarely visited but there had been weeks of dry weather and this encouraged a party of climbers, led by A. R. Thomson, to attempt the first descent. They had not gone far when they came across Mr Crump 'just below the Bridge Rock, sitting sideways and gazing down the ghyll. He was conscious and able to walk a little.' For nearly three weeks he had had no food. He would undoubtedly have died had the weather not been unusually warm and had he not been close to running water.

In March that year the Pinnacle Club had been formed, exclusively for women climbers. Its chief begetter was Mrs 'Pat' Kelly who explained: 'Perhaps we got tired of being taken in hand by men climbers, kind and helpful though they might be ... As in other walks of life, women wanted to find their own feet.' She believed that women would only attain high standards if, as she had done, they acquired the confidence to lead or solo hard routes. Her own climbing was as good as ever. Yet, on 17 April 1922, scrambling down the Heather Terrace on Tryfan which is nothing more than a rough path for walkers, she stepped on a loose stone, fell and was killed. H. M. Kelly was with another party on the other side of the mountain. His climbing diary makes no mention of the terrible and astonishing accident.

It was in 1922 that the Fell and Rock Climbing Club decided to publish guide books. In this respect, the Snowdonia men, inspired by Winthrop Young, had been well ahead of them; Archer Thomson's little books on Lliwedd and the Ogwen District had come out before the war. For a further decade and more the Lake District climbers had had to make do with handwritten and uncollated accounts in the various books in the various valley centres and with new-route descriptions in the club's *Journal*. Now, it was felt, the time had come to gather all this material together in an organised form.

Between 1922 and 1926 five slim volumes were published, under the overall editorship of R. S. T. Chorley. They were octavo-sized and cased in leatherette in the club's distinctive dark red. In order of appearance, they were: *Doe Crags and Coniston*, by George Bower who was on the losing side in the continuing controversy about how Dow should be spelt; *Pillar Rock and Neighbouring Climbs* by H. M. Kelly; *The Scawfell Group* by Holland: a book that brought together *Great Gable* and *Borrowdale*, the former by H. S. Gross and the latter by A. R. Thomson; and a final volume incorporating *Great Langdale, Buttermere and Outlying Climbs* dealt with, respectively, by George Basterfield, A. R. Thomson and R. S. T. Chorley. Bower's contribution was individualistic. He described Woodhouse's Route as 'Difficult in and owing to boots'. He recommended the use of rubbers on the harder climbs and for Eliminate B 'rubbers; insurance policy; 80-foot rope'. At one point in his account of the Girdle

Traverse he added a warning: 'Note. The hyacinths grow 60 feet below the traverse, and great care is required to keep them at this distance.' But it was Kelly's book that proved most influential. He opted for precision, using a graduated rope to get an accurate, instead of a subjective estimate of the length of each pitch. His system of giving a concise pitch-by-pitch account of the nature of the climb and its particular problems and solutions has been generally adopted and prevails to this day.

In the summer of 1924 an issue was finally resolved that had concerned the club since the end of the war – the provision of a worthy memorial to the members who had not come home. In 1919 a committee member H. P. Cain said 'Let's buy a fell' and when this idea was put to the Annual General Meeting it was accepted unanimously. The club offered £50 to Lord Lonsdale for Pillar Rock but he refused to sell. They tried to get Napes Needle but the negotiations fell through. Finally, after much hard work by the club Secretary Darwin Leighton and H. P. Cain, they struck a remarkable deal. Mr H. W. Walker of Seascale agreed to sell, for £400, a vast acreage of the high ground on all sides of the Sty Head pass, embracing twelve fells – among them Broad Crag, Kirk Fell, Brandreth, Glaramara, Great End, and at the centre, Great Gable. The money was quickly raised from the club members and the title deeds were handed over to the National Trust, in effect to the nation.

The next question was the particular form the memorial should take and it was Dr Howard Somervell of Ambleside who came up with the answer. He proposed a bronze tablet inscribed with the names of the fallen, to be set up on the summit rocks of Great Gable. In the event a more elaborate tablet was cast in bronze with a relief model of the land acquired, beneath that an inscription saying it was for 'the use and enjoyment of the people of our land for all time', and beneath that the names of those who were remembered.

It had all taken a long time but on 8 June 1924 some 500 people assembled in the mist and rain on the summit of Great Gable. The club President, Dr A. W. Wakefield, spoke briefly and unveiled the memorial: Geoffrey Winthrop Young, whose lost leg had not halted his mountaineering, pronounced an eloquent tribute; Godfrey Solly read Psalm 121, 'I will lift up mine eyes unto the hills ...'; Cain read the inscription on the tablet and the names below it; two buglers sounded the Last Post.

There has been a memorial ceremony there every November since that day and it is regularly attended, often in defiance of the weather, by several hundred people. In 1987, although the day was grey and the summit in cloud, as many as 500 people heard a few words from Desmond Oliver and then, at 11 am, stood for two minutes in silence that was total and very moving.

Two years after the unveiling on Great Gable the club organised a much more light-hearted commemoration on the summit of Pillar Rock. It was the centenary of John Atkinson's first ascent of the Rock and scores of people went to Ennerdale (about to be transformed by the Forestry Commission's conifer planting) and followed the Old West route: '... public orators, children, dogs, maidens and grey-haired ladies, as well as strong bearded men with boots, led by a cheerful person in a top hat, all chattering and clattering upwards, roped or unroped, as the fancy took them'.

On the wider mountaineering scene the first half of the 1920s was most notable for the three British expeditions to Everest. The first of these, in 1921, was a prolonged reconnaissance during which George Mallory, who had survived the war unscathed as an artillery officer, discovered the key to the mountain's northern approaches and established himself in the public mind as the man of Everest. Next year saw the first serious attempt to reach the summit. Mallory was there again, of course, and this time there were two Lake District men in the party, Dr Howard Somervell and Dr A. W. Wakefield. The latter was badly affected by altitude but Somervell proved himself a strong and enduring climber and a good companion. So when another attempt was planned for 1924 Somervell was again invited and so were Noel Odell (the last man to see Mallory and Irvine alive), Bentley Beetham whose health let him down, and Jack de Vere Hazard who apparently behaved in a strange and unhelpful manner. No approach, it seems, was made to the two best climbers in Britain at that time, C. D. Frankland and H. M. Kelly. Perhaps it was felt that, for all their mastery of rock routes on modest mountains, they had insufficient experience of snow and ice climbing at altitude. Perhaps it was feared that Kelly might try to take command. He was disappointed not to be asked and consoled himself with a month's hard climbing in Norway that summer.

After the death of his wife H. M. Kelly had spent much time with his close friends, the Eden-Smiths who lived at Grange-over-Sands. Mrs Eden-Smith, whose name was Blanche (although most people called her 'Bessie' and Kelly usually referred to her as 'G', which was short for the angel Gabriel and referred to her habit of keeping records), became a keen and highly competent climber. Those who remember her say she was the kindest, gentlest of women. They also agree that, though they spent much time together over many years, there was never any hint of the romantic in the attachment between her and Kelly.

For the latter half of 1922 and the first part of the following year Kelly devoted himself to his Pillar guide book. He repeated the established routes, measuring and taking notes, and created a few new ones including the Appian Way on the west face of Low Man. The job completed, he turned his attention to an old problem, Tophet Wall above the scree of Great Hell Gate on Great Gable.

He had first explored the route in August 1920 with R. E. W. Pritchard. He failed, narrowly, to climb the initial crackline so they scrambled higher up the scree and then traversed on to the face. Protected by a top rope, Kelly climbed down to the point he had almost reached from below, then climbed up again. His diary reads: 'Climbed back to Pritchard testing a good piton (about one-third of the way *en route*) and found it quite safe – useful as a belay if pitch is led. Did not explore any further than this.' It is not known who banged this piton in. These metal spikes with a hole at the end to take a karabiner, which are hammered into cracks to provide supplementary holds or protection for the leader, had been used for many years in the Alps and the Dolomites where the routes are very long and speed is important. But, except for the metal nails that the Reverend James Jackson employed on Pillar Rock, this seems to mark their first appearance in the Lake District. Their use, or abuse, on the crags was to be a source of heated contention in the 1960s.

Two years later, on 14 July 1923, Kelly and Pritchard returned to the attack during what Kelly called 'the one fine week of that atrocious year'. In fact, the day they chose was so excessively hot that it took them three hours to reach the foot of the wall from Wasdale Head. Once again they evaded the steep crack at the bottom and traversed on to the face from higher up the scree to reach the route at the top of what is now the second pitch. The only possible belay they found was what Kelly called a 'ridiculous stump of juniper bush' and above them loomed a short but very steep wall with tiny holds. Kelly led off and, to his surprise, quickly reached the top and traversed left to a shallow niche where he belayed to 'an even more absurd root of juniper'. They pressed on until overhanging rock above forced them to traverse to the right, 'the cream of the climbing so far'. At the last serious problem, the final narrow crack, they had to make another detour and do some vigorous scraping out of loose stones before it could be climbed. That was the end of the difficulties and they moved easily on to the top but Kelly was dissatisfied because they had not done the direct start to the route.

This was accomplished two years later by Michael de Selincourt, a science student with a natural aptitude for climbing but a flippant attitude towards it. He liked to deflate the over-earnest. According to Ivan Waller, who was a friend of his, de Selincourt arrived at Tophet Wall one August morning in 1925 and found a group of Fell and Rock Club men studying the direct start. Before they could move he walked up to the foot of the route and fluently soloed the first two pitches. Also according to Waller, de Selincourt gave up climbing soon after on the grounds that when it was easy it bored him and when it was difficult it frightened him and he did not care for either condition.

Although he loved Pillar best of all and did much pioneering on the Napes face of Gable, Kelly's undoubted masterpiece was on Scafell Crag.

Moss Ghyll Grooves follows the airy line of the leftwards-slanting slabs from the dark recesses of the ghyll on to the exposed rocks high above the Great Flake on C.B. It is 260 feet long and graded Severe (Hard), though Tom Price says it is 'a Severe with the hallmarks of a Very Severe' and Kelly himself reckoned it 'probably slightly harder than Botterill's Slab'. He led the first ascent on 1 July 1926 with Blanche Eden-Smith as his second and a comparative beginner J. B. Kilshaw, as last man.

He had prospected the first part of the climb seven years before. Now, with the rock dry and the sun shining, he determined to try, though not before further reconnaissance. They went up the Penrith Climb and Kelly noted: 'Explored Moss Ghyll Grooves from above. Self climbed down to first groove and descended it about 15 to 20 feet, gardening *en route*. Saw enough to satisfy me that lower portion might be linked up with this, a matter of about 30 feet. Rejoined others.' They had lunch, during which a sharp thunder shower made them anxious. But it passed quickly and by the time they had descended the Keswick Brothers' route and reached the foot of the grooves, the rock above had dried out.

They were careful to make sure the leader had all possible protection from below before he tackled the crux moves. Mrs Eden-Smith gave a graphic description in the Fell and Rock *Journal*:

> From a very narrow foothold on the centre of the slab, a left-hand movement had to be made upward and outward to a small but level stance (the Pedestal) on the extreme edge, about two strides away. The difficulty lay in the fact that there was nothing to stride on and no handhold except a small protuberance about the size of a damson stone, on which moreover hands had to be changed somehow. Twice Kelly tried it and came down to the grass for a rest from the toe-cramping foothold from which the movement must start. The third time he went straight for it and seemed just to flow over those two 'holdless' strides to the Pedestal, where, at last, both feet could rest at once. The earnest pathos in his voice, as he besought his followers to do their best when their turns came, was ominously indicative of what he thought of the place!

Kelly's account was published in the Rucksack Club *Journal*:

> A pedestal some six feet away on the left looked hopeful but it seemed hardly attainable, as the intervening space appeared destitute of even the minutest holds. A very close survey, however, did reveal something of the sort for I got across somehow. An upright – but far from moral – flake of diminutive proportions was used for the left foot, thought it was rather high up and far away; and a still more immoral rugosity was found for the left hand.
> To balance, in transit, by the aid of these two points of attachment, was a ticklish business, and a breathless moment followed as a rapid change of hands was made, so that the left could reach forward to the pedestal and lodgement be gained thereon.

There was much climbing still ahead, including one or two dramatic steps out on to the open face, but the chief difficulty was overcome and

Kelly had already visited the higher section.

Three days later the same trio, with the Wood-Johnson brothers, made the second ascent. Ernest Wood-Johnson was the last man, designated to take photographs. He later wrote:

> At the top Kelly was very pleased and suggested a grand tour of Scafell. That day we did all the V.S.s except the C.B. and Kelly, unconsciously, taught us more than we had taught ourselves in the previous years ... It was the first time we had not led ourselves and he took us from the scrambling style to precision and delight in smooth movement. The final climb was the first descent of Hopkinson's Gully. I went first and told H.M.K. that I couldn't see any holds. He replied: 'Well, just keep going down.' So I learnt how to do what looked impossible to me. After that marvellous day we were friends for good.

In 1928 G. G. (Graham) Macphee led, from the rear, the first descent of Moss Ghyll Grooves, which some had said was 'irreversible'. Macphee was a wealthy dental consultant from Liverpool and a dedicated climber, and it was his ambition to be able to write in the climbers' book in the valley 'MGG–GGM'.

It was at Easter 1928 that Kelly produced his final burst of new-route-making. His diary shows his relish for climbing entirely undiminished. On 11 April he and H. G. Knight and three others, one of them A. E. Field, a veteran of the earliest days, went to Great Gable and climbed Eagle's Nest by the Ordinary route, descended the Arrowhead ridge, climbed Abbey Buttress and descended Ling Chimney, then three of them climbed Eagle's Nest Direct and descended the Ordinary. Feeling pleasantly 'run in', Kelly and Knight then tackled a new route, Long John, which is graded Very Severe (Mild) although the opening move of the final pitch is Very Severe (Hard). Kelly led the first half but his short stature made the higher part impossible for him and Knight took over. Kelly's account makes mention of a piton in position in the adjoining Ling Chimney and throws light on his ethical attitudes:

> The wall was now tackled and very soon the leader [Knight] was forced to go to the edge of Eagle's Nest Ordinary on the left in his search for holds. Some feet higher, to relieve the great strain, a traverse on good holds was made to the piton in Ling's Chimney. From here the leader was only able to climb the centre of the remainder of the wall because of his height (6' 1") and long reach, and even then touched the edge of Ling's once. He thinks, however, this would be unnecessary now he knows what follows. In any case Ling's should be *verboten* except for the stop at the piton. The second man (5' 7½") found it quite impossible to make anything of the wall direct and traversed back to the edge of Eagle's Nest Ordinary. Good holds took him up some few feet, after which he was able to get back on to the face of the wall again.

The two men were reunited at the Wastwater Hotel at the end of the month and were joined by W. G. Standring. On 27 April, after some prospecting, they created the Kern Knotts Chain, an exploring and traversing route more than 400 feet in length and graded Very Severe

(Hard). They worked their way, with Knight leading and Kelly in the equally demanding position in the rear, from high up on the Flake Climb, round the Buttress, across Kern Knotts Crack just above the Sentry Box, then across the wall to the Innominate Crack which they ascended. Kelly concluded: 'The climb is a study in small holds and has many exposed and severe sections. Fortunately at some points there are adequate and reassuring belays.'

Next day they went to Pillar Rock to tackle the Grooved Wall on the side of Walker's Gully, which they had already inspected. First they climbed the North-east Climb and Standring spent 2½ hours on a top rope giving the long groove and the ledges below it what Kelly called 'a final sweep up'. Altogether they had spent some eight hours cleaning up the route: 'There was enough earth sent down into Ennerdale', Kelly commented, 'to provide soil for the whole of the reafforestation scheme.'

Kelly led off and did most of the route, including the very hard move over the overhang at the foot of the long groove. He wrote in his diary: 'The crux of the climb is to effect a lodgement in the Long Groove. (A spike, high up, proved a perfect blessing on the occasion of this ascent, but we are afraid its life may be short. We hung a loop or rope over it to use as a stirrup and it would seem quite impossible to surmount the overhang without some such aid.) Strenuous climbing up the groove brings one to a fine belay.' In fact, the doubtful spike lasted thirty-eight years before it disappeared.

The day after that they went back to Kern Knotts and reversed the Chain, doing it from right to left this time. Then they walked along to Napes Needle and, with Knight leading, made the first ascent of the Direct Obverse route from the gap.

The decade that followed the end of the First World War had seen a remarkable renaissance in Lakeland climbing. In their *Short History*, published in the Fell and Rock *Journal* for 1936–7, Kelly and J. H. Doughty summed it up in these words:

> It was now becoming clear that climbing had entered upon a fundamentally new phase. What had been regarded a few years before as the unapproachable plane of performance attainable by occasional gifted geniuses like Jones, Botterill, Herford, was now looked upon rather as the norm by which our leading climbers measured their own achievements. Virgin rock was approached in a new spirit of confidence and enterprise. It was not that the best men were any better than the giants of the past, but they were more numerous, while the standard of ability among climbers in general had increased enormously.

There were many reasons for this. The spread of motor-cycles and cars made the crags more accessible. The Everest expeditions had aroused great public interest. More and more books about climbing, abroad and at home, were published – Winthrop Young's *Mountain Craft* and several by George Abraham. Even the film-makers were beginning to take an interest; the Abraham brothers helped to make a five-minute travelogue about climbing Napes Needle for Pathé in the early 1920s. Those who found themselves attracted to the new sport were greatly helped by the special guide books of the Fell and Rock Climbing Club and greatly encouraged by rubber-soled shoes and sensible safety techniques with the rope. They were encouraged, too, by the advice and example of the leading men of the time, among whom H. M. Kelly was the foremost.

Throughout this period the Lake District's leadership in the sport was undisputed. But the situation was about to change.

—·6·—

The Men From Wales
1928–1936

CLIMBING in North Wales had not enjoyed a post-war resurgence in any way comparable with that in the Lake District, but the opening of Helyg, the Climbers' Club hut in the Ogwen valley, towards the end of 1925, stimulated fresh interest and achievement.

On the day the hut was officially opened two Cambridge students who had been climbing on Idwal Slabs, Jack Longland and Ivan Waller, stopped to find out what was going on and were promptly enrolled as club members. Within two years Waller, who was studying engineering, had created his classic Belle Vue Bastion on Tryfan and made the first ascent of the Fallen Block Crack on Clogwyn y Ddysgl. In 1928 Longland (later Sir Jack and variously noted for his work on Everest, in education and as a broadcaster) made the impressive route that bears his name on the West Buttress of Clogwyn du'r Arddu.

This big sombre cliff, affectionately known to generations of climbers as 'Cloggy', had long been regarded as out of bounds. In his *British Mountain Climbs*, first published in 1909 but several times reprinted, George Abraham had pronounced: 'It cannot be said that this imposing mass possesses much prolonged interest for the rock climber. It has been truly said that the easy places are too easy and the difficult places are impossible.'

The appearance of a new generation of thrusting young climbers on the crags of Snowdonia, especially 'Cloggy', in the late 1920s showed – for neither the first nor the last time – how rash it is to use the word 'impossible' when speaking of climbing. In 1927 Fred Pigott and Morley Wood, both of the Rucksack Club, made a route on the East Buttress. The year after, Longland made a longer and more forbidding route up the West Buttress. The year after that, a young bank clerk from Liverpool, C. F. Kirkus, paid his first visit to 'Cloggy' and, with A. B. Hargreaves in support, made the second ascent of Longland's Climb.

Colin Kirkus was to be a leading figure, in Lake District as well as North Wales climbing, for the next few years. He had started scrambling in Snowdonia as a boy. By the age of seventeen, with George Abraham's *British Mountain Climbs* as his 'Bible', he was exploring the crags, often alone and carrying an 80-foot length of line to lassoo flakes or abseil off if the going got too tough. 'Though wrong as a policy', he later wrote, 'this early solo climbing taught me an immense amount. I knew that if I made a mistake I had no one to help me; I had to rely entirely on my own skill and my own judgement.' He fell several times but, luckily, was not seriously injured. He thoroughly explored Helsby Crag, the sandstone outcrop close to his Wallasey home. He had something of Kelly's voracious appetite for the sport. One Sunday afternoon in 1932 he cycled the twenty miles to Helsby, soloed 42 climbs, then cycled back. He wrote to A. W. ('Alf') Bridge: 'I lost 4 lbs over that show, but my finger muscles should now be as good as yours after 1,500 feet of Helsby climbing ...'

Kirkus cycled to Snowdonia, too, and when he was there he either bivouacked or stayed at Helyg. He could not afford anything else. Alf Bridge wrote:

> I remember, one day in winter, being on Clogwyn du'r Arddu with Colin as we almost forced the route now known as Vember. We were in boots and the sole of one of Colin's boots had come adrift from the upper and he had tied the two parts together with string. Of course, we had very little money, using 6-inch nails as pitons. We had to work up to noon each Saturday and we did without mid-week lunches to gain a little extra for the week-end. We preferred it that way and any form of subsidised climbing would have been declined.

The old feeling, always stronger in Wales than in the Lake District, that climbing was a sport exclusively for men of comfortable background and considerable education was beginning to be eroded.

A. B. (Alan) Hargreaves, who seconded Kirkus on their second ascent of Longland's Climb, came from Blackburn. He was some six years older than Kirkus and, not much over five feet, several inches shorter. He had trained as an engineer, then moved to Liverpool to learn to be a chartered accountant. The Wayfarers' Club was advertising for members so he joined, went with them to Helsby and Snowdonia and served a long climbing apprenticeship. Where Kirkus was a natural, Hargreaves had to learn it all the hard way. When they came together it was to form one of the great partnerships, each complementing the other – the bold, inventive leader and the careful, methodical, reliable support. Writing of Hargreaves, Kirkus said: 'A belay to him is an engineering problem, not to be used until it is as perfect as possible. He delights in constructing safe anchorages in the most appalling situations.'

When Kirkus was killed in the Second World War, Hargreaves wrote in the Climbers' Club *Journal*:

He was care, skill and confidence embodied ... There was nothing showy about his climbing, in fact he liked to take things slowly and was occasionally awkward and ungainly in his movements. He was not temperamental and never got rattled under even the most difficult circumstances. His principle physical characteristic was his extraordinary endurance and insensibility when having to sustain himself on small awkwardly-shaped holds for a long time and for a long distance. One never saw him flapping about, kicking with his feet or hauling himself up by main force. Everything seemed to go according to plan, up or down ... It did not seem to matter to him what he had on his feet or whether he had anything on them at all. Cold and wet did not seem to affect him as much as it did other people...

As a man he was a delightful companion on the hills, full of fun and interest in the things about him. He was kindliness itself and also most unassuming about his climbing ... To those who did not know him well he may have appeared dull, but this was not so – he was a simple soul, not much interested in the complicated ways of modern life, finding his escape and true expression in his mountaineering.

Hargreaves's description is confirmed by a reading of the book that Kirkus published in 1941, *Let's Go Climbing*. It is a short work, written in a plain and unpretentious style, enlivened by many stories of his own adventures and misadventures, giving the reader sound technical guidance and much wise advice and, above all, a convincing account of the delights he found in climbing and wanted others to share. He describes the pleasures of Alpine mountaineering in perfect weather, the pains of hard going at Himalayan altitudes (he was in the Gangotri region in 1933) and the joys that could be found on the cliffs of home:

To be poised on a steep smooth face, concentrating with every nerve, and then to stretch cautiously up and to come unexpectedly on a large handhold which solves the problem – that seems to be the most thrillingly satisfying moment of your life each time it happens.

For most kinds of rock climbing he recommends tricouni nails: 'You can choose the tiniest hold, fit one nail in it and know that you are safe.' But for the hardest pitches, when the rock is dry, he suggests rubbers: 'The cheaper and lighter they are, the better ... Wear them with only one pair of stockings and see that they fit very tightly.' He advises novices to 'learn to climb down from the very beginning of your career', and when they come to lead climbing he says: 'It is no disgrace to turn back; but it is a disgrace to fall off, whether you hurt yourself or not.' Towards the end of the book he writes: 'Your main object in climbing should be enjoyment, not achievement.' He also writes: 'Personally I prefer Wales to the Lake District ... It is probably just a question of where you start. Each gives equally good rock climbing, but the Welsh mountains certainly are real mountains; there are no sharp rocky peaks in the Lake District to compare with Tryfan or Crib Goch. On the other hand the Lakeland valleys are more beautiful.'

A. B. Hargreaves left Liverpool in 1931 to take a job, which he held for the rest of his working life, as secretary/accountant to a firm of launderers and dry cleaners based on Barrow-in-Furness. He immediately joined the Fell and Rock and was dismayed to find that many of its members had no notion of the exciting developments taking place in Wales. 'So I decided to set about educating them,' he says.

Although he never led a new route, 'A. B. H.', as he is generally known, is one of the most important figures in the story of Lakeland climbing. He is also known as 'the little man', sometimes (and not always as a joke) as 'the nasty little man'. Like other very small men, he made – and still makes, in his mid-eighties – an entirely disproportionate impact. He is wiry, bright of eye and strong of voice, and strong of mind as well. He gives the impression of an intensity of vigour, physical and mental, that he only keeps in control by an equally intense assertion of willpower. His manner is direct and definite. He has firm views and is ever ready to state them forcefully and back them up with evidence. In 1933 he wrote an article for the Fell and Rock *Journal*, describing the explosion of climbing activity in North Wales and claiming that 'although the statement may be distasteful, and even unbelievable, to the loyal Fell and Rock-er, that country is, and has been since about the year 1929, the centre of gravity of rock climbing in these islands'.

He compares the standards of climbing in the two regions and concludes that Snowdonia, with Colin Kirkus and Menlove Edwards to the fore, is in the ascendant:

> The principal advantages of the harder Welsh climbs over those of the Lake District are that they are usually longer, generally less artificial, and almost invariably better provided with natural hazards, such as quantities of grass, loose rock, bad rock and long distances between belays, requiring a really all-round technique. To some, of course, these are not advantages at all, and such are welcome to the comparatively clean, much smaller Lake District crags, constructed of perfect rock and well sprinkled with belays. On the other hand, when once one has tasted the joys of negotiating in conscious safety pitches which, in the Lake District, would be written off as unjustifiably dangerous, one is inclined to be bored with climbs, the only reason for falling off which would be just letting go.

It seems odd that A. B. Hargreaves should have found it necessary to say all this in 1933 since the leading North Wales men had already been impressing themselves, very forcefully, on the Lakeland scene for more than three years.

Colin Kirkus had started inauspiciously. On Good Friday 1930 he fell from the South America Crack on the Great Central Route on Dow Crag, hit the wall fifty feet below and fell a further twenty feet before the rope held him. His second, Hargreaves, had both hands 'burnt and torn almost to the bone' by the friction of the running rope. Kirkus suffered nothing worse than a broken toe and carried on climbing.

He was back in the Lake District in May the following year to open up what was virtually a new and major climbing ground. Although

climbers had been active on Scafell Crag since the earliest days of the
sport, nothing of any note had been done on the other side of the Mickledore Gap, on the massive bulging cliffs of the East Buttress. They
must have seen them frequently and wondered about the possibilities
there. Perhaps they were repelled by the bleakness and steepness of the
prospect and the usual wet and greasy state of the rock. Whatever the
reason, in half a century of climbing only two routes had been made –
Mickledore Chimney at the northern end and Slime Chimney at the
southern, neither of them of much merit. Between these two lines of
weakness lies nearly a quarter of a mile of high and forbidding rock,
specially designed by nature, it would seem, to attract the interest of
men who had trained on 'Cloggy'.

The first serious route on Scafell's East Buttress was made by Kirkus
in May 1931. It is called Mickledore Grooves, graded Very Severe and
described in the guide book as 'A bold lead, opening up a new phase in
Scafell's history.' Ivan Waller was second on the rope, Marco Pallis
third. Waller remembers Kirkus as an effective but inelegant climber:
'He pottered. He'd a funny way of standing to rest on a foot hold and
flapping his hands against his thighs. Then he'd potter to another hold
and stand there for a bit. He did it in a series of moves, like playing
chess, like the lead climbers of the 1980s.'

In an article he wrote for the Fell and Rock *Journal* nearly fifty years
later, Waller recalled the climb:

> Colin was a thin untidy-looking lad with wiry hair and slightly sunken features.
> He looked neither strong nor athletic, and quite unprepossessing. In fact he was
> incredibly tough, determined and completely dedicated to the mountains. We
> had set off from Langdale and there had been the ritual swim in Angle Tarn...
>
> On arrival at the foot of East Buttress, then unclimbed, Colin led the first two
> pitches just as if he was on a well-trodden route. Each pitch had a strenuous
> fingery move which I thoroughly enjoyed... For the main pitch the second man
> sits on a good ledge with an overhanging wall above, behind which goes the slab
> up which the pitch starts. After about a quarter of an hour Colin made an
> excursion to the left edge of the slab and his head appeared above me. He was
> happy and relaxed and assured me that all was going well. After a further half
> hour all the rope was out, Colin was at the top and it was my turn to follow.
>
> I imagined during those 45 minutes that Colin must have found various ledges
> where he could rest and was surprised to find the difficulty sustained throughout
> without anywhere to stand in real comfort. Colin had just pottered from hold to
> hold in a completely relaxed manner where many climbers would have been
> thoroughly gripped.

It was a run-out of the rope of 140 feet. Kirkus had not reconnoitred
the route beforehand and had no protection from running belays of any
kind. He and Waller were so exhilarated by the climb that they then
went round and climbed Kelly's Moss Ghyll Grooves 'which by contrast
seemed very easy and we climbed at great speed with enormous enjoyment'.

The 300-foot West Face of Pillar Rock in Ennerdale. The Rock was a favourite playground for the pioneer climbers and well into this century but it is not so popular now, partly because it is a walk of several miles from the nearest car park, partly because it takes a long time to dry out after rain. But it offers the climber a range of long, steep and sustained routes, ranging in difficulty from the Abraham brothers' New West (1901) to Geoff Cram's Gondor (1967) which is graded Extremely Severe 2. (Photo by the Abraham brothers.)

(*Far left*) The proud Westmorland siblings of Penrith, with their trusty poles, in a picture taken a[t] their ascent of Pillar Roc[k] July 1873. Annie, on the [left,] waited at the foot of the [crag] while the others, Edward[,] May and Tom (the fathe[r of] 'Rusty' Westmorland), scrambled up the Rock, probably on its eastern si[de,] put their names on the lis[t in] the summit bottle and sa[ng] 'God save the Queen'.

(*Left*) The man with the gesture and the mutton-chop whiskers is John Wi[lson] Robinson of Lorton. His companion is George Seatree of Penrith. They were the first local men t[o] join in the new sport in t[he] 1880s, and in June 1885 [they] took a tent and an 'Alpi[ne] rope' to Pillar Rock. It w[as] the first time rock climbe[rs] had used either in the La[ke] District. The picture is a [fake] and was shot in Keswick[.] (Photo by the Abraham brothers.)

Taken in the 1890s, the picture shows climbers scrambling about, unro[ped] on the summit of Scafell Pinnacle. The dark, rightwards-slanting gull[y] holds an early and easy climbing route called Professor's Chimney in honour of John, the elde[st of] the five brilliant Hopkin[son] brothers of Manchester, who were all keen cragsm[en.] At the top of the gully is [the] Jordan Gap. (Photo by [the] Abraham brothers.)

Napes Needle, Great Gable. Haskett Smith made the first ascent, solo, in June 1886, following the Wasdale Crack route which these climbers are using. Although it is only 55 feet and graded no higher than Very Difficult (Hard), pictures of climbers on this pinnacle did more than anything else to attract recruits to the sport. (Photo by the Abraham brothers.)

A. E. Field reaching the top of Eagle's Nest Ridge Direct on Great Gable. It was the first route climbed in the Lake District which is still in the Very Severe grade. Godfrey Solly, a solicitor from Merseyside, led its first ascent in 1892. He and his companions were so impressed by its danger they wondered whether or not to let it be known they had done it. (Photo by the Abraham brothers.)

Curving Crack on the face of Scafell Pinnacle overlooking Deep Ghyll. This is probably the first picture ever taken of a new Lake District route being made. Jones' Route from Deep Ghyll was first ascended on 20 April 1896. O. G. Jones can be seen, in his niche and white shirt, at the top of the crack; George Abraham strikes a dynamic pose halfway up. 'We composed our limbs', Jones wrote, 'to a photographic quiescence.' (Photo by Ashley Abraham.)

Soon after he finally made his first ascent of Kern Knotts Crack on Great Gable in 1897, O. G. Jones
did it again, with the reassurance of a top rope, for his photographer friends. The 'Sentry Box' is the
wider part of the crack, below Jones. The much thinner crack line to the right, Innominate Crack,
was not climbed until after the First World War. Many climbers now consider it easier than Kern
Knotts Crack. It is certainly much easier to protect the leader's progress with nut-runner belays.
(Photo by the Abraham brothers.)

The house party at the Sun Hotel, Coniston, after the second annual dinner of the Fell and Rock Climbing Club of the English Lake District. The picture was taken, by Alan Craig, on 22 November 1908. The people are: (*Standing at back*) H. Livingstone, J. G. Howard, J. Hanks, T. Thackeray, J. H. Burman, S. H. Gordon, A. S. Thompson. (*Standing*) B. H. Witty, F. B. Kershaw, W. A. Woodsend, H. Harland, H. Bishop, J. H. Buckley, C. Graysen, G. H. Charter, E. Hope, C. H. Oliverson. (*Seated*) H. B. Lyon, G. B. Bryant, W. C. Slingsby, G. Seatree, C. B. Phillip, L. J. Oppenheimer, D. Leighton, P. S. Minor, E. T. Thorpe. (*On ground*) A. Craig, E. H. P. Scantlebury, R. Lamb, A. P. Abraham, W. T. Palmer, R. B. Domony, F. C. Clitheroe.

Two pages of advertisement from early Fell and Rock Club Journals. The left-hand page appeared in the first ever Journal, in 1907; the other was two years later.

Three men on the Abbey Buttress of Great Gable, first climbed by Fred Botterill in 1909. Years after the tragic accident on Scafell Pinnacle Face, many climbers were still using hopelessly ineffective rope techniques. The leader here is not belayed to the rock behind him and merely passes the active rope hopefully behind a flake. (Photo by the Abraham brothers.)

George Sansom, with the pipe, and Siegfried Herford taking tea and drying out their boots and rope.

The first Girdle Traverse of Scafell Crag was completed over two days in September 1912. When they set off, leftwards, from alongside Deep Ghyll, Sansom was leading, H. B. Gibson was the middle man, and Herford climbed last. (Photos by W. B. Brunskill.)

Sansom and Herford on Jones'
Route Direct from Lord's Rake,
Scafell Pinnacle Face, first climbed
by O. G. Jones in April 1898:
Sansom traversing leftwards along
the Gangway, with Herford below.

Herford makes the delicate
'Mantleshelf' move near the top of
the climb. Sansom usually led this
pitch as they reckoned the move
was easier for a shorter man. Asked
how he did it, Sansom said:
'Imagine there is a foot hold on the
wall, two feet up. Step up on it
with your right foot and put your
left knee on the Mantleshelf.'
(Photos by W. B. Brunskill.)

The Central Buttress of Scafell Crag. The Central Buttress climb, first ascended by Herford and Sansom in April 1914, kept its place for many years as the hardest climb in the Lake District. It is 475 feet long and still graded Very Severe (Hard).

Soon after he led the first ascent, Herford repeated the crux for the photographers. His white-sweatered figure can be made out, nearing the top of the Great Flake. On this occasion he was protected by a top rope from H. C. Bowen.

Just to the left of the climbers is Botterill's Slab. The gully, casting a shadow, on the right side of the picture is Moss Ghyll, with the left-slanting slabs of Moss Ghyll Grooves catching the sun above it. (Photo by the Abraham brothers.)

The first ascent of Moss Ghyll Grooves was led by
H. M. Kelly on 1 July 1926. Three days later he led
the second ascent and these pictures were taken.
(*Above left*) Kelly nears the top of the 80-foot third
pitch.

(*Left*) Mrs Blanche Eden-Smith, who seconded
Kelly on the first ascent, did so again on the second.
Here she makes the awkward leftward stride while
Kelly gives her a tight rope from the 'Look Out'.
(Photos by Ernest Wood-Johnson.)

(*Above right*) Maurice Linnell leading and A. T.
Hargreaves paying out the rope on the first ascent
of the Overhanging Wall on Scafell East Buttress
on 23 July 1933. It was at the crux of this route
that Linnell hammered in a piton, used it to aid
his upward progress and offered no apology.

(*Above left*) George Basterfield on the edge nails of his boots and Kern Knotts Crack.

(*Above right*) G. R. Speaker, in his famous black beret, on the Girdle Traverse of Dow Crag.

(*Right*) Sid Cross reconnoitring Tower Buttress on Scafell Crag. Soon after, in April 1938, he led H. M. Kelly and two others up The Rampart. (Photos from the Fell and Rock Club Archives.)

Mabel Barker in action on Dow Crag, 1930.

C. D. Frankland at Pillar Rock, 1924.

Millican Dalton prepares one of his brews for Jean Brown and Mabel Barker.
(These three photos from the Mabel Barker collection.)

Millican Dalton, troglodyte and 'Professor of Adventure', sockless and without a belay, brings a client up a climb.

Dalton navigating his home-made raft, Rogue Herries, towards Derwentwater. (Both photos by Maysons, Keswick.)

Two leading Lake District guides in action: Stanley Watson of Borrowdale using the layback technique on Amen Corner, Gimmer Crag. (Photo by the Abraham brothers.)

Jim Cameron of Coniston on the edge of Lower Scout Crag, Langdale.

The message – that the North Wales men had arrived, in devastating form – was further rubbed in three months later when John Menlove Edwards turned up at Wasdale Head and made an unaided ascent of the Great Flake on Central Buttress. On the first and all subsequent assaults on C.B. the leader had only conquered the Flake by using the second man, firmly secured to the chockstone, as foot holds. At the end of August 1931 – more than seventeen years after the first ascent – Edwards did it free, in nailed boots, using the layback method, virtually unprotected and apparently without great difficulty.

Edwards, like Kirkus, lived in Liverpool – he was twenty-one years old, studying medicine at the university – and had learned his climbing in North Wales. He was a more fluent and graceful mover than Kirkus and had an even greater relish for steep and slimy vegetation. But on this day on Scafell Crag the rock was clean and dry and the sun was shining. It had not rained for ten days. Edwards's problems were psychological rather than physical for when they reached the foot of the cliff they found another party ahead of them and were waiting and watching when one man, attempting the Flake without aid, had a narrow escape.

The party ahead – Alf Bridge, Maurice Linnell and A. B. Hargreaves – was a strong one. They had bivouacked at the foot of the crag, breakfasted well and felt so confident they then soloed to the Oval. Bridge, who was a steeplejack and very strong in the arms and shoulders, was determined to make the first unaided ascent of the Great Flake and did not even pause to put a loop round the chockstone and thread his climbing rope through it. He advanced boldly, grasped the edge of the Flake in both hands, threw himself into a layback and immediately his feet shot off the wall opposite and he fell. By a near-miracle he managed to seize the chockstone with his left hand as he fell past and by sheer strength he arrested his fall.

There was more than mere luck in this escape. Alf Bridge was a Manchester man and a regular on the local gritstone where he had spent much time practising what he called 'the technique of falling'. He got so good at it he could drop twenty-five feet and more without hurting himself. He said that when the climber knew he was about to fall, and he usually does, he should look down and make for the softest possible landing place. Perhaps Bridge turned as he fell from the Flake and saw the top of the chockstone and realised that was where his salvation lay. Certainly he was too shattered to try again. He tied himself to the chockstone and the party climbed the Flake in the traditional manner.

Menlove Edwards and his companions, Marco Pallis and Bill Stally-brass (a fellow-member of Liverpool University Climbing Club), had seen it all. Edwards may have been relieved that the chance of making the first unaided ascent was still his, but the manner of it can hardly have been reassuring. Bill Stallybrass described what happened next:

> Our party was soon on the Oval. As last man on the rope, I was carrying a spare 100-foot line. In my haste to catch up with the others, I had left my rubbers behind and was climbing in stockinged feet. At the foot of the Flake, Menlove quickly arranged some slings and brought me up to him. Our whole performance was hair-raisingly chaotic. For some reason I was still carrying the spare line. I gripped hold of Menlove's shoulders and we both swung out from the rock. He seemed to be only very loosely tied-in. My strength was by then running out. I seized hold of a spare rope which Menlove had secured to the chockstone and lowered myself until I could jam my body into the crack and take a rest. Menlove meanwhile was making fresh arrangements with the rope. Suddenly he called out: 'I'm going to have a go!' Next moment he was laybacking steadily up the crack, unbelayed, and was soon at the top. It was an astonishing feat of courage after witnessing Alf Bridge's near-disaster.

When he heard about it Kirkus wrote promptly to Edwards:

> Congratulations on C.B.. It was a most marvellous achievement ... I have sometimes thought of it, but I expect I would have funked the beastly thing when I got under it. To do it straight off without exploration was a marvellous feat. Three cheers for the Climbers' Club!

There were no cheers from the Fell and Rock. Its *Journal*, published at the end of the year, makes no mention of Edwards's achievement or of Kirkus's Mickledore Grooves.

The pioneering work of Kirkus on Scafell's East Buttress was soon being developed further by new men, most of them from Kendal or from Manchester.

Maurice Linnell was born in Stockport in 1909 but the family soon moved to the Kendal area and, not being much good at team games, Maurice took to fell walking. He attended the mass centenary climb of Pillar Rock in 1926. Three years later, when he was studying chemistry in Manchester, he went with a group from the University Mountaineering Club and climbed with H. M. Kelly, leading him up the South-west Climb on Pillar. During his student years in Manchester he spent much time on the gritstone outcrops, often soloing, sometimes making new routes. A formidable climber with great confidence and all-round technique, he was also an odd-looking one. He wore spectacles and a suit – 'last year's office suit', he said, 'is this year's climbing suit'. Ivan Waller describes a day on the upper pitches of C.B. 'when Maurice Linnell appeared on the scene, looking as if he had just stepped out of an office with his neat appearance, lithe figure and metal-rimmed spectacles. While we were climbing up from the V-Ledge Linnell, having greeted us, proceeded to solo the first ascent of the Bayonet-Shaped Crack alongside us.'

One of Linnell's regular companions on the gritstone crags was A. T. (Albert) Hargreaves, not to be confused with and in no way related to A. B. (Alan) Hargreaves though they were both Lancashiremen and both played influential parts in Lake District climbing over many years. A. T. Hargreaves, six years older than Linnell, came from Rochdale. In the mid-1920s, by which time he had a job as a salesman for Nestlé's Milk, he took to gritstone climbing and got to know Linnell, Alf Bridge and many others. He had a company car which gave him easy access to the Lake District.

In 1929, with Graham Macphee from Liverpool, he went to investigate the rarely visited Deer Bield Crag in Far Easedale. Only one route had been made on this steep little cliff, the Chimney. They climbed it and then explored the central buttress area, only to be driven off by wet rock. A few weeks later they returned to study the possibilities of the crack which bounds the central buttress on its left-hand side. Hargreaves roped down from the top and cleared away a mass of loose boulders from the stance at the foot of the top pitch. But once again the rock was too wet. They were back once more on 9 February 1930 to find the conditions perfect. Hargreaves climbed about eighty feet up without much difficulty but then he came to the crux of the climb, the narrow and very strenuous chimney. He tried to find ways round the problem but failed and by this time he was too exhausted to continue. So another week passed before he returned yet again, with Macphee in support. This time, after a struggle lasting four hours, they succeeded. The route is generally graded Very Severe (Hard) nowadays though modern climbers can protect themselves with running belays at the key points, something Hargreaves had to manage without.

The next year A. T. Hargreaves and Linnell made the first descent of Gimmer Crack. This route, which is graded Very Severe (Mild), had been first ascended in May 1928 by A. B. Reynolds, an active figure in these years who did most of his climbing bare-foot. Linnell had done the first ascent in nailed boots on a wet November day in 1931.

In April 1931 Linnell and Alf Bridge met in their favourite Manchester café and, over their coffees, wondered where 'the best opportunities for some further exploration' lay in the Lake District. One of them raised the question of Pillar Rock and the prospects of making a girdle traverse. They determined to try.

They camped in Wasdale during Whit Week and on two days, Friday and Saturday, made an exhaustive reconnaissance across the west face of High Man and on to the Low Man, gardening vigorously as they went, and prospecting their line across the north face. They went up the North Climb to the Split Blocks, then looked for a way to the right. They spotted a crack that would take them to some promising grass ledges, so Linnell set off. His account, published in the Rucksack Club *Journal*, shows how useful – if disconcerting – Bridge's leaping techniques could be:

> The crack is very steep and contains a good deal of grass, and while I was
> thoughtfully hurling the more accessible sods and stones into Ennerdale, Bridge,
> who was exploring the almost perpendicular wall to my left, attracted my attention
> by suddenly jumping down the 15 feet or so which he had gained. However, he
> said it would go so we roped up and attacked it.

They were now confident that they could string their long and complicated route together so they set off on Sunday morning, with A. B.
Hargreaves. Linnell and Bridge took turns leading. The route begins by
climbing the first five pitches of the South-west Climb, then edges its
way high up across the west face. All went well until they reached the
Appian Way when there was a very heavy shower of rain and Linnell
and Hargreaves pulled stockings over their rubbers. They carried on
across the north face, concluding with the final pitch of the Grooved
Wall.

The route is some 1,300 feet long, graded Very Severe and regarded
as a classic because it cleverly contrives to include many of the finest
pitches on Pillar Rock. Linnell wrote:

> The whole course, which can be made to total 28 pitches, took seven hours for
> the first party of three. It contains several very severe parts, and maintains a good
> height on rock which is very steep and exposed, but there is nothing desperate
> about it. It provides sustained interest and enjoyment for a whole day's climbing.

Linnell ended his account with a paragraph that reveals the generosity
of spirit which, for the most part, characterised the climbers of those
days:

> But we had one regret, and that was that H. M. Kelly had not been with us. We
> had not seen him for some time and he knew nothing of our plans. We had hoped
> to work out the route and then get Kelly to come with us to Pillar for the first
> complete traverse. However, to end a perfect day at Wasdale, glasses were raised
> as Bridge proposed the toast – 'To the man who made a girdle of Pillar possible'.

In fact, Kelly was not far away, staying in Langdale, and during the
holiday he led the first ascent of the Central Route on Bowfell Buttress.

In 1932 the old firm of A. T. Hargreaves and Graham Macphee
produced two new routes, the Nor'-nor'-west on Pillar and Sinister Slabs
on Bowfell. But the great event of that year took place on the East
Buttress of Scafell, when Linnell led the first ascent of the route he named
the Great Eastern. His companion was a young man who had repaired
his boots and hero-worshipped him for years.

It used to be widely supposed that it was not until after the Second
World War, with the advent of Joe Brown and Don Whillans and their
mates in the Rock and Ice Club, that the working class made any impact
on the rock-climbing story. It is not so. During and before that war a
quarryman from Little Langdale called Jim Birkett and a coal-miner
from West Cumbria called Bill Peascod were climbing hard and making
impressive new routes. And years before them, a couple of working-class

lads from Kendal had taken to the sport with enthusiasm and ignorance. One of them worked in an engineering shop, the other for his father who was a cobbler. The first was called Charlie Tatham, the other Sid Cross.

Sid Cross was the youngest of five children. Born in Kendal in 1913 he went to the local council school and left at the age of fourteen to work, unpaid, in his father's shop. Within a year he and Charlie Tatham were cycling into Kentmere each Sunday morning to scramble about on the rock. They used a rope that Charlie 'borrowed' from his father's garage and which was used, on other days, by a firm of undertakers, to lower the coffins into the ground. They saved up for a Beale's 80-foot Alpine rope, which cost just over 10s (50p), and started rock climbing. They could not afford guide books so they read up about the routes in Kendal public library. On their feet they wore either cheap plimsolls ('pumps') or old football boots which Sid converted by removing the studs and replacing them with triple-hob nails.

They hid the rope in a rucksack until they were out of range of home but on the fells took turns carrying it across one shoulder and feeling proud.

Their first route was the Crescent Climb on Pavey Ark, followed by Gwynne's Chimney. They found it easy. Of the traverse on the Crescent, Tatham said, 'I could have pushed a wheel-barrow across.' Soon they were doing Severes on Gimmer Crag though they had no idea how the rope should be deployed.

One day in 1931 they climbed the Crack on Gimmer and discovered a loose hand hold on the top pitch which they carefully circumvented. A week later, once again on top of Gimmer, they met two older climbers who had just come up. As Sid Cross recalls it, he asked 'Have you just done the Crack?'

> They looked at us suspiciously – we were very scruffy – and said, 'What's it to do with you?'
> We explained about the loose hold and then they became friendly and chatted.
> 'What are you going to do now?' they asked.
> 'Hiatus.'
> 'Where are you from?'
> 'Kendal.'
> 'You don't know anyone called Linnell?'
> 'I've mended his shoes.'
> 'He's our climbing partner.'
> They only half-believed us about Hiatus, so we led them up it.

In fact, they did rather more than that. Alf Bridge, writing in the Rucksack Club *Journal*, recalled the meeting and went on:

> These two shook us by proceeding up Hiatus (or what they *said* was Hiatus – it had actually a very severe direct finish discovered by themselves) using as belays, when they did use any, things like the 'coffin' at the beginning of the traverse

(A.B.H. very ostentatiously taking cover in the cave meanwhile) and eventually asking us when *we* reached the top, duly impressed, how to tie a bowline!

Alf Bridge goes on to say:

> That was an excellent day's fun, and I shall treasure the memory of overhearing our young acquaintances describe Hargreaves and myself as 'a pair of doddering old devils' because we suggested that they might with advantage use a thread belay while their No. 1 was doing the second pitch (traverse) of the Crack!

It has sometimes been argued that the first working-class climbers had to contend not just with the crags but also with the social prejudices of their middle-class predecessors. They were, it is said, snubbed and made to feel unwelcome and excluded from club membership. The idea springs not from any historical evidence but from latter-day notions about the proper conduct of class warfare according to Karl Marx. All the early working-class climbers agree that it did not happen like that. Sid Cross says:

> There was never any need for any of them to have taken to Charlie and me. We were scruffy and ignorant – and we were often rude about them, calling them 'the Pilgrim bloody Fathers' and things like that. But they made a bit of a fuss of us – encouraged us, gave us useful tips, bought us shandies. It's mountains – that's what mountains do. I never found anything but friendliness with any of them. That's what the mountains are!

About a week after their encounter with Bridge and Hargreaves, Sid Cross and Charlie Tatham were on Gimmer Crag again. They studied a crack and wondered if it would go and tossed up for who should try it, protected by a top rope. Tatham won so Cross soloed up A Route:

> There was an old fellow soloing up B Route. I saw him and thought 'Silly old bugger'. Anyway, I got to the top and threw the rope down to Charlie and he tied on and I shouted 'O.K.'. And a voice behind me said, 'Young man, don't you think you'd better tie on? There's a nice boulder here. Put your rope round that'. He showed me how to do it and I brought Charlie up. The 'silly old bugger' was George Basterfield, a lovely man.

One Saturday afternoon in August 1932 Maurice Linnell picked Sid Cross up in Kendal and drove him up Langdale in the sidecar of his Royal Enfield motorbike. Tatham should have been with them but he had injured himself playing soccer. They parked at the Old Dungeon Ghyll hotel and had a few drinks. Then in the dark they walked up Mickleden and Rossett Ghyll to Angle Tarn where they bivouacked. Cross did not get much sleep as he had no sleeping bag. He was not sorry when Linnell resumed the march before dawn so that they could see the sunrise from the summit of Scafell Pike. Then they descended to Mickledore and Cross slept again, wrapped in an old rug, while Linnell went off to survey a possible route on the East Buttress. It was the Great Eastern Route, 230 feet long and graded Very Severe (Mild). Sid Cross says:

Linnell was experimenting with a diet – he seemed to eat nothing but sugar. We got cracking and he just did it. It was a lovely day and it went very well. I was just someone to hold the rope while he climbed up into quite unknown regions of cracks, bulges and slabs. As I watched him climb, in between contemplating the scenery, I thought he was fortunate in finding holds wherever he wanted them.

The new route completed, they went round the corner to Scafell Crag where Cross led Botterill's Slab, then Linnell led the way up Moss Ghyll to look for a variation to Moss Ghyll Grooves:

Linnell tackled the second groove out of the ghyll. I saw very little of him after he left me, with a belay that kept slipping off, but I could hear him. It was very slimy in places and he was having a desperate struggle. I spent about an hour whistling and singing and being bombarded with sods. Now and again I put my belay back on the rounded knob. Very near the top Linnell was really struggling. A. B. Hargreaves, who was watching from above, insisted on giving him a top rope. I think he felt that 'young bugger down below' couldn't be trusted to hold a fall. So Linnell couldn't claim a first ascent. But it was a terrific lead all the same, completely unseen.

The summer of 1933 was exceptionally fine and Linnell took the opportunity to make further conquests on the East Buttress. The first was Overhanging Wall, graded Very Severe (Hard). Halfway up the second pitch, he ran into difficulties:

Above me was nothing but overhang with a few scanty holds; but to the right a sort of scoop, with a holdless, vertical back wall, and quite an inadequate crack at the far side to pull across into. There was only one thing for it, and it was an eventuality for which I had come prepared. I inserted a piton in the little crack, and inserted it well and truly with a hammer. Nor was it only put there as a safeguard; by pulling on it sideways, downwards, outwards and upwards, and finally planting a foot on it, I was able, with a struggle, to reach the little ledge. I offer no apologies; those who prefer to climb the place unaided are cordially invited to remove the piton and do so.

Linnell's piton, which he had had made for him by colleagues at work, was still in place in the early 1970s.

Its use caused some apprehension. The new routes on the East Buttress, and the piton, were mentioned in the 1933 Fell and Rock *Journal*. In his Editor's Notes, G. R. Speaker, who was under the misapprehension that the piton had been used solely to protect the leader, wrote:

At a time when rock and ice climbers abroad have adopted new engineering tactics, and are climbing more and more with the aid of pitons, the admirable restraint shown by the leaders on the more severe of our courses is as commendable as it is reassuring. To a great many of us the general introduction of mechanised climbing would rob this wonderful and noble pursuit of ours of a great deal of the force of its appeal and of its charm.

Linnell's companion on the climb had been A. T. Hargreaves and a few weeks later they reversed roles and Hargreaves led the first ascent of Morning Wall on the East Buttress. A few weeks after that, with another companion, Harry Pearson of the Manchester University group, Linnell returned to the crag he was making his own.

First he led the way up his Overhanging Wall route, pausing briefly to knock his piton further in with a plasterer's hammer. From the top of the third pitch he created a variation finish known as The White Slab. Then they descended the Great Eastern route till they reached the stance at the top of the third pitch there. He had another variation finish in mind, up The Yellow Slab. It is a ferocious climb, steep and strenuous, often on tiny holds and, for much of the way, poised over a fearsome overhang. Early on Linnell knocked a piton in to protect an awkward move over a bulge, thought about it, then removed the piton and made the move anyway. Higher up, with Pearson balanced far beneath him on a very uncomfortable and inadequate stance, it took him three attempts before he finally conquered the hand-jamming crack at the top of The Yellow Slab. When Pearson's turn came and he reached the foot of the crack he was not greatly reassured to hear Linnell call: 'All it needs is lots of guts.'

Linnell certainly had that as well as skill, strength and great determination. His climbs were comparable to the hardest routes of his greatest predecessors, Herford and Kelly, but, unlike them, he was doing them without elaborate preparation. They had tackled their more testing new routes only after long and thorough reconnaissance, usually protected by a top rope, clearing away the dangerous rubbish, assuring themselves that it was possible, sometimes even rehearsing the exact sequence of moves that would solve the problem. Linnell simply studied the crag from the bottom, worked out a line in his mind, then had a go – a very committing method.

The Yellow Slab variation, graded Very Severe (Hard), was his last new route in Lakeland. A few months later, at Easter 1934, he went camping with Colin Kirkus on the north-western shoulder of Ben Nevis. Kirkus was leading up a snow climb when a step gave way and he fell. He plunged over a cliff and the shock of the fall pulled Linnell from his ice axe belay. When they finally came to a halt, 200 feet further down, Kirkus was badly injured and Linnell was dead, strangled by the climbing rope. He was buried in Glen Nevis.

In June that year, all in the course of a fortnight's holiday, a new man burst briefly but very productively on the Lakeland scene. His name was F. G. (Graham) Balcombe. He was beginning a distinguished career with the Post Office. His impact on Lake District climbing has been described as 'meteoric' – in proper tribute to the abruptness of his appearance and departure, the shortness of his stay and the brilliance of his achievement.

Balcombe began rock climbing with the Co-operative Holiday Association's Mountaineering Club. He took to holidaying in the Lake

District and working his way through the routes in the guide books, usually with a colleague from work, Jack Sheppard. At the start of their 1934 holiday they met C. J. Astley Cooper, working on a new guide book to Great Gable, who was so impressed with Balcombe's climbing he asked him to help. Balcombe responded by creating six new routes on Gable in the next few days. Three of them were on the Napes crags – a variation to the Rainbow Ridge route, Lucifer Ridge and Hell Gate Pillar which is graded Very Severe (Mild). Then they moved across to the Kern Knotts area and, with Astley Cooper seconding, he created the short but very exposed route which he called Buttonhook because he used a piece of wire to thread the rope behind a small chockstone. It is graded Very Severe (Hard).

The next day, 8 June, they went to Gable Crag on the northern side of the mountain. Balcombe recorded it laconically:

> Met Astley on Moses Trod. On starting up the scoop as an easy variant to the first pitch, Astley dropped a pile of boulders on himself hurting his chest and arm muscles. Temporarily *hors-de-combat*. Took over lead and removed heaps of grass and muck with a slater's hammer. A full day's work – six hours approximately and made a fine climb of it. Some rain and mist.

The route was the classic Engineer's Slabs which was not repeated until eleven years later.

Next day they returned to the same spot and Balcombe and Sheppard made another new route, Unfinished Arête, just to the right.

They spent a few days repeating established classics on Pillar Rock and Scafell Crag, then, at the end of this astonishing holiday, Balcombe made his final contribution. It came about inadvertently. Sheppard had turned his ankle and Balcombe went to tackle the Central Buttress on Scafell with J. E. B. ('Jerry') Wright and J. R. ('Bobby') Files. The rock was so wet they climbed in stockinged feet and opted for the traditional method at the Great Flake. Loops were fixed round the chockstone and Bobby Files secured himself to them to give Balcombe a hand. Above the Flake they discovered they had left their guide book at the foot of the crag and that no one knew where the route went. So Balcombe devised the Direct Finish. 'I regarded it', he said many years later, 'as an escape route and was astonished to learn later of the clamour in the local and national press.'

It was not Balcombe but Jerry Wright who had given the story to the newspapers and it led to some inaccurate and lurid accounts. The *Daily Telegraph* man began his piece:

> I have just heard the story of one of the most daring and arduous rock climbing expeditions ever undertaken in the British Isles. Anyone who has been on Scafell Pike will have seen the gigantic precipice which towers for a thousand feet above the Mickledore chasm . . .

As far as is known Balcombe made only one more climbing visit to the Lakes – in 1936 when he introduced a group of leading German climbers to C.B. and one of them used two pitons on the Direct Finish.

Balcombe lived in Somerset and he returned home from this trip with a number of German pitons in his rucksack. He used seven of them, soon afterwards, when pioneering the Piton Route in the Avon Gorge. But by this time he was more interested in caving than climbing. Again with Jack Sheppard in support, he began to explore underground, using home-made diving suits and air tubes fashioned out of garden hose-pipes. From now on he devoted his leisure energies to pot-holing, writing a book about his Wookey Hole explorations and founding the Cave Diving Group.

Jerry Wright was already widely known, to some notorious, as 'the Keswick guide'. He was the most obtrusive and controversial of those who made a living out of mountain guiding in the Lake District. But he was not the first. Before the First World War the man from Dauphiné, Gaspard, had been in regular attendance at the Wastwater Hotel. The eccentric Millican Dalton had started guiding before the war, and after it set the pattern for his subsequent life – wintering in the south, in huts in Epping Forest and the New Forest, and spending the rest of the year in Borrowdale, camping at High Lodore and later taking over a cave system on Castle Crag.

Millican Dalton was a 'drop-out' long before the word was coined and the welfare state made it comparatively comfortable. He lived frugally and happily, doing the things he wanted to do in places where he wanted to be. He proclaimed himself 'Professor of Adventure' and for a modest fee would take clients camping, sailing and climbing, promising them 'Mountain Rapid Shooting, Rafting, Hair-breadth escapes'. In fact, the routes he climbed were never very hard, though they were rendered more exciting by the fact that he rarely bothered to belay. He was teetotal and vegetarian. His main expenses were Woodbine cigarettes and coffee, both of which he consumed incessantly. He was stimulating company, with strong views on almost everything, a great admirer of Bernard Shaw, left-wing and pacifist, contemptuous of conventional, urban, consumer society. Once a week he went shopping in Keswick on his old and battered bicycle, painted bright blue. He was lean and bearded. He habitually wore a broad-brimmed hat with a pheasant's feather for decoration, nailed boots, no socks and self-made jackets and breeches that were tattered, weathered and leathery. His skin was weathered and leathery too, and since he hardly ever washed it was generally judged advisable to stay up-wind of him. It is hard to imagine a greater contrast with Jerry Wright.

A note in the Fell and Rock *Journal* for 1927 says:

We have received a pamphlet entitled *The Fell Guide to the English Lakes*, by Mr. J. E. B. Wright, the Keswick guide ... Mr. Wright appears to be energetic and enthusiastic, and to have taken pains to qualify himself for his work. If his propaganda methods smack of American advertising and the cheap press, that is perhaps only to be expected in our modern age. Walking tours up the well-known peaks are naturally the principal activity, but there is also a rock climbing department. Here some of the fees sound high, especially when one remembers the moderate charge formerly made for the services of Gaspard at Wasdale Head. Five guineas per day for each guide for selected courses on the Pillar Rock (selected by Mr. Wright) makes rock climbing a sport for plutocrats, instead of what it essentially is, the most democratic of all recreations.

The next year the *Journal* attacked Jerry Wright on new grounds. There had been a fatal accident on the fells and Wright's remarks at the inquest, about the nature of climbing and the folly of soloing, had been reported – or, as he claimed, misreported – in the press. Wright had even organised a public meeting at Friar's Crag, Keswick, to protest against solo climbing and fell walking. The *Journal* editor, Katharine Chorley, said that 'a good deal of indignant feeling was, we think, quite rightly aroused' among Club members by Wright's actions. She discussed the pros and cons of solo climbing and concluded: 'Everyone has a right to push his or her own climbing opinions. We have no desire to advocate mountaineering Mussolinism. Nevertheless we agree wholeheartedly with the criticism that a public meeting is not a seemly occasion for climbers to argue their domestic controversies.' She also wrote: 'We, who have had the good fortune to inherit a tradition of Lakeland climbing, so totally alien in its genesis and ideals, have naturally felt alarmed at the introduction into Cumberland and Westmorland of Alpine finance and Trans-Atlantic propaganda.'

But Wright was not to be deterred. He was enterprising and efficient and before long he had an organisation, the Lakeland Mountain Guides, and a regular clientèle. He operated, at first, from Seatoller House in Borrowdale. The staple of his business was fell walking and he would lead assorted large groups along the paths, with an attendant – it is said – to open the gates for him. He did not do the harder rock climbs but on routes graded up to Severe he was capable and safe. By all accounts, he was a good instructor. Bobby Files paid four guineas for a four-day introductory course on rock climbing in 1929 and was impressed by Wright's careful methods and the way he instilled confidence. The first climb they did was Oliverson's on Gimmer and Files loved it from the first moment. A fellow-student on the course was H. W. ('Bill') Tilman who was soon to become famous for his exploits on much higher mountains.

If clients wanted to do very hard routes Wright would engage the services of top-class men. Charlie Wilson of Carlisle and his friend Charles ('Chuck') Hudson of Ambleside were taking parties up C.B. in the late 1930s. Wilson recalls:

> I quite admired Jerry Wright. He was a professional. He would assemble his course, 20 adults or so, often at the Waverley Hotel in Keswick, and before the end of the first evening he knew all their names and had them feeling like a group. 'Chuck' and I did the first guided ascent of C.B. I led to the chockstone, tied myself on, then 'Chuck' shot up the Flake. Then the clients would start coming up, one by one, climbing over me. If they fell off I would give the rope a swing and 'Chuck' would haul them back on to the holds.

Wright confined himself to a few classic routes like the North Climb and the New West on Pillar, Needle Ridge and Napes Needle and Eagle's Nest Ridge Direct on Great Gable. He did them all scores of times. Sometimes, to impress his clients, he would race up and down the Needle. His record time was sixty-five seconds.

Almost everything about him, it seems, was calculated to offend the old stagers – his stunt climbing, his skills at self-promotion and publicity, the fact that he was attracting all sorts of new people to the hallowed ground. But the charge most frequently levelled against him was that he was turning what should be a holiday pastime into a profession. There was nothing very logical about the criticism. No one had complained about Gaspard or Millican Dalton and they took money for guiding. Perhaps they were found acceptable because they charged their clients less and were not so obtrusive and organised about it. More professionals appeared in the 1930s – Jim Cameron at Coniston, Stanley Watson in Borrowdale – and there was no consensus of feeling against them. They were much better climbers than Wright but they were also much quieter about it. In the final analysis it seems clear that it was not what Wright did that upset people, so much as the manner in which he did it. And in his defence it can justly be claimed that he gave countless beginners a sound introduction to the fells and crags, through his own guiding, his organisation of the Mountaineering Association after the Second World War and also through his books, *The Craft of Climbing* and *The Technique of Mountaineering*.

At Easter 1936 there was a celebratory gathering at Wasdale Head. It was the fiftieth anniversary of the first ascent of Napes Needle, which some regarded as the true starting moment of the sport. The climb's 'onlie begetter', Walter Parry Haskett Smith, was seventy-six years old by this time but had kept himself reasonably fit by regular walks with the London section of the Fell and Rock Club. Invited to return to Wasdale Head and repeat his historic climb, this time with a roped companion fore and aft, he agreed promptly.

The first ascent had been made towards the end of June but the Club decided that the jubilee climb should be made at the Easter weekend, presumably so that more members would be able to attend. Unfortunately, this meant the old gentleman had to contend not only with his advancing years but also with hostile weather conditions.

On Good Friday he was driven up from London in a small open car and when he arrived at last at Wastwater Hotel his limbs were stiff and his eyes streaming. The club President, Professor R. S. T. (later Lord) Chorley, and the editor of the club *Journal*, G. R. Speaker, were there to greet him. Next day they planned to take him on a trial climb on Pillar Rock but he had to turn back when he got as far as Robinson's Cairn. Easter Sunday morning, the day of the climb, dawned cold and blustery and there were occasional snow flurries. Although his eyes were by now badly inflamed, Haskett Smith and his escorts made their way slowly up the Sty Head path and then along the climbers' traverse to the foot of the Needle, where some 300 people were assembled to cheer them on.

Chorley climbed first, in nailed boots, following the original Wasdale Crack route. Haskett Smith, in rubbers, was second and Speaker kept close behind him, carefully guiding his feet on to the holds. Before long Haskett Smith appeared on the top. One of the spectators shouted, 'Tell us a story.' 'There is no other story', he called down. 'This is the top storey.'

Chorley paid tribute to Haskett Smith and went on: 'And in praising him let us also praise those famous men who took the torch from him and who have passed it on from hand to hand until it came to those who in the present day worthily maintain the tradition.' Haskett Smith thanked everyone and thought he might not be fit enough to repeat the climb after a further fifty years. In fact he died ten years later.

Other figures from the first days of the sport were still sometimes to be seen. It was in 1936 that the Abraham brothers had their last climb together, their own New West on Pillar Rock, and George carried on climbing for several years after that. A. E. Field was occasionally out, and in 1939 Godfrey Solly, the creator of Eagle's Nest Ridge Direct, marked the fiftieth anniversary of his first ascent of Pillar Rock by leading up the Slab and Notch route 'with cheerful ease'. Among those on the rope behind him was the man who had been with him on the first ascent, the Reverend Edmund Freeman of Whitehaven. From the next generation of pioneers, George Sansom, whose love for the Lake District never faded, still enjoyed climbing – he did Napes Needle with his eldest son, John, in 1939. There were, indeed, those who believed that the spirit of Sansom's great partner, Siegfried Herford, still roamed the fells. C. F. Holland, who had a mystical turn of mind, claimed that he often met him when he was walking alone. And A. B. Reynolds, a Quaker, chatted briefly at Esk Hause with a young man of striking appearance (wearing a polo-neck sweater) who suddenly disappeared and whom he subsequently recognized, from a photograph, as Herford.

The mid-1930s mark the halfway stage in this story.

In some ways the sport had hardly changed in half a century. Most climbers, tramping up the fell side to the crags, would have been virtually indistinguishable from their pioneer predecessors. Raffish scruffiness, in the Haskett Smith style, was still the prevailing fashion, though there were a few who thought A. B. Hargreaves took it altogether too far. They wore old tweed jackets and breeches, with thick woollen stockings and nailed boots – though many would be carrying a pair of plimsolls in the rucksack. They no longer carried ice axes all the year round but the vital piece of equipment was exactly the same, the Manilla hemp 'Alpine' rope with the red strands.

Once on the climb, only one or two points of difference would be noticeable. If the rock was dry most of them would be wearing rubber-soled shoes. Some might be using line in place of the thick hemp rope. More care would be taken over the secure anchoring of the stationary man and, as he pulled the rope in or paid it out, he would be passing it over one shoulder for extra friction.

These improvements made for safer climbing – for everyone but the leader. For him there was little more protection than there had been fifty years before. If he fell, from any distance above the second man, he would be very lucky to avoid death or serious injury. The old golden rule – 'the leader must not fall' – still held. But it was not always observed.

There were more people climbing, of course. What had been an exclusive pastime for a few dozen men had become the sport of several hundreds of men and women. And a higher proportion of them were inexperienced. Internal combustion, better roads, the growth of tourism, the appearance of youth hostels – all these meant that more young people were escaping from their urban surroundings to find adventure in the fells. As a result, there were many more climbing accidents. In the first twenty-one years of rock climbing in the Lake District there was not a single fatal accident. By the mid-1930s the death rate, for roped climbers, was running at well over one every year.

In 1933 a brother and sister fell to their deaths on the east face of Pillar Rock, and a lead climber who fell from Kern Knotts Crack suffered 'serious spinal injury'. But the year before had been worse. Two men fell from Tophet Bastion and one was killed, the other badly injured. Two seventeen-year-old lads, completely without experience, fell while trying to find a way down Gimmer Crag and one of them was killed. An accident on Dow Crag makes it clear that careful belaying methods were by no means universal. Dr John Brogden of Hartlepool, who had done a good deal of climbing, was leading two others – Bill Tilman, who had already conquered Mount Kenya with Eric Shipton, and a schoolteacher called Vera Brown – up Jones's Route. It is not a hard climb but the weather was bad, cold and windy. Brogden had reached the grassy ledge at the top and Tilman was only a few feet below him, on a poor belay, when Miss Brown, traversing from the Bandstand, slipped and fell. Tilman was immediately pulled off and Brogden, who cannot have been anchored, fell sixty feet or so on to the scree of Easter Gully. Brogden was killed and the others were terribly injured. When he recovered consciousness Tilman, with fractured vertebrae, crawled the four miles of rough ground back to Coniston to raise the alarm. It was a remarkable feat of willpower and endurance and it took him four hours. But it enabled rescuers to reach Miss Brown in time to save her life. The doctors told Tilman he would never climb again but three months later he was in the Alps, proving them wrong.

Each new accident inspired the newspapers to sensational and inaccurate accounts with banner headlines of the 'Mountain Madness' type. Normally the press paid little attention to rock climbing and the climbers were happy that it should be so. But the death of King Albert of the Belgians in 1934, rock climbing near Namur, created a great *furor* and led to calls for the banning of the sport. The local papers were as bad, in this respect, as the 'gutter' nationals. The editor of *The West Cumberland Times*, the appropriately-named Mr A. E. Inkpen, was fiercely opposed to climbing. J. W. Nicholas, who took over the editorship in 1936, took the same line and it was not until after the Second World War when Frank Carruthers, a climber himself, got the job that the paper's attitude became sympathetic and informed. The public remained almost unanimous in its conviction that rock climbers were crazy and many continued to imagine that the crags were climbed simply by swarming up ropes, lassoed to a flake above or held in place by some obscure kind of Indian rope trick.

But if the public were as ignorant as ever, the enthusiasts had easy access to much more information than their predecessors. They no longer had to ferret it out by word of mouth or by searching through the pages of the hotel climbing books. Between 1935 and 1938 the Fell and Rock issued its second series of guide books, rigorously edited by H. M. Kelly and illustrated, with great clarity, by the line drawings of William Heaton Cooper. Kelly imposed his succinct, factual, pitch-by-pitch style and condensed the information into four pocket-sized volumes: *Pillar Rock and Neighbourhood* which he wrote himself; *Scafell Group*, the work of A. T. Hargreaves; a volume covering *Great Gable, Borrowdale and Buttermere*; and a fourth embracing *Dow Crag, Great Langdale and Outlying Crags*.

There was another way in which things had changed. The first climbers had concentrated almost exclusively on the three climbing grounds they could easily reach from Wasdale Head – Scafell, Pillar Rock and the Napes cliffs of Great Gable. Gradually the ripples had spread outwards and in the 1920s and '30s many new areas were opened up:

Pike's Crag by Kelly and his friends; Boat Howe on Kirkfell where George Basterfield launched the tradition of giving the routes nautical names; in Ennerdale, the Mosedale Buttresses and Black Crag; in Borrowdale where Bentley Beetham uncovered several scattered crags and climbed them; and, further north, the Castle Rock of Triermain above Thirlmere and the gabbro outcrops on the eastern slopes of Carrock Fell.

The Castle Rock, which was to play an important part in this story, is splendidly visible from the main road through the Lake District. As Graham Macphee said in an article in the club *Journal* for 1929, 'It is surprising that in this age of intensive rock climbing in the Lake District nobody seems to have climbed the Castle Rock. None of the experts who were consulted had ever even heard of the crag.' Macphee determined, as he put it, to 'explore its scansorial possibilities' and the redoubtable Mabel Barker of Caldbeck joined him. They failed to make much impression on the main central face, which is high and very steep everywhere and overhanging in places, so transferred their attention to the easier South Crag. In 1928 four new routes were made there, one of them – the Slab Climb – led by Mabel Barker. The next year A. T. Hargreaves led Macphee up the Direct Route, which is graded Very Severe (Mild).

Dr Mabel Barker was not the first woman to lead a new route in Britain. The credit for that goes to Mrs E. H. Daniell, a West Country novelist, who led the first ascent of Hope on Idwal Slabs in Snowdonia in 1915. But Mabel Barker did notch up an impressive list. In 1925 she became the first woman to climb Central Buttress; she was the first to traverse the Cuillin Ridge on Skye; and starting in 1927 she created a number of short climbs, several of them graded Severe, on the slopes of Carrock Fell near her home. She lived in Caldbeck and, although she died nearly thirty years ago, she is still remembered, vividly and with affection, as a notable eccenric.

Born at Silloth on the Solway Firth, she studied geography at Oxford, then took a B.Sc. in geology at London University. After the war she went to the University of Montpellier where she was awarded a doctorate of literature for a thesis she wrote, in French, arguing her advanced views on education. Back in Cumberland she acquired a terraced row of cottages in Caldbeck and converted them into a school, partly for boarders and also for local boys and girls. She ran the school as a prototype outdoor pursuits centre, teaching the children about the environment and the importance of protecting it, taking them walking and scrambling about on the fells. They also learnt French.

She was a striking, gipsy-like figure, slim and lean-featured, with a beaky nose and a weather-beaten complexion and long black hair, tightly coiled at the back. Though she seemed to subsist almost exclusively on cigarettes and strong tea, she kept very fit. On the crags she was a neat,

balanced climber with impressive powers of endurance and unquenchable enthusiasm. In 1936, at the age of fifty, she took part – with Ieuan
Banner Mendus and Jack Carswell – in the first descent of C.B.

Jack Carswell had grown up in Workington on the coast, fascinated
by the sight of Grasmoor fifteen miles away. At the age of twelve he
would set off early on Sunday morning, walk to Loweswater, scramble
up Melbreak, then walk home again – a round trip of nearly thirty miles.
He left school at fourteen and went to work with a firm of boiler-makers.
He read O. G. Jones's book over and over again until he knew the old
classic routes intimately, although he had never seen them. It was not
until 1932, when he met a young Welshman called Banner Mendus who
had come to work in a solicitor's office in Workington, that he began
climbing. On Saturday afternoons, the week's work done, they would
cycle to Ennerdale or Borrowdale – the rope hidden in a rucksack – and
work their way conscientiously up through the grades in the climbers'
guide books, to pedal home again on Sunday night. Carswell took to
climbing like a duck to water and he remembers his first encounter with
Mabel Barker as if it were yesterday:

> One of the most delightful things I know is to be climbing on the Pinnacle Face
> of Scafell in the late afternoon in summer when the sun is on the rocks and all is
> warm and beautiful. You needn't do any particular route. You can just wander
> about. We were doing that on just such a day in 1934 when we heard some people
> singing in Moss Ghyll. It sounded wonderful. So we went over and found Mabel
> Barker with a group of German students, all singing German songs. She was
> camping with them at Seathwaite, which she did every year, and taking them
> climbing.

After that the three of them did much climbing together, climbing down
as well as up, and in the summer of 1936 Carswell proposed that they
should attempt the descent of C.B.

They did it on Sunday 21 June, a day of perfect weather. Mabel
Barker led – 'I had all the fun of working out the route backwards' –
with Mendus in the middle and Carswell in the key station in the rear.
As they descended towards the Great Flake they heard the voices of a
party coming up – A. T. Hargreaves and his wife Ruth, Sid Cross and
'Jammy' Nelson who derived her nickname, apparently, at school, from
the French *jamais* because she would never do what she was expected to
do. The descenders waited on Jeffcoat's Ledge and let the others step
over them. Mabel Barker cadged some cigarettes from them as they
passed.

Banner Mendus went first across the top of the Great Flake, with
Carswell close behind. Carswell wedged his leg firmly inside the Flake
and paid the rope cautiously out as Mendus edged his way down to the
chockstone and tied himself to it. Mabel Barker then climbed past them

both, protected by two ropes, and down to the Oval. Then it was Carswell's turn:

> I had been perched on the Flake for so long that I was stiff and sore, so I took a short rest before commencing the descent. This I found less trying than the ascent, because by getting the right shoulder in the Crack one can use sundry small holds on the inside, sufficient to control a descent but not of much help when overcoming the excessive friction of an ascent.

The story illustrates that there were several women, by this time, operating at a high standard. Blanche Eden-Smith was still climbing with Kelly and often leading. Brenda Ritchie led many hard routes. In June 1939 'Jammy' Nelson became the first woman to lead Central Buttress.

But the greatest change in the sport in its first half-century lay in the social background of the climbers. For two decades and more it had been an occasional though compelling holiday pastime for a handful of professional men from the great population centres of England, most of them highly educated. Many keen climbers were still of this description but increasingly, in the years before the outbreak of the Second World War, the leadership of the sport was being assumed by a very different breed of men. They left school as soon as possible and worked hard in factories and shops and offices and they had very litle money. But they lived near the crags and were able to spend every weekend climbing. Carswell and Mendus cycled in from Workington. Charlie Wilson, who worked in a sweet factory in Carlisle, had to pedal even further. From Kendal came Sid Cross and Charlie Tatham and their friends. From Barrow there was a larger contingent, now called 'the Barrow boys'. George Basterfield was still their leader and their ranks had been reinforced by the transfer of A. T. Hargreaves to Barrow. One of their recruits, in the late 1920s, was Harry Griffin, a trainee journalist on the local paper who was to write more words – as newspaper columnist and the author of many books – about the Lake District than anyone else. In an article he called 'Nostalgia for Nails' he recalled those days:

> What wonderful spacious days they were in the late 1920s and early 1930s – carefree, youthful days on uncrowded crags, so long before even the threat of war. Outside holiday times, the Lake District, in those uncomplicated days, could still be regarded as a quiet, fairly secluded paradise with few motor cars, no caravan sites or litter baskets, uneroded tracks and the four-in-hands going over the passes...
> My introduction to 'proper' climbing had been provided by George Basterfield, that kindliest of men, who happened to be the Mayor of Barrow at the time. Plucking up my courage, I went to see the great man in the Mayor's Parlour to ask his advice and George not only told me how to get my boots nailed – by George Stephens at Coniston – but actually offered to take me climbing on Dow Crag the following Sunday ... On the way up to the crag from the old quarries above Torver, George pointed out many of the routes on the cliff and, somewhere near the quartz cairn, stopped, looked at the ground and told me, with confidence,

who would be climbing that day. In those days climbers used distinctive types of nailing – sometimes with nails of their own manufacture – and George, studying the imprints of the nails on the track, knew exactly who we would meet on the crag ...

The day proved even more rewarding and exciting than I anticipated. I can clearly remember looking down between my legs at the screes while climbing the final crack on A Buttress and thinking that this was the most wonderful experience of my young life. All at once, climbing seemed the only thing that mattered.

There was rivalry between the various groups but it was light-hearted. Sometimes, inevitably, there was friction: some felt intimidated by Kelly's commanding manner; George Bower did not care for women climbers; Graham Macphee and A. B. Hargreaves could not stand each other; many disliked the brashness of Jerry Wright, the Keswick guide. But generally speaking, and to a remarkable extent, the friendly, happy spirit of the pioneers still prevailed, fifty years on. They encouraged and advised newcomers. They helped each other and, if there was trouble, they would turn out in all weathers to spend the night on search and rescue work. Climbing was still uncluttered and – except for the odd, very rare piton – done without artificial aids. The crags were uncluttered, too, and free, still offering endless opportunities to those who liked to explore new ground. When new routes were made, details would be given in the club *Journal* but the motivation was co-operative, not competitive. They wanted others to know the pleasure they had found.

— • 7 •—

New Men, New Crags
1936–1947

FOR THE Fell and Rock Climbing Club the mid-1930s were years of some anxiety.

In the first place, it was a period of fierce battles to protect the Lake District from the depredations of the developer. Five thousand acres of the Buttermere valley came up for sale and money had to be hurriedly raised to buy the land for the National Trust. There was talk of a road from Borrowdale to Wasdale Head by way of Sty Head Pass. The Forestry Commission planned to blanket much of Eskdale and Dunnerdale with dark and gloomy conifers, planted in straight lines. Great areas of Lakeland fell side had already been transformed by the introduction of millions of fast-growing, profit-making spruce and larch – the slopes above Thirlmere and Bassenthwaite Lake, the length of Ennerdale above the lake. The Fell and Rock threw its weight unreservedly behind the forces of conservation, led by the Council for the Preservation of Rural England and the newly formed Friends of the Lake District. It was among those arguing that the District should be designated a national park, with special powers to preserve its unique character.

Of more immediate concern to the club was the state of the sport of rock climbing. These were years when young continental climbers were making remarkable new routes on the Alpine North walls. But in the Lake District, after the initial burst of activity on Scafell East Buttress, little had happened. By the middle of the decade few new routes were being done and hardly any of them by members of the club. It was a similar problem to that which had troubled the Climbers' Club in North Wales after the First World War, and the Fell and Rock turned to the same solution. A club hut was built at Brackenclose in Wasdale Head.

It was not the first climbing hut in the Lake District. In 1930 the Wayfarers' Club of Liverpool had opened their Robertson Lamb hut in Langdale. Not long after that, the stone-built house on the summit of

134

Dunmail Raise was converted for the use of Roman Catholics who wanted to go fell walking or climbing. It was named the Achille Ratti hut in honour of the priest/Alpinist who became Pope Pius XI.

But members of the Fell and Rock who wanted to holiday near the crags yet in reasonable comfort had to book into hotels or farmhouses. Many of these places were inexpensive and several became famous for their hospitality – the Jopsons of Thorneythwaite, the Edmondsons of Seathwaite, Mrs Birkett of Gillerthwaite, Mrs Bryan and Miss Pirie at Parkgate, Coniston, and others. However low their prices, however, they were beyond the means of the working-class lads from Penrith or Workington who wanted to spend every weekend climbing. It was for them that the club decided to build its own hut.

The job was thoroughly done, built by Wasdale men with local stone, and Brackenclose was ceremonially opened in October 1937. A. T. Hargreaves was made Warden and H. M. Kelly kept the accounts. The charge for staying one night was two shillings (10p).

A. T. Hargreaves ran the hut on a tight rein but it proved a great success and remains in active service to this day. The Fell and Rock now has four more huts – Raw Head in Langdale, Hasness in Buttermere, Salving House in Borrowdale and Beetham Cottage at Brothers Water. But for all its effectiveness, it was not from Brackenclose – nor, indeed, from within the club at all – that the next breakthrough in Lake District climbing was to come.

It was the work, primarily, of a coal-miner from Workington and a quarryman from Little Langdale, Bill Peascod and Jim Birkett respectively.

Robert James Birkett has lived all his life in the Lake District and never wanted anything else. His father ran a small farm, then worked for the council, looking after a stretch of valley road. Jim left the village school to be an apprentice 'river' in the slate quarry, learning to split the blocks with a hammer and chisel. It was the collector's passion for birds' eggs that took him to the cliff faces. He would borrow the rope his grandfather used to fix loads to the farm carts, and lower himself down the crags to steal eggs. A market gardener in Hawkshead, Jim Tyson, who was a climber, taught him how to protect himself with sensible belays and the proper knots. Many years later Jim Birkett came to regret his egg-stealing escapades and devoted himself, in contrition and with equal passion, to the protection of wildlife and especially the birds and their nests.

In 1936, when he was twenty-two, he teamed up with a fellow-quarryman, Billy Jenkinson, and went to try rock climbing. They had no guide book but Birkett had seen the Abraham photographs and when they visited Kern Knotts he immediately recognised the Crack as an established route. So they climbed it. It was an impressive way to start.

Next year Birkett led his first new route, Tarsus on Dove Crag, a Severe which he named in commemoration of the pigeon's shinbone (tarsus) that he found on a ledge. Over the next dozen years he was to add nearly fifty routes to the Lake District list, most of them of the highest aesthetic as well as technical quality, one of them the first climb in the District to be graded Extremely Severe.

Bill Peascod appeared on the climbing scene a year or two after Birkett. The son of a Maryport coal-miner, he left school at fourteen and went to work, for just under £1 a week, at a Workington pit. Soon he was working at the coal-face alongside his father, swinging a pick to fill twenty tubs of coal a day. He had already discovered the fells, cycling to Buttermere early one morning, after the night shift:

> As I breasted the hill the whole panorama of the beautiful valley began to unfold. Below me Loweswater and the hazy fells slept in a gentle dawn. From high up on Fang's Brow I could hear the valley sounds – voices of man and beast – the 'clip-clop' of a draught horse. Apart from them all was still and totally at peace. After a night spent in the darkness and turmoil, amongst the sweat and stink of stale air, pit ponies and one's own pit shirt, my discovery of Western Lakeland set my senses in a whirl.

Before long he was fell walking every Sunday and, by means of his other escape route – the public library – learning about climbing from the books of O. G. Jones and George Abraham. Somehow he got a 50-foot length of hemp rope and with this, in the summer of 1938, he soloed Central Gully on Great End and the Sphinx Ridge on the Napes, trailing the rope behind him in the hope that, if he should fall, it might catch on something and save him. Next year he led his first Severe. The year after that he was making routes of his own on the crags of Buttermere, at and around the Very Severe standard.

The two men had much in common. They came from humble homes, were given the minimum education the law allowed, and had to work hard and long, manually, for little pay. Their work gave them strength – in the arms and fingers, in physical endurance, and in temperament too, the capacity to think calmly and move surely in the most testing circumstances. Each made his own way to climbing and each found, with delight, that he had a natural aptitude for it. They were both men of lively and practical intelligence. Birkett applied it to the wildlife around him and became an authority on Lakeland flora and fauna. Peascod studied hard and became a mining engineer, an expert in underground ventilation, a teacher, and in his middle age developed a high talent as a landscape painter.

In many ways, though, they were very different. Jim Birkett was – as he still is – a man of reserve, modest and shy and disinclined to reveal much about his feelings. He does not appear on television and rarely agrees to be interviewed. When he does talk, he will answer questions directly, with palpable honesty and much laughter, but briefly, without gossip or elaboration:

> I kept myself very fit when I was climbing – never smoked – drank very rarely and never a lot – used to work out with friends at a gym in Keswick. I never took photographs and I never wrote my climbs up – you're taking time from the rock when you're writing about it. And I never competed. The only thing I competed with was the rock ... I never joined any of the clubs. I'm not a joiner. Most folk join the clubs so they can use the huts but I'd no need for that – I live here. It's rubbish to say the Fell and Rock rejected me because I was a quarryman. They had cobblers and carpenters and coal miners as members. I didn't ask to join. But when I met them on the crags they were always friendly and helpful ...
>
> There's no common sense in climbing. I've never encouraged anyone, even my own boys, to start. It's up to each individual. But I loved it. You do feel very good after a hard climb.

Bill Peascod, by contrast, was extrovert and convivial, an enthusiastic drinker of beer and malt whisky, an entertaining *raconteur*, and – by his own admission – 'not much given to modesty'. He was clubbable – a member of the Fell and Rock for forty-five years, until his death by a coronary, climbing on Clogwyn du'r Arddu, in 1985. He lived in Australia for many years and on his return home in 1980 resumed his Lakeland climbing as if there had been no interruption, got Birkett's son Bill to introduce him to the new climbs and techniques, appeared in television films and wrote his autobiography, *Journey after Dawn*. It is an evocative, sometimes romantic book, full of the sort of self-revelation that would be anathema to Jim Birkett.

They never climbed together but Peascod saw Birkett on Buttonhook in the early 1940s and remembered his 'combination of grace, delicacy and considerable physical strength'. Peascod had the strength but no one would describe his climbing as graceful. He had nothing of Birkett's fluidity of movement but he had an easy balance and could move across delicate slabs both nimbly and neatly. He was altogether noisier than Birkett, keeping up an almost continuous flow of banter or comment as he climbed, often delighted, sometimes – when the conditions were bad – loaded with scabrous invective. His climbing meant much to him. Writing a long time after the event, he recalled one of his finest first ascents with these words:

> Of course there are harder climbs, probably even steeper or longer or better climbs – but for me there is only one Eagle Front and it hasn't really got much to do with hardness, steepness or any of the other objective assessments. It is to do with a lad of 20 crawling out of a dirty hole in the ground, out of a monstrous soul-destroying existence to freedom and air and space, to grab life by the tail and to swing it round the head like a stone tied to the end of a rope.

Peascod cheerfully adopted the new equipment and methods when they came along but Jim Birkett preferred the old-fashioned ways. He used a hemp rope and usually carried a couple of slings, home-made from farmer's rope, for fixing belays. Sometimes, if the going was hard and the rock dry, he would wear Woolworth's black rubber 'pumps', but this was rare. On the vast majority of his climbs, he wore heavy boots, ringed with 'waisted clinker' nails – made of soft steel and grooved in the middle so that each nail offered two projecting points to the rock. Those who saw him climb agree that he was the finest exponent of the now-lost art of climbing in nails. 'He moved like a ballet dancer', Charlie Wilson says. 'He left no scratches on the rock, just a tiny point where the nail had bitten in.' Harry Griffin can recall no one who climbed with such balance and poise, moving with easy confidence, applying the edge nails to the tiniest wrinkles in the rock, using smooth momentum to keep in contact in places where the rock was unreliable or covered in slime. Birkett's own comments are characteristically self-effacing:

> I remember Ruth Hargreaves remarking, when I was climbing Central Buttress in nails, that it looked like I was climbing on ball bearings. But I thought they were the bee's knees. I hardly realised it had anything to do with me. I thought it was the boots that were getting me up the routes.

Birkett also remarked: 'Anyone who works with his hands gains a strong grip; that's more important than pulling power. It's how you can grasp a tiny hold and hang on that's important. Once I can get fingers over something, the rest will usually follow.'

He never had a fall. He knew his limits and was careful to keep within them. It was a rule with him never to make a move unless he knew he could reverse it. It was another rule always to be master of the situation.

He made his first classic new route on 1 May 1938 and called it May Day. It is on Scafell East Buttress and still graded Very Severe (Hard). A recent historian of the period, John Wilkinson, reckons it 'was the hardest climb in the Lakes at that time and was to remain so for over a decade'. Birkett's companions on that first ascent were Charlie Wilson from Carlisle and 'Chuck' Hudson of Ambleside. It was Wilson who spotted the line. He also brought with him a few pitons which his blacksmith uncle had made out of the axle tree of an old Ford.

It is not clear from subsequent accounts how many pitons Birkett banged into the cracks. One says there were four, another says three, yet another mentions only two. But pitons were undoubtedly used, though only for protection, not to help the climbing. Perhaps he was influenced by the knowledge that Linnell had used a piton on the nearby Overhanging Wall. Whatever the reason, he regretted the action: 'I was young and daft and thought I'd have a go at this pegging business. Perhaps I was a bit overwhelmed by the occasion. Because there was certainly no need for them. They didn't help the climbing at any point.' He never used pitons again.

In August that year Birkett created another classic on the same crag, the Buttress girdle, 750 feet of well-sustained severity. His companion this time was Len Muscroft, a fitter from Carlisle and the most dependable of seconds: 'I felt I could do anything', Birkett says, 'with Len on the other end of the rope.'

Next year Birkett turned his attention to another forbidding cliff. No routes had been made on the big North Buttress of Castle Rock of Triermain, though there had been several attempts. The eagle-eyed Charlie Wilson, always on the look-out for such things, spotted what looked like a challenging but possible line, tending leftwards across the face of the crag: 'I knew I couldn't lead the gangway', he says, 'so I got Jim to do it.' The third man on the rope was Len Muscroft.

On the early part of the climb Birkett experimented with a new idea for protection. He took some pebbles along in a pocket and when he saw a convenient crack, he would wedge a pebble in it and then thread a length of line behind the pebble to afford a running belay. It cannot have been very reassuring. The line was not strong. Birkett once said: 'I wouldn't trust my mother's washing on it.' But he advanced steadily and smoothly and had no trouble with what is now regarded as the crux of the climb – the committing step from the pinnacle to the foot of the gangway. He judged the whole route 'easy for a Very Severe'. But Overhanging Bastion was seen by many climbers as something of a psychological breakthrough and, perhaps because the cliff is so visible from the road, much was made of it by the newspapers. One headline said 'Lakeland Everest Conquered'.

Three weeks later, on 22 April 1939, the same team, in the same order of ascent, made an adjoining route, Zigzag, which is also in the Very Severe grade.

Soon after that Birkett had a road accident – his motor cycling was far more dangerous than his climbing – and was out of action for a while. But he came back in 1940 to make the North-west Arête on Gimmer and two new routes on the Napes, Eagle's Crack and Tophet Grooves (which was not repeated for seven years). In 1941, with Vic Veevers as his second, he created the F Route on Gimmer.

Other men were making routes of quality in these years: Alf Mullen with his Tricouni Slab on Scafell: Sid Cross with Citadel on Pike's Crag and The Prow of the Boat on Boat Howe; Jim Haggas with Hangover on Dove Crag and his impressive Gordian Knot on the untouched central mass of White Ghyll. But the most intensive assault was that made by Bill Peascod in his beloved Buttermere.

At first Peascod climbed alone and secretively, hiding the rope in his rucksack so that his fellow-miners would not think him 'bonkers'. On Grey Crags in 1939 G. R. Speaker – 'a gentleman in every sense of the word' – protected him up his first Severe, gave him advice and proposed him for membership of the Fell and Rock. Through the club Peascod found another Workington man who was keen on climbing, Bert Beck, who taught English at the grammar school. They made a good partnership – Peascod always leading and not to be deterred by bad weather or unstable and slimy ground, Beck perfectly contented with the supporting role and entirely reliable. Beck also had a Morris Tourer which was old and draughty but as reliable as himself. Soon they were spending every Sunday in Buttermere. Within weeks of climbing his first Severe, Peascod was leading them. Before the end of 1939 he had made his first new route. Next year he created six, five of them Very Severe. It is a measure of his natural skill and boldness that the first four Very Severes he climbed were routes of his own devising, first ascents. He is still honoured by rock climbers, more than anything else, for the best of his 1940 creations, Eagle Front.

Peascod made most of his routes simply by looking up at the crag, working out a likely line in his mind and then setting off to see if it would go. But Eagle Crag, high up in Birkness Combe, looks forbidding, big and dark and steep – it rarely gets the sun and is usually wet. So, together with Beck and another Workington man, Gordon Connor, Peascod traversed across the middle of the face, moving leftwards and making a close inspection of the cliff above. As they moved on to new ground they discovered the characteristic snags of the crag – ledges that had looked comfortable proved small and awkwardly sloping, the holds were small and sloping too, the belays were discouraging. At one point, while Peascod edged his way delicately across, Beck had to sit on the small boulder he was belayed to, simply to keep it in place. But they did the route and were reassured by what they had seen. The wall above the Terrace and the final crack that led to the summit slope both looked climbable. This was 9 June, a few days after the fall of France and the escape of the remnants of the British army from Dunkirk.

A fortnight later, on 23 June 1940, Peascod and Beck made the attempt. The weather was fine and the rock unusually dry so they wore Woolworth's plimsolls. Peascod climbed the initial rib easily, then tackled the long and serious second pitch:

> Safeguards in the form of slings were generally difficult to arrange on this huge face ... Our supplies of slings were fairly limited anyway (running only to one each) but I had managed to get one in position on the gangway. It was made of thick rope and it came off before I got to the top of the pitch ... The situation was breathtaking. We were on ground that no man had ever climbed before. We had ascended a pitch that would be most difficult to descend – and we didn't have enough rope to abseil. From the big belay on the top of pitch two a few awkward moves followed and then the angle eased. I could see the Terrace above me, we had reached the half-way point. My heart was singing as I climbed on to it!

Now he was on ground he had climbed before, until the final crack which he was delighted to find 'loaded with splendid hidden handholds'.

The route was done and he called it Eagle Front. He graded it Very Severe, but tentatively because he had never done an established VS and did not know how standards were assessed. He had not read any of the guide books. More than forty years later, writing his autobiography, he felt that his youthful ignorance had been a help:

> Because nobody had been up the front of Eagle Crag nobody was able to tell us it was steep and exposed; that it didn't run to sharp incut holds; that the belays were noticeable more through their absence than their quality; that when it came to using serviceable protection points, one may as well have left the slings and karabiners at home and saved oneself the job of carrying them up the mountain – because useful and positive flakes and threads were not readily available. But nobody was there to tell us – so we just went out and did the climbs.

In 1941 Peascod added nine more new routes to the Buttermere list, among them Dexter Wall, Suaviter and Fortiter on Grey Crag, the unstable V Gully on Haystacks and Resurrection Route on High Crag. But he also got married that year and Bert Beck went into the Royal Artillery, and, although he did not stop climbing altogether, the pace of Peascod's creativity diminished for a couple of years.

It was very quiet on the crags throughout the war years. Most of the climbers were in the forces, and strict petrol rationing made it impossible for those who were left to get to the mountains regularly, if they lived any distance away. The only new routes were those made by local men, like Peascod, who had reserved occupations or by men, like Bentley Beetham, who were too old to be conscripted into the armed forces.

The impact of the Second World War was nothing like so damaging to the sport as that of the First had been. The casualty list was much shorter and confined, oddly and almost exclusively, to the RAF. Sid Thompson, a gritstone expert who created Crow's Nest Direct on Gimmer in 1940, was shot down and killed. So, too, was Gordon Connor, Peascod's sometime climbing partner from Workington, who served as a rear-gunner in a Lancaster bomber. Colin Kirkus, the man who had opened up the East Buttress of Scafell but whose finest climbing period had been ended by the accident on Ben Nevis in 1934, became a navigator and bomb-aimer with the Pathfinder Squadron. On his twenty-fifth raid, over Bremen in September 1942, his plane was shot down and he was killed. He was only thirty-two. In his last letter to Alf Bridge he had said: 'I wish I could go back to the hills again, but I shan't really enjoy them until after the war, when all this business is behind me instead of just ahead.'

In the month of Kirkus's death over Germany, one of the leading and best-liked members of the Fell and Rock Club, Gustave Robert Speaker, fell from Eagle's Nest West Chimney on Great Gable and was killed. He was sixty-seven. He had started mountaineering in the Alps before the

First World War and had been a familiar figure – tall and lean, invariably wearing a black beret and a serious expression that belied his fun-loving character – on the crags of Lakeland since the summer of 1919. His enthusiasm was infectious and many beginners were grateful for his wise and generous encouragement. And he was a great club man, particularly attached to the Fell and Rock – he edited the *Journal* from 1953 to his death and was President 1937–9.

Speaker's educational background was scientific and in his mid-twenties he had founded an asbestos business, which he ran on enlightened profit-sharing lines and with great success. Despite his technical and practical abilities, he approached mountaineering in the high, spiritual style of the early Snowdonia men. Lecturing to the Rucksack Club in 1935, he stated his faith:

> Our acquisitive, over-industrialised social order has allowed mechanism to predominate, to the virtual exclusion of the divine thought principle behind it. From that position there is no escape until, instead of allowing ourselves to remain bent down towards the earth, we straighten our backs and turn our faces heavenwards. Thus out of the very excess of mechanism comes the desire to climb to free our brickbound souls. It is a deep craving for beauty, truth and happiness.

In several ways, in fact, the Second World War made considerable contributions to the progress of the sport.

The RAF set up a Mountain Rescue Service to recover air crew who had been forced down in mountainous parts of Britain. They had teams in Scotland, North Wales and the Lake District. It was a pointer to future development and the start of the close and beneficient co-operation between the RAF and local mountain rescue teams which has been maintained ever since.

The army trained its élite assault troops, the Commandos, in the arts of moving and surviving in very hostile circumstances and taught them how to climb up cliffs and how to abseil down them. The man in charge of this was Frank Smythe of pre-war Everest fame and one of his instructors was Major John Hunt, who was to be made famous by Mount Everest after the war. Another instructor was Alf Bridge. Yet another, amazingly, was C. F. Holland who had taken part in the first ascent of Central Buttress before the outbreak of the First World War, fought with distinction and been wounded in that war and now – 'by an adept alteration to his birth certificate' – contrived to get himself re-enlisted into The Buffs. Soon after the war, he described the experience:

> I was at first rather alarmed at the prospect of taking over the responsibility of piloting wild youths up cliffs, especially as I doubted my ability to lead after so long a period away from the rocks. I found, however, that I need not have worried. The wild youths of my imagination were conspicuous by their absence; the average age of the men was probably 25 or so, and though undoubtedly high-spirited, they were much easier to get on with, and infinitely more sober, than the old

sweats of the battalion I had originally joined. What struck me most forcibly was their great modesty, the refusal to regard themselves as anything out of the ordinary, or as superior in any way to other units. The inspired articles that appeared about them from time to time aroused their derision, and indeed anger, and the publicity given them was deplored by officers and men alike.

The Commando mountain warfare courses – held in the Scottish Highlands, Snowdonia and on the sea cliffs of Cornwall, with occasional visits to the Lake District crags – were influential. The army was not at all inhibited by 'ethical' considerations and perfectly happy to use every technical aid it could lay its hands on. As a result, items of equipment that had been in common use in Europe for decades but generally eschewed by British climbers – karabiners, pitons and piton hammers, étriers, even grappling irons – were now brought heavily to bear on British rock. Furthermore, the Commandos were issued with Vibram boots which had thick and moulded rubber soles, serrated to act like nails and catch on tiny holds. Their military advantage was that they were silent but they were also reassuringly adhesive to the rock in all but the slimiest of conditions. These boots and snap-link karabiners were to be key elements in the armoury of the post-war British rock climber. The war brought another important breakthrough in equipment – the introduction of the artificial fibre, nylon rope to replace the old natural fibre hemp. It was quickly realised that nylon rope was not only lighter than hemp but also stronger and less likely to break, and more elastic and less given to awkward kinking when wet. All these were advantageous qualities and soon after the end of the war the old Manilla 'Alpine' rope was, except as a quaint 'period piece', no longer used. Even more important, however, than all these advances in equipment was the fact that the Commando training, together with the extensive propaganda treatment it was given, awakened the imaginations of countless young men to the 'macho' excitements of climbing.

The war did much to encourage the belief, which had been gaining ground in the pre-war years, that outdoor adventure sports were in some way 'character-forming'. It came to be widely accepted that they inculcated what were known as 'leadership qualities' – self-knowledge and self-discipline, the ability to make sensible decisions in trying cir-cumstances, a capacity for patient endurance and selfless comradeship. The reforming educationalist Kurt Hahn had already, before the war, established his school at Gordonstoun in the far north of Scotland on these principles. In March 1942 Geoffrey Winthrop Young, who was an educationalist and a great admirer of Hahn's ideas, wrote a letter to *The Times*. He contended that the war would be decided 'by the quality of our man-power'; the Commando training, he said, showed this was generally acknowledged; but such training should begin before con-scription, in the schools: '... it is essential that the training be begun early, and that it contain those elements which can toughen the moral as well as the physical fibre and which can continue to provoke the individual to always sterner progress'. The call was well-timed. There was a powerful national urge, not only for stronger and better soldiers who would win the war but also for stronger and better citizens to build the 'brave new world' that would follow. What did emerge after the war was an array of schemes to involve climbing and mountaineering in the educational process – the Outward Bound movement, local authority outdoor pursuits centres, the Duke of Edinburgh's Award Scheme, and others.

Winthrop Young also used the spirit of the time to achieve a long-nurtured ambition. For decades he had argued the need for some central body to represent the interests of British mountaineers and climbers. He had a good case and he was a persuasive man, but his plans had foundered on the regional character of the sport in Britain. In most other countries the sport had always been centrally organised, a national club with – as required – regional branches. But Britain was spattered with small, local clubs which were jealous of their independence and resistant to any idea of centralised control. Most sizeable towns within reach of the mountains had their own clubs, and even the bigger organisations were strictly regional – the Fell and Rock for the Lake District, the Climbers' Club for North Wales.

But in 1943, when he was President of the Alpine Club, Winthrop Young succeeded in arranging a meeting of twenty representatives of the leading British climbing clubs. It took place at the Alpine Club in London in February 1944. Two members of the Fell and Rock were there. Winthrop Young argued that the war effort was hindered by the fact that there was no central authority to advise the armed forces on mountaineering matters. Such a body, he said, would also help mountaineering, enabling it to speak with weight when its interests were threatened and to promote properly regulated training schemes. He won the day. The meeting agreed to set up a Standing Advisory Committee and this soon became the British Mountaineering Council. Although the Scots promptly asserted their autonomy and set up their own Mountaineering Council, the BMC survived into peacetime and flourishes to this day. It now embraces over 250 clubs and there are more joining all the time. It protects their interests on environmental issues, questions of access to the crags, disputes over rights-of-way, and so on. It supervises training for mountain leadership. It tests new equipment. It represents Britain on the international scene. Fears that such a body would lead to rigid and repressive control from above have proved happily unfounded.

More than forty years on, Winthrop Young's innovations – the use of climbing in education, and the BMC – remain very much in evidence.

They are also perennial subjects for discussion, sometimes heated, whenever two or three climbers are gathered together.

In the Lake District the year 1944 was largely uneventful. In August the Fell and Rock opened its second club hut, Raw Head in Langdale. In September a new route, Windy Ridge, was made on the Ennerdale face of Great Gable. It is graded Severe and is not particularly distinguished. It requires a mention only because it was the first new route made in Lakeland by a man who was to make many very significant ones in the next few years.

Arthur Dolphin came from the Bradford region and studied metallurgy at Leeds University. There have been many strong climbers who have failed to look the part but Dolphin must be a leading contender as the unlikeliest-looking of them all. He was tall, lanky and scruffy, self-effacing in manner and, to all appearances, physically frail. Jim Birkett remembers him as 'long, thin and anaemic – with a permanent drip on the end of his nose'.

He came from a sporting family – his uncle, also called Arthur Dolphin, kept wicket for Yorkshire and England – but looked so sickly as a child that his parents encouraged him to walk the moors. Soon he was scrambling up the gritstone outcrops. By the age of thirteen he could lead the hardest routes on Almscliff. The year after, on his first visit to the Lakes, he led the Girdle Traverse of Dow Crag.

Dolphin was another 'natural', one of those enviable climbers who made the hardest moves look easy. Charlie Wilson says he was 'a real natural mover'. Bill Peascod first came across him on Almscliff, climbing in walking shoes, and said '. . . but one got the impression that it wouldn't have mattered terribly much if they had been scuba diving flippers; they would have presented little problem to Arthur. He was brilliant.'

He was a man of paradoxes. A meticulous climber, he was little concerned with his appearance or equipment. Sometimes he wore rubbers on his feet, sometimes nailed boots, often whatever he happened to be wearing. Later, when he was making his great routes, he usually wore Dunlop Green Flash running shoes. He adopted the nylon rope when it appeared and would carry a few nylon slings for running belays. But he used them sparingly. Bill Birkett says he was 'the last of the great unprotected leaders'.

There were other paradoxes. For all his apparent feebleness, he had great strength, especially in the fingers. His modest, gentle manner cloaked an intense determination. He was friendliness itself, liked and admired by everyone, but he was also highly competitive – not in rivalry with other climbers but against himself, striving to improve his standards like a golfer fighting to lower his handicap. Although he was quiet and unassertive in company, he was intelligent and could – as he showed in the naming of his routes – be witty.

Dolphin was back in the Lake District in 1945 to produce three more climbs – Nocturne on Gimmer and two routes on the Tophet Wall of Great Gable, Tophet Girdle and Demon Wall. But his finest contributions were to come after the war. In the meantime, both Peascod and Birkett were back in inventive action.

In 1944 Birkett concentrated his attention chiefly on Esk Buttress, the isolated crag that overlooks upper Eskdale, where he put up five new routes. The year after he returned to the East Buttress of Scafell to make a series of quality discoveries on the eastern wing of the crag, among them Gremlin's Groove and South Chimney. On 1 August 1945 he led Len Muscroft up Hollin Groove on White Ghyll in Langdale, the crag that was to be his favourite playground in the next few years.

After two years of comparative inactivity Bill Peascod was busy again in Buttermere in 1945, especially on Grey Crag. The next year, together with a demobilised Bert Beck, he went exploring and discovered two new crags. First they made two routes, Sinister Grooves and Honister Wall, on the steep slaty cliffs of Buckstone How, high up on the Buttermere side of Honister Pass. In June they investigated the formidable face of Eagle Crag in Borrowdale, on the spur that separates Greenup and Langstrath. They began with the classic Falconer's Crack and followed this up with The Great Stair and Postern Gate.

Statistically speaking, though, there was nothing in this period to compare with the achievements of the veteran Bentley Beetham in Borrowdale.

He had been born in 1886, the year Haskett Smith made the first ascent of Napes Needle. Educated at Barnard Castle School, a public school for boys, he then spent all his working life there as a teacher, much of it as the Second Master. He was a keen naturalist and published several books on his great interest, British bird life.

He started climbing soon after the First World War. In 1921 he seconded Bower on the first ascent of Innominate Crack on Kern Knotts, and seconded Frankland on the second ascent of Central Buttress. Three years later he was invited to join the Everest expedition. He went but an attack of sciatica prevented him from going above Camp 3. He did not return to the Himalayas but climbed regularly and hard in Norway and the Alps, the Tyrol and the Tatras, and in the High Atlas of Morocco.

Those who remember him give conflicting accounts of his character. To Jim Birkett he seemed 'a bit of a nut-case'. Ivan Waller did not like him but confesses that Beetham reciprocated the feeling and may have had some justification. Sid Cross often disagreed with Beetham on matters of mountaineering principle but always found him 'a real gentleman, an enlightened man'. Several others speak of him with affection as 'a tremendous character, delightful company, a lovely man'. On certain

(*Above left*) Bert Beck and Bill Peascod, schoolteacher and coal miner from Workington, at the top of Honister Pass in the summer of 1940, with Beck's Morris Tourer. It was Peascod, often with Beck in support, who opened up the climbing in and around Buttermere before, during and after World War Two. (*Above right*) Jim Birkett, quarryman, who made many new routes, most of them in his native Langdale area and all of them in nailed boots.

(*Above left*) Bill Peascod leading the first ascent of Resurrection on High Crag, Buttermere, 7 September 1941. (*Above right*) Higher up the route, Peascod approaches the slimy, mossy wall which was the reason why he chose to climb in nailed boots. (Photos by Austin Barton.)

On 12 April 1936, when he was 77
and this picture was taken, Hasket
Smith marked the 50th
anniversary of his first ascent of
Napes Needle by doing it again.

He followed the original route but
this time he was closely attended,
with Professor R. S. T. Chorley
above him and G. R. Speaker
below.

Past the mantleshelf move on to the top block, he is almost there.

When he reached the top one of the spectators shouted 'Tell us a story'. 'There is no other story', the old gentleman called down. 'This is the top storey.'
(Photos from the Mabel Barker collection.)

Jack Carswell, nicely poised on Kern Knotts Crack.

Bentley Beetham exploring Shepherd's Crag, with Derwentwater and Skiddaw beyond.
(Both photos by Austin Barton.)

Arthur Dolphin (inset)

The first ascent of Kipling Groove
on Gimmer Crag, 17 May 1948.
J. B. Lockwood waits on the belay
while Dolphin wrestles with the
exposed crux moves near the point
where Joe Brown later hammered
in his controversial piton. (Photo
from the Marie Blake Collection.

...an ('Tubby') Austin, the
...ding Langdale new-router for
...rly twenty years after World
...ar Two and the fiercest
...ender of the Lake District's
... climbing tradition.

...Yorkshire limestone, however,
...vas prepared to use pitons, for
...ection. He was not concerned
...ut sartorial elegance, another
...ng Lake District tradition.
...otos from the Brian Evans
...ection.)

Chris Bonington on the fierce second pitch of the Medlar on Raven Crag, Thirlmere, August 1964. The route was spotted by Martin Boysen and he led through to complete it. He also named it in honour of a rare medlar tree they found at the top of the first pitch. The climb is graded Extremely Severe 3 and gets three stars for quality. (From the Chris Bonington collection.)

eoff Oliver leading the Direct Route on Castle
ock, Thirlmere, first climbed in 1930 by A. T.
argreaves and Graham Macphee and now
aded Very Severe (Mild). (From the Geoff
liver collection.)

elow) A rogues' gallery of Borrowdale climbers
the 1960s, the years of the 'Keswick iron men'.
ney are watching the Welsh interloper Pete
ew, leading an early ascent of Praying Mantis
Goat Crag. From left to right: Paul Ross, Brian
nderson, Gordon Dyke (half-hidden), Dennis
glish, Joe Griffin and Mike Thompson.
nderson went on to lead the first ascent of The
t Race, using much aid, so the date must have
en 11 April 1966. Ross and Thompson were
obably already planning their maverick guide
Borrowdale climbing which came out in the
nmer of that year. (Photo by Ken Wilson.)

(*Above*) Don Whillans and Chris Bonington in 1984 when Bonington made his *Lakeland Rock* series of films and Whillans re-climbed his classic Dovedale Groove on Dove Crag, more than thirty years after the first ascent.

Pete Livesey, whose Borrowdale routes in 1974 gave an impetus to Lake District climbing, comparable to that of Whillans and Joe Brown twenty years before. (Both pictures from the Adrian Bailey collection.)

Chris Gore inserts a 'friend' for a running belay to protect him through the crux moves on Livesey's Footless Crow on Goat Crag. The route is graded Extremely Severe 5, the first of that standard in the Lake District. (Photo by Al Phizacklea.)

Bridging across the steep groove above the overhang. The whole route is some 60 feet in length.

Colin Downer, with two ropes, nut runners and a chalk bag, sets off to lead the first ascent of Desmond Decker, an 'extreme' on Car Park Buttress, Grange Crags, Borrowdale, after weeks of vigorous gardening. The date is 10 March 1984. Since he has been unable to protect himself with any runners, Chris Bacon and Ray McHaffie stand ready to break his fall if Downer comes off from the gymnastic crux move (5c) over the bulge. He named the route partly out of respect for the pop singer of that name, partly out of concern about the chances of 'hitting the deck'.

Bob Wightman on the sensational 90-foot top pitch of Fallout on Esk Buttress, first ascended by Bill Birkett and Andy Hyslop in 1979. The route is graded E4 and this top pitch, which is meagrely protected, has the technical grading 6a. (Photo by Al Phizacklea.)

Pete Whillance and Dave Armstrong rest on their belays and consider the problems above them on the crux pitch of Incantations on Tophet Wall, Great Gable, the route they made in 1984 for Bonington's film series *Lakeland Rock*.

Armstrong finally succeeds in reaching the pre-placed piton which gave them 'ethical' misgivings but which now gave Whillance a greater sense of security on the pitch above.

The 60-foot slab overhangs severely and is some 200 feet above the foot of the crag. The climb is graded E6 and the technical grading of this pitch is 6b. (From the Bonington collection.)

Paul Cornforth making the first ascent of Superdupont (E5 6c) on the limestone of Chapel Head Scar in 1985. The route is 150 feet high and there are five in-place bolts for protection.

Martin Atkinson making the second ascent of Torture Board (E6 6c) on Reecastle, Watendlath valley in September 1987. (Photos by Al Phizacklea.)

points there is no dispute. He did great work over many years in introducing boys to the pleasures of fell walking and climbing. Stocky in build and tough in mind as well as in body, he was a resourceful and determined climber. He was also the most assiduous and ruthless of mountain gardeners. When he was opening up a new crag for climbing, as he did many, Beetham would take a spade, a big saw, an axe, an ice axe, and, most ominous of all, a box of matches. Anything that came between him and the rock would be dug, sawn, hacked, scraped or simply burnt away. It would have driven modern environmentalists berserk with outrage. But no one seems to have complained at the time, even though Beetham's methods were notorious. He was suspected of being behind the fire which removed 'a fairly liberal mantle of vegetation' from the Lower Crag in White Ghyll, Langdale, in the early 1950s. There were also dark suspicions that his was the arsonist hand behind the great conflagration of Greatend Crag in Borrowdale in 1940. But in the 1953 climbers' guide to the Borrowdale area, Beetham blandly wrote:

> That Greatend has remained unnoticed and unused so long must be on account of the quite exceptionally heavy vegetation – sphagnum, bilberry, heather, birch, rowan and oak which clothed and hid it. It was this density of the vertical jungle that produced the remarkable forest fire which raged here for more than a week in 1940. Not until the botanical drapery had been partially removed did the cliff face emerge and at last attract the climbers' eye ...
>
> The present state of the crag is transitional. The soil was left sterile, but life is quickly re-establishing itself on ledges and in crannies, and climbers should make the most of the place while the rocks are thus fortuitously cleared.

It will probably never be known exactly how 'fortuitous' it was, but it is a matter of historical fact that the first routes on Greatend Crag were made by Beetham, though not until ten years or so after the great fire.

Up to 1936 only twenty-five climbs had been made in the Borrowdale area. There was a general feeling among the early climbers that the cliffs there were too low to be of much interest, the climbs too easy and the crags too wet. In 1936 the mountaineering club of Barnard Castle School, the Goldsborough Club, acquired the lease of a corrugated iron hut near Mountain View, the row of cottages near Seatoller. Beetham, of course, was the club's moving spirit and the hut became his Lake District headquarters. He took parties of boys there every holiday, and for their purposes it was the ideal spot. The crags were conveniently close to the valley and rarely visited by climbers. The rocks were no wetter than elsewhere, on average, and many of them dried out faster than most. And climbs could be found to suit all levels of ability. Between 1936 and 1959 Beetham created more than seventy new routes in Borrowdale.

They are all short, by Scafell standards, and many are very easy. Others are contrived. Beetham became adept at linking short steep rock problems together with intervening scrambles up vegetated slopes and scree. Many climbers were not impressed by this. They liked committing climbs, where a high standard of difficulty is maintained for a long time and there are no escape routes. Others disapproved because the crags were too close to the road, so little or no fell walking was required and no mountain summits were gained. It was not 'real mountaineering'.

But Beetham was undeterred. He found virtue in the fact that many of his routes were complex and artificial. They called, he said, for accurate route-finding and were thus good training for the Alps: 'This purity of purpose to follow the given route becomes more and more important on these newer climbs, since any departure from them savours not of exploration but of retreat, for it results in the avoidance of the very difficulties which are the *raison d'être* of the expedition.'

He was over fifty years old when he began the great Borrowdale breakthrough and well into his sixties when he finished. The majority of his first ascents were made solo and throughout the period he was suffering from an increasingly painful ankle, the result of a fall in the *Grandes Jorasses*. He had one serious accident in Borrowdale. He fell while climbing Raven Crag Gully and broke his skull in six places. He was unconscious for three weeks. Then he recovered and resumed his climbing.

For all the criticisms, few would deny the value and the magnitude of his achievement. He opened up many new crags and created dozens of fine climbs at many levels of difficulty – Monolith Crack and Shepherd's Gully, both on Shepherd's Crag and both graded Very Severe (Mild); Ardus and Chamonix, in the Severe range; down to climbs like Little Chamonix and Corvus which, however humbly graded, are varied and delightful and still among the most popular climbs in Britain.

The first significant development, after the end of the Second World War, was not in climbing but in mountain rescue.

Up till now, when someone was reported injured or missing in the mountains, a search and rescue party would be hastily assembled on a volunteer basis – local farmers, shepherds, climbers, perhaps the local doctor, often the local policeman – and they would do their best. But there was no organisation, no co-ordination, no established procedure, no special equipment. Most of those who went out, often at night and in foul weather, were not climbers.

Just before Christmas 1946 a man called Eric Sivyer, who was a climber, arrived at the Holiday Fellowship house at Monk Coniston to take charge of sporting activities. He went out alone one afternoon, with his rope, and did not return at night-fall. The police were notified and a massive search operation was organised. They concentrated at first on Dow Crag, then spread out to comb the slopes around Levers Water. It was not until three days later that Sivyer's body was found at the foot of a gully on Yewdale Crag, just above the road north of Coniston.

When the bill for the police operation reached the Treasurer's Department of the local authority, sharp questions were asked. Why should policemen, without climbing experience or equipment, be expected to undertake such work? Why should the rate-payers be required to meet the cost? Harry Griffin, returned from the Burma campaign to resume his career as a journalist, wrote an article for the *Lancashire Evening Post* saying that the time had come for some form of organised rescue service. A Hawkshead councillor, having read the article, called a public meeting in Coniston. From this, the first mountain rescue team in the Lake District emerged.

It was, at first, very loosely organised – a group of men, fell walkers rather than rock climbers, who were prepared to turn out when the call came. Their leader, from the start and for more than thirty years, was an expert climber, Jim Cameron.

Born in 1898 at Barrow-in-Furness, he worked in the Vickers shipyards throughout the First World War, becoming a foreman boilermaker. After the war he took to the vagabond life, exploring the Lake District mountains and the Scottish Highlands, then making his haphazard way across Canada, picking up odd jobs as he went along. Back in England he worked as a waiter in various hotels and would often stand in for Youth Hostel wardens. At Black Sail Youth Hostel in 1933 he met the artist, William Heaton Cooper, and was introduced to rock climbing.

He loved it from the first. Nearly six foot tall, lean and tough and almost fanatically fit, he made an excellent climber, neat and sure-footed in movement, never hurried or flurried, always cheerful and confident. He was a very good climbing guide, too. He would take people out in small groups or singly. His charges were modest – £3 a day for a single client – and he had the gift of inspiring others with his confidence. He had great charm and was normally easy-going, though he could be severe if he thought people were treating the mountains with insufficient respect. He did not care for Jerry Wright, the Keswick guide, whom he considered an ego-maniac. 'If you treat the rocks properly', he would say, 'they will treat you properly.' One of his minor eccentricities was to wear a tie when he climbed. His widow, Betty, says he was the only man she knew who dressed up to go climbing.

When the Second World War broke out he went back to work at Vickers as a plater and foreman. He and his wife lived at Torver and managed to go climbing, usually on Dow Crag, most weekends. He wore Woolworth's plimsolls on dry rock and at other times boots nailed with the soft metal waisted clinkers. Though he climbed at a high standard he was not interested in making new routes. He created only three climbs – Black Buttress, Quest and Alasdair, all on Dow Crag and none of them particularly notable.

As soon as the war ended he left his regular job and went back to mountain guiding. When Coniston rescue team was formed he was the obvious choice as leader. What was not so predictable was that he would also be the team's first casualty.

In the summer of 1947 he was leading a client, a young naval officer, up the Necklace Route on Dow. The client fell off and, though Jim Cameron was able to hold him, his own belay rope snapped under the strain and he was pulled from his stance. He fell more than seventy feet and it was thought, when his team of rescuers reached the spot, that he had broken his pelvis. In fact, his injuries were not so serious. Both he and his client were recovering within a few days.

The other important name in the early history of Lakeland mountain rescue is that of 'Rusty' Westmorland.

The son of one of the pioneer 'Pillarites', Westmorland had been climbing and making new routes in the Lake District before 1914. He was in Canada, working as a surveyor in the Rockies, when the First World War broke out. He enlisted in a Canadian Territorial regiment and served in France and Belgium as a transport officer. He stayed in the Canadian army after the war, making the most of the generous scope he was given for the active outdoor life he loved, horse-riding and ski-ing, camping, trekking and climbing. For all his fitness, though, he suffered much ill health. When he was invalided out of the army in 1944, by which time he was a Lieutenant-Colonel, he returned to his native country, to live at Threlkeld near Keswick. Some thirty years later, asked how he had come to be involved in mountain rescue, he told this story:

> It was my 60th birthday, April 24 1946. It was a horrible day – a strong cold wind, then rain and sleet and snow. I'd climbed Arrowhead Ridge on Gable and was making my way along the climbers' traverse when I met a couple of lads who said: 'There's a man up there with a broken leg.' So I went up Hell Gate, then climbed down the Shark's Fin, and there, on a ledge, I found Wilf Noyce. He'd fallen near the top of Tophet Bastion and broken his leg. His companion, Claude Elliott, had got him out of the wind and gone for help. He was very cold so I gave him some extra clothing, then went off to find more people.
>
> Two girls had come up from Wasdale Head with a stretcher. Then Claude Elliott arrived with Bobby Files, James Yule and two other climbers. That made six men. We got back to Noyce and tied him on to the stretcher. We hadn't a long enough rope to lower him to the foot of the crag so we had to haul him upwards. It took us three hours to get him to the top. Bobby Files was in charge. Elliott and I, each leading out a rope, would climb about 20 feet. Then the other four, on the word, would haul the stretcher up, very gradually, while we held the ropes tight. It was pitch dark by this time – still blowing a gale and sleeting. When we were nearly at the top we could hear a big group, who'd come up to help, shouting below us in the dark. We shouted but couldn't make them hear. So we made our way, very slowly, down Hell Gate and when we got to the bottom of the scree run there wasn't a soul there. And they hadn't left anything for us – not a blanket, no food, not a light!

So we had to carry on slowly down, over very rough ground. At one point, when Bobby Files and I were on the front of the stretcher, I couldn't find the ground with my foot. I said to Bobby: 'I don't know if it's a ten-foot drop or two inches.' So he came round and lifted me down and it was only a few inches.

When we finally got to Burnthwaite we put Noyce down by the Aga. Mrs Ullock looked at us and said: 'You all look gey tired.' I said: 'Well, we've been out for 20 hours.' And that's when she made the famous remark: 'Ay, it's far less trouble when they kill theirsells.' Which is true, isn't it?

Anyway I was fed up with this party having come up and then not even leaving a couple of people to help or some food or anything. I saw Colonel Morton, the magistrate, soon after and said I didn't think much of the party the police had sent up. He said: 'I don't see why the police – who aren't climbers and haven't got the equipment – why they should have to go up and rescue those damn-fool climbers who fall off.' He had a point.

I didn't do anything immediately but when I heard Jim Cameron had started a team in Coniston, I put an appeal in *The Keswick Reminder* asking for volunteers to form a Keswick mountain rescue team. There were 36 replies, four of them from doctors.

Wilf Noyce, who had done much hard climbing in North Wales and the Alps, recovered completely and made an important contribution to the success of the 1953 Everest expedition. But he was accident-prone. He fell to his death in the Pamirs in 1962.

'Rusty' Westmorland's military background saw to it that the Keswick team was soon much more highly organised than the one in Coniston. There were regular training sessions. Everyone learnt first aid. 'Rusty' was in charge for a further twenty-seven years and in 1965 was awarded the OBE for his work.

There have been many changes in the last forty years. There are now fourteen mountain rescue teams in the Lake District and the hills nearby. They are equipped with four-wheel-drive vehicles and ambulance vans, together with a sophisticated array of radio and medical and climbing equipment. They use search dogs and can call in the RAF helicopters. They have well-practised techniques for getting stretchers safely down the steepest cliffs. They answer an average of well over 200 call-outs each year. No one could say how many lives have been saved because they are there, but it must be many.

The teams are still chiefly funded by public contributions. They are still staffed entirely by unpaid volunteers. And, in contrast to many other countries where an accident in the mountains can end up with an enormous bill for rescue, their services are still freely given.

— 8 —

The Great Leap Forward
1947–1959

THE CREATOR of a new climb has the right to choose its name, though there are many who see this more as a burden than a privilege.

For all their high education and wide reading, the early climbers were disappointingly pedestrian in their choice of names. They often invoked the points of the compass so that Pillar Rock acquired an Old West and a New West, a North Climb and a North-east Climb, reaching the ultimate absurdities of the Nor'-nor'-west and the South-west-by-west. Sometimes, more appropriately, they referred to outstanding features of the rock, which led – taking Pillar once again as the example – to the Slab and Notch, Long Chimney, the Rib and Slab Climb and Kelly's Grooved Wall. When these sources of inspiration failed, more desperate solutions were sought, numerical or alphabetical. For many years the names, Route 1 and Route 2, were preferred to the more vivid Sodom and Gomorrah. On Green Gable the Greek alphabet was brought to bear with Alpha, Beta, Gamma etc. And, despite their contempt for self-promotion, the early climbers contrived to scatter their names across the crags in generous profusion. This was especially so on Scafell Crag which offers a considerable, though incomplete, roll-call of the pioneers: Slingsby's Chimney, Collier's Climb, Botterill's Slab, Sansom's Traverse and others, including several mentions of O. G. Jones and the Hopkinsons. They preserved their reputation for modesty by protesting that their companions on the first ascent had insisted on the name.

Other mountain regions of Britain took a more inventive and literary line. In North Wales, before the outbreak of the First World War, Geoffrey Winthrop Young called one of his Lliwedd routes the Purple Passage, explaining that 'it was that kind of passage and better left out'. He named the Solomon Climb to mark the fact that it bisected a feature known as the Quartz Babe. Morley Wood of the Rucksack Club was even more intriguingly allusive. He had two reasons for giving a route

152

on Castle Naze the name Pilgrim's Progress. The first, more obvious one
was that it led to a feature called Paradise Corner. The other was that
he had found it 'interesting but steep', which was Huckleberry Finn's
comment on Bunyan's book.

Gradually, the Lake District men began to look for brighter names.
George Basterfield made two routes on Boat Howe in 1925 and called
them Sea Wall Arête and Starboard Chimney, establishing that crag's
tradition of nautical nomenclature. It was the 'Barrow boys' who led the
way towards a more light-hearted and imaginative approach. In 1929
A.B. Reynolds cocked an effective snook at the cumbersomely titled
Oxford and Cambridge Buttress with his Borstal Buttress on Bowfell;
Bert Gross was referring to the deleted expletives which accompanied
the first ascent when he named Asterisk on Gimmer; and on the same
crag in the same year Graham Macphee called his route Joas, which was
said to stand for 'just one awful sweat'.

In the 1930s the working-class men arrived on the scene and carried
on the livelier tradition. On Pike's Crag, Sid Cross created Urchin's
Groove and the Citadel; Jim Birkett came up with Afterthought and
Frustration on Esk Buttress and Gremlin's Groove on Scafell's East
Buttress; and the coal-miner, Bill Peascod, brought a touch of classical
class to Grey Crags, Buttermere, with Suaviter and Fortiter. In 1940
Jim Haggas made his route on the upper crag of White Ghyll and called
it The Gordian Knot, which was apt and was to have an impressive
progeny.

It was the quarryman, Jim Birkett, who established the 'knotty'
dynasty of routes on White Ghyll. For several years after the end of the
Second World War, the 'old guard' – Birkett, Peascod and Beetham –
remained the chief creators of new climbs. With characteristic modesty,
Birkett claimed to be past his best but the decline was not apparent to
anyone else. He still wore his trusty nailed boots. His regular second was
still the trusty Len Muscroft. In 1945 they climbed Hollin Groove on
White Ghyll's Lower Crag, which had been cleared of its blanketing
vegetation by a fire, the cause of which has never been discovered. In
1946 they created White Ghyll Wall and White Ghyll Traverse. In May
1947 Birkett led the way up one of the classics of the Lower Crag, a steep
seventy-foot pitch to a good belay ledge, then a delicate and committing
traverse leftwards, an awkward stride on to a rib of rock, up an overhanging bulge, and then steep airy rock face to the top. He christened
the route Slip Knot, in recognition of Jim Haggas's pioneering work and
also of the exciting verticality of the climb.

In 1948 the same pair made two more routes on White Ghyll, Haste
Not and Granny Knot. And the year after they added three more – Why
Not, Perhaps Not and Do Not.

Though Birkett was making White Ghyll his speciality, he did not ignore opportunities elsewhere. He and Muscroft climbed Leopard's Crawl on Dow Crag which the guide book describes as 'A bold lead with a nasty landing' and 'not well protected'. When they did it, it was not protected at all. Even so, they only reckoned it Severe. Today it is graded Very Severe (Hard). They also advanced the exploration of Castle Rock of Triermain. In 1947 they created two routes there in the Very Severe category, May Day Cracks and Flying Buttress. And in June 1949 Birkett led the first climb in the Lake District to be graded Extremely Severe. He called it Harlot Face: 'I found it hard', he says. 'Hence the name!'

Bill Peascod was active, too, on Buckstone How in Buttermere and Miners' Crag in Newlands. By the late 1940s he had more time and energy for climbing. He had qualified as a colliery manager and did some lecturing at Workington Technical College. No longer exercising his muscles at the coal-face, he kept a rigorous three-times-a-week weight training schedule. 'For my part', he wrote in his autobiography, '1948 was the beginning of a very satisfactory period of climbing which lasted pretty well up until my departure for Australia in August 1952. It was (I realised years later) the time when I did my best climbing, when confidence was backed up by experience and good physical condition, when anything might have happened...'

He was also being more adventurous, by this time, in his naming of routes. He had spotted a possible line on Buckstone How when he was girdling the crag, in the winter of 1948, with Bert Beck. Beck gave up hard climbing soon after, but at Whitsun 1951 Peascod returned to the cliff with a new partner, Brian Blake, a geography graduate from Cambridge who was now warden of a youth centre in Maryport. They spent two days reconnoitring the route they had in mind, then went for it, Peascod leading. At one point, halfway up the upper wall, Blake had to leave his secure belay and climb up a few feet so that his leader could stand on his shoulders and reach the next hand holds. This is how Peascod described the final pitch:

> When Brian reached me I moved out up the wall to the left then, in about 20 feet, moved back once more to the right, via a delightful, though short, traverse, into the shattered groove immediately above the third line of overhangs. The left hand wall of this groove led straight to the top of the crag – it was all air and light and joy.
>
> We called the climb 'Cleopatra'. The date was May 18, 1951. It was one of the best new climbs I ever did ... What is it that Shakespeare said about 'Age cannot wither her nor custom stale her infinite variety'...?

Peascod gives no reason for the name. David Craig, the writer and teacher who did the climb with Peascod many years later, suggests it might have been because the rock there has 'a tawny front' and is 'wrinkled deep in time'. Whatever the reason, Peascod's other three outstanding new routes of that year were all given the names of what he called 'notorious ladies'.

In July, with Stan Dirkin as his second, he climbed Jezebel on Miners' Crag – it was, incidentally, Peascod and a fellow-miner and sometime climbing partner, Graham Rushworth, who had christened this crag. On 10 August, with Brian Blake, he did Delilah on High Crag Buttress, Buttermere. And next day the same team made a new route on the North Buttress of Shepherd's Crag in Borrowdale and called it Eve, which was the name of the barmaid at the Scafell Hotel so they were able to celebrate with free pints that evening.

Soon after, Peascod got a job in Australia, teaching mining, and it was to be twenty-six years before he returned to live once again in the Lake District. Not long before he left, he found himself climbing Overhanging Bastion in the wake of a party led by Arthur Dolphin:

> We laughed and joked all the way up the climb. After doing the 'gangway' and stepping around and up the flaky overhang Arthur had his team wedged in behind the yew tree awaiting my arrival. All was lightheartedness and laughter. As I went up the final overhang and having to do some fancy footwork on the loose flakes that were around, because I could not reach the holds that long-legged Arthur had attained, I cried out in mock horror for them to pass me down a handhold. I made some crack about Arthur's length and he said with a grin, 'It's being so short that keeps you down in our class'.

Dolphin's time was cruelly short but it was he who formed the vital link between the old order – Birkett and Peascod and others who had started climbing before the war – and the surging wave of new young men that was to carry the sport powerfully forwards in the 1950s. He gave himself a little more protection, using nylon rope and threading thin nylon slings around chockstones, than his immediate predecessors had used, but he consistently climbed at a higher level of difficulty and danger. In his naming of routes he was more ingenious than any of his predecessors.

In May 1947, during the Whitsun weekend, he made three new routes in three consecutive days, culminating in the varied and sometimes strenuous Whit's End on Gimmer. In August that year, exploring the eastern wall of Pavey Ark, he tried to follow the line which – more than ten years later – was climbed and called Astra. He made for a prominent corner that seemed to offer the solution but when he got there found the rock formidably smooth and his position horribly exposed. So he adopted an easier line and, because the alternative had seemed unacceptable, called it Hobson's Choice.

On three days in May 1948 he produced three more new routes. On 15 May he led J.B. Lockwood and J. Bloor up Samaritan Corner on Gimmer, so called because it was often passed by. Next day he took the same company up Alph on Pavey Ark, named after the meandering river in Coleridge's poem 'Kubla Khan'. Then on 17 May he produced what is widely regarded as his masterpiece, though it is by no means the highest graded of his routes.

For some time leading climbers had been considering the possibilities of the challenging North-west face of Gimmer Crag. There was no route on it between Gimmer Crack on the left-hand side, conquered by A. Reynolds and G. Macphee in 1928, and F Route which Jim Birkett climbed in 1941. Birkett was particularly interested – this was his stamping-ground – and in 1948 he abseiled down and cleared away some of the débris on the likeliest line. He reckoned it could be done and told Dolphin about it.

Dolphin, who was working on the 1950 revision of the Fell and Rock guide book for the Great Langdale area, was inspired to go and see for himself. He top-roped down it more than once, inspected it thoroughly, then – with J. B. Lockwood in support – went to make the attempt. He did it – in three superb and varied pitches – protecting himself, very sparsely, with his slings of nylon line. He called it Kipling Groove because even he found it 'Ruddy 'ard'.

In the guide book he described the route as '175 feet. Very Severe. Extreme severity and a high degree of exposure combine to make the route perhaps the most serious undertaking in the district.' His account makes it clear that at the first very hard section, halfway up the second pitch and just below the overhang, he did not use the overhang as an 'undercling' hand hold but hand-traversed leftwards before reaching that point, using a line of small flakes for hand holds. The hardest part of the whole route is more than halfway up the final pitch, involving a sensational swing out on to a brutally exposed slab, above the great overhang. Dolphin wrote: 'The next move is the crux. A strenuous arm-pull brings a diagonal crack above the overhang within reach, followed by a horizontal crack a little higher to the right. The latter is used first to surmount the overhang and then as a mantelshelf, footholds being almost non-existent . . .'

Kipling Groove is one of those rare routes which, immediately and lastingly, attain legendary status. It is a beautiful, unremitting line that, even with the most advanced protection techniques, still has the feel of a serious undertaking. Its first ascent was a formidable achievement. It was rapidly established as the climb you had to lead, if you were an ambitious rock climber. From the first it attracted stories around itself.

The first of these – that Birkett was offended when Dolphin 'snatched' the route from his grasp – was nonsense. Such rivalry as there had been between the two was entirely friendly. Each greatly respected the other, for his climbing and for his honesty about it. Birkett was wise enough to know that he could not dominate the vanguard of the sport for ever, and to recognise the new generation when it emerged. Now he says: 'We were great friends, though we never climbed together. Arthur was a very good man, a real gentleman and a perfect climber. And he rode a motorbike and that gave him a head-start with me.' At the time he said: 'It's true we were both looking at the wall on Gimmer and Arthur was the first to climb it, but it really didn't matter a jot who climbed it first.'

The second ascent came quickly and mysteriously. A member of the Creagh Dhu Mountaineering Club in Glasgow, George Shields, rushed down to the Lake District, climbed the route and went away again.

It was the third ascent that made rock-climbing history.

Joe Brown, a plumber's apprentice from the slums of Manchester, was nineteen years old and the leading light of that city's thrusting group of enthusiastic young climbers. They learned on the outcrop crags close to home and went, whenever they could, to North Wales, climbing on Clogwyn du'r Arddu and the cliffs of Llanberis Pass. There were very occasional forays to the Lake District, too, and between 1948 and 1951 they made a point of repeating most of Dolphin's new routes in the Langdale region.

Some time in the winter of 1949–50 Brown went to Gimmer Crag with one of his mates and did Kipling Groove. It was a wet day and when he got to the final pitch, just below the crux moves, he considered the prospect so serious that he hammered a piton into a crack and clipped his climbing rope to it to afford secure protection. The news spread fast and created consternation. Dennis Gray in his climbing autobiography *Rope Boy* says:

> One Sunday night in the winter of 1950, the door of the café swung open and in came Harold Drasdo, obviously the bearer of news. He had just hitch-hiked from Langdale where Joe Brown had repeated Kipling's Groove, placing a piton in the climb to protect the hardest moves. This was a bombshell. Brown putting a piton into a climb previously led free? We couldn't believe it . . .

Gray and Drasdo and their climbing companions were known as 'the Bradford lads'. Dolphin was their hero. In their eyes, Brown's piton was 'a Red Rose affront'. One of their number, Peter Greenwood, determined to reverse the trans-Pennine insult. A week after Brown's ascent, Greenwood and Fred Williams made the fourth ascent and spent a lot of time trying to wrench the piton out. But Brown was noted for the thoroughness of his workmanship and Williams had forgotten to bring the piton hammer. So they had to leave the piton in place and content themselves with not using it, in the proper Yorkshire manner. Pete Greenwood says:

> I did the climb without using the piton but every time I did the route after that I did use it, for protection. There's no doubt – it's saved a lot of lives.
>
> But the point is this. Kipling Groove was THE route and this man Dolphin had done it clean. Then along comes another man and knocks in a piton. As far as we were concerned, if the weather was too bad and he found he couldn't do it, he should have come back down again. If you can't do it, don't spoil it. Leave it.

Now, instead of having a long, hundred-and-odd foot run-out of the rope, with a hard crux at the end and no protection, it's been made into a route that you can fall off and be safe, a pedestrian route.

Nearly forty years on the ethics of Joe's piton can still arouse intense and convoluted debate among climbers. The route is now graded Very Severe (Hard) but it is given three stars, the top rating for overall quality. Mick Burke writing in the mid-'70s for Ken Wilson's *Hard Rock* said:

Eventually, Kipling became a trade route for the hard men. But it claimed its victims. Pat Walsh took a big fall trying to exit leftwards from the peg. Paddy Hunt wore through one of his ropes when he lost contact with the rock. I saw one climber fall off the crux three times before he gave up and went home. There was always a good crowd in the North-west Gully to watch for any action. Even with the peg in place, it was still a 60-foot fall before the rope came tight. Oh yes, a good route, Kipling: good to do and good to watch someone else doing. The Langdale climbers were very proud of it. They used to get very annoyed with anyone who treated the climb badly.

If Dolphin had any feelings about the Brown piton, he kept them to himself. He continued to make new routes and find apt names for them – Baskerville and Stewpot on East Raven Crag in Langdale, Russet Groove and Inferno on White Ghyll. In June 1951 he confirmed his leadership by solving a problem that had tantalised climbers for years – Deer Bield Buttress in Easedale. He did it with A. D. Brown and it is the first route he made which is still graded Extremely Severe. Bill Birkett, in *Lakeland's Greatest Pioneers*, says it is 'a technical masterpiece, boldly climbing up the stark slaty rock ... another plumb line, comparable to, but harder than, the great Kipling Groove'.

Other fine achievements followed. In October that year, again with A. D. Brown, he created Rubicon Groove on Bowfell. In May 1952 he and Pete Greenwood, alternating the lead, did two new routes on the East Buttress of Scafell on successive weekends. The first was named Pegasus. Greenwood recalls:

It was a really hot, beautiful summer's day. Arthur set off and found it so easy he shouted down, 'I've found the first Severe on the East Buttress'. But then it got harder and harder. I led through and was ages on the next pitch – it was full of loose stuff that I had to clear away with my hands. Then I came down and Arthur had a go and he cheated, lassooed a litle spike and did it that way. It was a good climb.

It is graded Very Severe (Hard). A week later they returned to the same area and climbed Hell's Groove, which is graded Extremely Severe:

Arthur showed it to me and said 'If you can get up the first first pitch, I'll do the next one'. I didn't find the overhanging crack very hard. Knee-jamming was a speciality of mine and I got such a solid knee-jam in the crack, I could take both hands off and lean out and feel over the overhang for the holds. But I got a shock when I got up that. It looked like a big comfortable ledge but there was nothing at all, just a little, narrow sloping thing. Arthur led through and did the next pitch with no real protection, not a runner except for one piton near the bottom which he pushed in by hand because we'd no hammer.

In the same year Dolphin, with Greenwood and D. Hopkin, climbed Sword of Damocles on Bowfell; then Dunmail Cracks on Deer Bield; then, with his girlfriend Marie Ball, Babylon on Far East Raven, Langdale, which brought his tally of Extremes up to four. In May 1953 he opened up an important new climbing ground – Raven Crag, Thirlmere – with a climb he called Communist Convert because it moves from left to right.

This was the year when a British expedition finally succeeded in climbing Mount Everest. Dolphin was disappointed that he had not been invited to join the team, presumably because he was known to suffer more than most from altitude sickness at around 10,000 feet above sea level. He had been told, though, that if the spring attempt failed, he would be a member of the next expedition. So, at the beginning of June 1953, before the news from Everest arrived, he went to the Alps, hoping to improve his performance at altitude.

He did. He spent several weeks working on a glaciological project on Monte Rosa, then climbed with a Belgian, André Colard. Towards the end of July, by which time he would have heard the Everest news, they climbed the south face of the *Dent du Géant*, with Dolphin doing most of the leading and cheerfully ignoring the in-place pitons. It was the first British ascent.

Dolphin was twenty-eight years old and going better than ever. He was engaged to marry Marie Ball and looking forward to starting a new job at Calder Hall on the Cumberland coast. But he fell from easy ground, on the shoulder below the *Dent du Géant*, and his body was found at the foot of a snow gully. He was buried at Courmayeur.

He had been a familiar and inspirational figure on the Pennine outcrops and on the igneous cliffs of the Lake District. His shock of almost white hair made him easily recognisable. It is surprising how many of the emergent young climbers of the post-war period can still remember their first sighting of Arthur Dolphin. Dennis Gray was eleven years old when he found his way to Hangingstones Quarry on Ilkley Moor and saw a group of climbers gazing at the quarry wall:

> A tall, athletic, white-haired man was balanced on what appeared to me a vertical holdless face. Nonchalantly he pulled a handkerchief out of his trouser pocket and blew his nose, to the delight of the watching climbers, and reminding me of a stage acrobat. He began to move upwards, and this was somehow immediately different from a stage show; his agility, grace of movement, control and, above all, the setting high above ground, with no apparent safety devices, sent a thrill through my young body such as I had never before experienced.

He was loved for his character as well as the quality and style of his climbing. Allan Austin, the leading Langdale climber of the 1960s, says:

'He was a super climber and he climbed openly. He hid nothing. All you want is a man who tells the truth and doesn't do anything he wouldn't tell his mates about. Dolphin was such a man.'

Dolphin's example was one of many factors that came together, in the years after the Second World War, to bring about the great explosion of interest and achievement that took place in the 1950s. The fighting men came home, many of them with vastly widened horizons. The idea that adventure in the open air was good for the individual character, and for society in general, had been promoted by the war. An Outward Bound School was opened at Eskdale in 1947 to introduce young people to the rigours and pleasures of movement in the mountains. The Fell and Rock Climbing Club launched a new series of pocket-sized climbing guides, once again edited by H. M. Kelly. They began with the Great Gable region in 1948 and over the years eight volumes were issued, including Bentley Beetham's *Borrowdale* and concluding with Harold Drasdo's *Eastern Crags* in 1959. Gradually, the wartime restrictions were eased. Petrol became more freely available and by the early 1950s working-class lads from industrial Lancashire and Yorkshire could get to North Wales or the Lake District at the weekend, by hitch-hiking or by motorbike. Once there, they could live cheaply in club huts – the Fell and Rock opened three between 1950 and 1954 – or, even more cheaply, packed together in barns or, for nothing at all, bivouacking under bridges or among boulders.

Achievements in the high Himalayas stimulated great interest in mountaineering. In 1950 a strong French expedition conquered Annapurna, the first of the world's giants to be climbed, and the book about it was exciting and moving and very popular. Three years later the British finally defeated Everest and a German-Austrian team climbed Nanga Parbat, and there were books and films about them. But from the point of view of British rock climbers, the key book of the period was J. E. Q. Barford's *Climbing in Britain*. Barford, an engineer who usually climbed in North Wales, was the first secretary of the British Mountaineering Association. Soon after it was formed in 1944, the Association decided that there was an urgent need for a simple, up-to-date book to guide the steps of those who wanted to try hill walking or rock climbing or snow and ice climbing in Britain. Barford was asked to write it and the book was published by Penguin Books, price one shilling (5p), in 1946. Within a few years it had sold more than 100,000 copies.

It has nothing of the colour and exhilaration of Colin Kirkus's book, but as a plain, factual, cool, clear introduction to the British mountains, which is what it was meant to be, it was an admirable piece of work, full of sound advice and useful information. For rock climbers Barford recommends the nylon rope but makes no mention of the moulded-rubber Vibram boots; nailed boots are advised, with rubber pumps 'for hard climbing in dry weather'. He says the lead climber should carry two or three slings, at least one of them of line, to fix running belays with the aid of karabiners. He describes pitons and says 'A leader may well carry two of these aids.' But he insists that they should be used only for protection and not to help the climbing – a usage, he says, which 'is common in some continental ranges, but is considered bad form in this country'.

Dennis Gray, later to become the National Officer for the British Mountaineering Council, was one of many thousands who had cause to be grateful for Barford's book. In *Rope Boy* he says he bought a copy in 1947 when he was twelve years old:

> I was not strong and was small for my age. Slowly I worked through the easier graded climbs on local outcrops, wearing triple hobs, using no running belays but climbing carefully and belaying well by accepted standards ... We all wanted to extend our experience, and from reading about mountains I wanted to be able to call myself a mountaineer. I listened with awe to stories of climbing in high mountains, and read and re-read the only text book on climbing I could afford: John Barford's *Climbing in Britain*.

Gray was growing up in Leeds but already a regular with the group of local enthusiasts who called themselves 'the Bradford lads'. It was one of several such groups that emerged in the industrial cities in the late 1940s. Others included the Creagh Dhu Club in Glasgow, the Valkyrie Club for Peak District climbers and, soon after, the Manchester-based Rock and Ice.

The 'Bradford lads' differed from the others in that they never organised themselves into a formal club. Gray writes: 'Radical in outlook, they were against everything which smacked of authority. Everyone had grown tired of the restrictions imposed by the war: we looked for freedom in our climbing and were not to be stopped in this quest.' Dolphin was their father-figure. The only woman member of the group was his fiancée, Marie Ball, who could lead Very Severes. Other members included Peter Greenwood, Harold and Neville Drasdo, Don Hopkin, Fred Williams and Alf Beanland. Most of them were from working-class families. They spent every spare moment on the outcrops near home and every weekend they hitch-hiked to the Lake District to climb in the Langdale valley, the most easily reached of the climbing grounds. They stayed in the Wall End Barn, off the Blea Tarn road, in cheap, companionable squalor. This is Dennis Gray's description:

> This ancient building was on the most generous scale and could accommodate dozens of climbers; people used the barn instead of camping because they couldn't afford tents. Originally the place was reasonably clean and tidy but when the climbing population boomed a short while later and the number using it increased enormously, conditions became definitely insanitary and even unhealthy. The floor was covered with bracken which slowly disintegrated to dust and was rarely replaced; it was always dark and in winter cold and draughty in the extreme.

> However, it was shelter and catered almost exclusively for climbers; there friendships were made and visiting climbers passed on information . . .
>
> There was real character in that climbers' slum, it was a finishing school of an unusual type. Philosophies were expounded and politics discussed, one learnt blues and folk songs well ahead of their popularity . . . There were no rules or regulations and things often went out of control; sometimes fights broke out, and only its damp stopped the place burning down on several occasions. If a climber and his girl friend stayed together in the barn, and many did, it was solely their affair. As long as the farmer had his one shilling a night per head, he left young climbers, often in their dozens, to run their own affairs.

During the 1950s a cult grew up around this new breed of climber. Its ideal was 'the hard man' – working class, made strong by physical work, capable of cheerfully enduring the most atrocious hardships, intensely loyal to his mates and suspicious of strangers, scruffy in person, anarchistic in attitude. Before long, stories of their outrageous conduct – their feats on the crags and their fights in the pubs – were circulating freely and growing wilder with every telling. There was more myth than truth in many of the tales but they sprang from an authentic base. They were very tough and they climbed very boldly and they had no automatic respect for their 'elders and betters', especially if they displayed Oxbridge accents and manners. Clan loyalty was paramount, which meant they would do anything for a mate but were quick to take offence at the behaviour of others. When they fought, they did so ferociously, pulling no punches. Among themselves, they competed ferociously. They developed a fine, laconic line in gallows-humour.

Three of the leading figures later described those days in autobiographies – Gray in *Rope Boy*, Joe Brown in *The Hard Years* and Don Whillans in *Portrait of a Mountaineer*. Brown was more than three years older than Whillans but both grew up in the slums of Manchester, in the depression of the '30s, then the years of wartime privation. They both hated school and left to work as plumbers' apprentices. Each of them found an exhilarating escape on the moors and gritstone crags, and then quickly discovered that they had great natural abilities as rock climbers.

Before he was sixteen Joe Brown – who had read Kirkus's book – had climbed the New West on Pillar and one of its short, Very Severe routes. He first went to North Wales at Christmas 1947 and before long he was leading impressive new routes on Clogwyn du'r Arddu and repeating the Dolphin routes in the Lake District. By 1950 he was a member of the Valkyrie Club, with a high and rising reputation.

It was about this time that he began to hear the name of Don Whillans:

> . . . even in 1951 the reputation of one of Britain's greatest mountaineers in the making had something of a mythical quality about it. A story was told that this exceptionally powerful lad had fallen from the top of Twin Eliminate at Laddow Rocks. He had jumped from wall to wall in springboard style, landing at the bottom, 50 feet below, in an upright position and without a mark on him.

On 22 April 1951 Don and his close friend Eric Worthington were walking along the lower tier of the Roaches, the gritstone edge near Leek in Staffordshire. They had done a little climbing but both were amazed to see a figure, comfortably perched on the nose of a bulging buttress, with 70 vertical feet beneath his boots: 'I couldn't believe it at first', Don wrote. 'The climber didn't seem to be in any trouble at all. He was inspecting a wide crack above him which went through two bulges.'

It was Joe Brown, making the first ascent of Valkyrie Direct Start. Whillans stopped to see Brown complete the climb, then watch 'Slim' Sorrell attempt to follow. When Sorrell failed, Whillans shouted up to ask if he could tie on and try. He did it. It was the beginning of what turned out to be perhaps the most productive partnership in the history of British rock climbing.

Though both of them were unusually strong, Joe was only five feet four inches tall and Don was an inch or so smaller. Other outstanding climbers of the time were also short – Dennis Gray, Ron Moseley, John Streetly – and the coincidence led to the belief that shortness of stature and muscular strength were the vital qualities. Geoffrey Sutton, writing in *Snowdon Biography* about the climbing scene in North Wales in the early 1950s, said:

> Up to this time there had been great climbers of every build: though there was a numerical bias in the direction of men of medium height and wiry or muscular frame, the hardest climbs had been available to and had been done by men of every build who possessed the necessary technique and determination. It is dangerous to make predictions, but it seems probable that future advances in rock climbing will be made by men of less than medium height but of strong and lithe physique, for apart from other considerations only such men have the power-to-weight ratio necessary, above all in the fingers, to climb safely up the angles and minute holds of the new ultra-Severes.

Unfortunately for the theory, the 1960s brought to the fore several men – Chris Bonington and Martin Boysen, for example – who were six feet tall or over and capable of climbing at the limits of the sport. Don Whillans spoke greater sense when he wrote: 'It seems to me that natural ability, an affinity with the rock and a desire to try for the impossible are qualities which will make a great climber, irrespective of physical characteristics, though, at the highest level of climbing, stamina and strength will always be essential.'

When it came to strength, what mattered most was the gripping power of the fingers. 'Give me the handholds', Don said, with his unfailing gift for the vivid, lapidary statement, 'and I'll show you the fancy foot-work.'

One of the myths that soon attached itself to them, especially to the Manchester group in the Rock and Ice, was that of persistent drunkenness and consequent disorderliness. Although Don Whillans, early in his career, was undoubtedly quick with his fists and, later on, showed an impressive capacity for beer, there was no basis for the accusations. For a long time they simply did not have enough money to drink. When they went to the pub, a jug of orange juice was made to last the whole group the whole evening. At other times, they subsisted chiefly on continuous brews of tea. If someone misbehaved, the camp punishment was to be given the next so-many billy-cans to make.

These impressions are confirmed by Sid Cross, who, by 1950, was running the Old Dungeon Ghyll hotel at the head of the Langdale valley. Immediately after the war he had decided to give up shoe-making and go into business, with his wife 'Jammy', as a publican. For £2,750 they acquired a run-down row of cottages in Eskdale, which was known as the Freemason's Arms but which had not operated as a pub for many years. A. T. Hargreaves, demobilised from the army and wanting – with his wife, Ruth – to live in the country and near the fells, asked if they could be partners. It was done and, with much hard labour, the four of them built up a thriving little concern.

Three years later, in 1949, Sid Cross heard that the Old Dungeon Ghyll was to be sold. He moved fast and he and 'Jammy' drove over Hardknott and Wrynose passes to establish the ODG as the climbers' rendezvous in Langdale. An old shippon was turned into a bar and there the climbers would meet each evening to talk about their routes and laugh and argue and sing songs round the piano. Sid Cross says:

> Everyone behaved marvellously. The Creagh Dhu lads came down one week every year and they gave no trouble at all. They always washed if they were going to have dinner. It was the same with the lads from Yorkshire and Lancashire. Joe Brown was charming. Ron Moseley was delightful. So was Don Whillans, though you could see he was very tough. I think he was the hardest man that was ever on the fells.

The nickname for Don was 'the Villain'. Some of the stories of his 'dobbings', often of obstructive and uniformed officials, were true, and he was held in some awe by his fellow-climbers. Brown tells the story:

> During the early fifties, when hordes of climbers slept rough in the Wall End barn, Whillans quelled a riot of noise late at night by shouting, 'Pipe down and go to sleep'. This order was greeted by indignant comments, such as, 'Who the bloody hell do you think you are!' Whillans replied in a whip-cracking voice, 'Whillans', and silence fell instantly upon the rowdy company.

North Wales was the usual climbing ground for the men of the Rock and Ice and it was there they made their most important rock routes. But they enjoyed the Lake District, too. Joe Brown thought the tradition of antagonism between the two regions was 'spurious and silly'. It is a measure of the quality of their climbing that, though their visits to the Lakes were only occasional, they notched up an impressive list of new routes.

Their most productive year was 1953. In March Whillans, Don Cowan and Joe Brown climbed Triermain Eliminate on Castle Rock, which is graded Extremely Severe and which the guide book describes as 'An extremely strenuous variation to the lower part of Harlot Face'. At the beginning of May the same trio went to Dove Crag and climbed another 'Extreme', Dovedale Groove. Whillans had spotted the steep crack line some time before and thought it looked interesting. They had a nylon rope and a few nylon slings with ex-War Department karabiners attached. Whillans, wearing gym shoes, led the first and harder pitch. The very first move, getting off the ground, is virtually impossible without aid, so he hung a sling on a flake of rock and stepped up in it. More than thirty years later, repeating the climb for the television cameras, he explained:

> When you're doing a climb for the first time, you do everything you can to conserve your energy. You don't know what's coming next – how hard it's going to be further up. So if you can fix yourself a nice little leg-up, you do it – to save the strength in your fingers and arms. It's all right for those who come later. They can read all about it in the guide book – they know what's ahead. But there was no guide book to this crag in 1953 – there were only three or four routes on it.

Higher up, Whillans and Brown, who led the second pitch, managed to insert stones into cracks and thread slings behind them to make running belays. The technique had been used before in the Lake District but it was now developed into a fine art. Before setting off on a climb they would put pebbles of varying shapes and sizes in their pockets. Brown often carried some in his balaclava. As practical craftsmen, they took pride in making their protection as solid as possible. It gave them the confidence to create routes, remarkable for their relentless rigour and exposure.

On 31 May Ron Moseley climbed Pendulum on Deer Bield Crag. He had prepared the way by abseiling down and hammering a piton in at the crux point on the second pitch. When he reached the place, he lassoed his peg with a sling and hung on to it as he swung himself across.

In October three new routes were made. Moseley led Ray Greenall up Dight on Gimmer Crag. Then, on successive days, Brown led Laugh Not on White Ghyll which is graded Very Severe (Hard), and Whillans and Moseley girdled Deer Bield Crag which is 340 feet long and graded Extremely Severe.

In the summer of 1955 – a few days after Joe Brown reached the summit of Kangchenjunga, the third highest mountain in the world – Whillans led the first ascent of Trinity on Scafell's East Buttress. In February the following year he went to Raven Crag, Thirlmere, with a new club recruit whose name was Joe Smith but who was known as 'Mortimore' or 'Morty' to avoid confusion with Joe Brown. Whillans wrote:

The route, which had been attempted first by Arthur Dolphin and later by Harold Drasdo, took a fine line up the cliff and included one or two exciting, exposed traverses. When Morty and I did it, the whole crag was plastered with snow although it was not frozen over. It was a magnificent climb which gave me great pleasure. We called it Delphinus.

In May 1956 Whillans and Pete Greenwood alternated the lead to complete Raven Traverse on the same crag.

In 1957 Ron Moseley used one point of aid to conquer the forbidding Phoenix on the East Buttress of Scafell. It is graded Extremely Severe and the guide book said it was 'a full grade harder than anything else on the crag'. In that year, too, Joe Brown produced perhaps the finest of his Lake District routes, Eliminot on White Ghyll, another 'Extreme' which the guide book called 'a masterly solution to a particularly improbable line'.

Finally, in April 1960, Whillans created his Lakeland masterpiece. In his description of the route, in *Hard Rock*, Chris Bonington says:

> Extol is rather like Whillans: direct, uncompromising and hard. It goes straight up the centre of Dove Crag, a cliff full of surprises. It's only 300 feet high and looks quite small as you approach it ...; but once you are on it, it feels big and serious... The climbing has a brutal character, more like that of Wales than of the Lakeland fells.

Whillans's companion on the first ascent was Colin Mortlock. At one point, it is said, Whillans had run the rope out its full length and could find no belay point, so Mortlock had to untie from his belay and they were both, for a few anxious minutes, climbing extreme rock at the same time. Some of the grooves were still wet from recent rain. For the Lake District, this was the ultimate statement from the Rock and Ice men, in both senses of the adjective. It was their last new route in the area, their sixth Extreme in seven years of intermittent activity. And it exemplified the new kind of climbing – a direct, natural line up the cliff face; demanding awkward and difficult moves at every stage; involving chimneys and grooves and overhanging walls and ridges; committing and unremitting.

By this time Don Whillans – as much for his character as for the quality of his climbing – had gained legendary status. In later years he concentrated increasingly on expedition mountaineering in the higher ranges and made himself, arguably, the finest British all-round mountaineer of all time. He turned his direct, vigorous intelligence to designing equipment and produced, among other things, the Whillans box (a high-altitude tent); the Whillans hammer, or 'Whammer', combining ice axe and peg hammer; and the webbing waist harness that became ubiquitous.

Both he and Joe Brown went to live in North Wales and did most of their rock climbing there. But Don was frequently away on expeditions; or exploring under-water; or motor-cycling long distances; or lecturing.

In 1984 he returned to Dove Crag to re-climb Dovedale Groove for a TV film series Chris Bonington was making. He was more than thirty years older than when he made the first ascent, and at least five stone heavier. The years of beer drinking and cigarette smoking and generally indulging himself had taken some toll. But, though the gymnastic ability of his earlier days was no longer in evidence, the strength and determination and methodical cool were undiminished. He moved up the initial, vertical wall with all the old neatness and, for all his bulk, delicacy. His verbal mastery was undiminished, too. 'It's all psychology, this climbing lark', he said. He surveyed the threaded sling he meant to use as a foot hold and commented: 'It's strong all right but is it 14 stone strong? We'll soon know.' And when he came to the bulge near the top of the wall, he said: 'The problem here is getting my belly over this overhanging bit.' He took one hand off the rock face and lifted his gut on to the bulge, chuckled and carried on.

He died of a heart attack in the summer of 1985.

Although they were outstanding, the Rock and Ice men were by no means the only creative climbers during the 1950s. Some of the 'Bradford lads' were very active – Harold Drasdo on the Eastern crags of the District, Dennis Gray and Pete Greenwood. In his later writings, Gray portrayed Greenwood as a mad, tearaway figure, constantly getting into fights and ready to take terrible risks on the crags to assuage his driving ambition. Greenwood, who later became a businessman, involved in building and property, thinks the picture a little exaggerated:

> I don't think I was mad, or particularly rebellious. I just liked a good time. I enjoyed climbing – in all kinds of conditions. They said I was competitive and I certainly climbed for achievement, I wanted to be the best. They also said I was a 'necker', took terrible chances. In modern terms, that was true. There wasn't much protection in those days – just natural runners. And the gear wasn't that good – ex-army karabiners. And nobody did any special training in those days – except by climbing. We did a lot of that.

He climbed a good deal with Whillans, in the Dolomites and the Lake District, and they got on well. But one day in 1956 he decided to give up climbing:

> I'm a spur-of-the-moment man. I was in digs on the Headlands in Keswick. I was getting married the week after and I thought I'd better concentrate on that, and making some money. Climbing was a dangerous game in those days – lots of friends had been killed. So I went out that morning and told Don I was giving it up and he could have all my gear. He told me I was a bloody idiot. But he took the gear.

Harold Drasdo made many routes throughout the 1950s and it was he who compiled the guide book to the *Eastern Crags* which came out in 1959. He is another who was vividly presented in *Rope Boy*, especially in Gray's account of the first ascent of North Crag Eliminate on Castle

Rock in September 1952. The Drasdo brothers had prospected the route and gardened some of it. Gray was invited to the attempted climb because he had just bought a 150-foot length of nylon rope. Harold led quickly up the first 140 feet, belayed to a yew tree and brought Gray – who was 16 and small for his age – up to join him.

> 'From here', he proudly announced, 'we employ an unusual method. First we climb the tree to its top branch, then launch ourselves at the overhang above, and climb it direct.'
> 'No kidding,' I gasped
> 'Actually, it's easy. We came this far the other week, our kid romped up it.'

Gray watched Drasdo do it but when he climbed up the tree he found he was too small to reach the rock. Drasdo's solution was prompt: 'Get the tree moving.' So he got it swaying backwards and forwards, then catapulted himself on to the overhang and clung on grimly. There were more dramas higher up but Drasdo fixed running belays whenever possible and banged a piton in near the top. The route is still graded Extremely Severe and the tree is still there and used, though the latest guide book (1987) describes it as 'wilting'.

Gray makes it clear that it was not only the Rock and Ice men who were devising improved techniques to protect the leader. Of Harold Drasdo, he writes: 'Once he got to grips with a problem he would go on trying until he was successful or exhausted. He was also a master of the new and revolutionary techniques of utilising carefully placed and contrived running belays.' The Rock and Ice men have also been credited with the virtual invention of another influential technique, hand jamming. This involves pushing the flattened hand into a crack, clenching the fist to lock it in position, then bending the arm to gain height. It involves the painful shredding of the hands but it is effective. Brown and Whillans and their friends certainly used the method, but Peter Harding was hand jamming up the Snowdonia cliffs before they arrived, and an entry in the old Climbing Book at the Wastwater Hotel suggests that the technique was not unknown fifty years before that. The note, signed by Ernest Baker and Horace Westmorland, is dated Easter 1910. It describes their conquest of the Western Crack on the crag at the head of Mosedale: 'First difficulty occurs where big step overhangs steep water-swept slab. Splinter under waterfall gives belay. Small loose chockstone gives a grip, and hand can be jammed in crack. First a shoulder from second man, then friction give foot hold and fingertip holds enable upper slab to be reached ...'

In 1954 Jim Birkett, with Harry Griffin seconding, made the last of his fifty Lake District routes – Kestrel Wall on Eagle Crag, Grisedale. As almost always, he was wearing nailed boots.

By this time, though, new gear was coming in. Most climbers had nylon ropes and carried loops of nylon sling, attached to karabiners made on the Continent. Nylon line, thin enough to thread round pebbles wedged inside very narrow cracks, made a lot of difference. Increasingly, they wore the moulded-rubber Vibram boots, named after their Italian inventor, Vitali Bramani. These began to be superseded in 1958 by a lighter and more efficient rock boot, designed by the French climber, Pierre Allain, for climbing on the sandstone crags at Fontainebleau. They were called P.A.s in his honour, though later they came to be known as E.B.s. They had wrap-around rubber soles and heels for maximum adhesion and a metal stiffener through them for greater rigidity. The old gym-shoe 'rubbers' were adhesive on dry rock but soft-soled and very 'bendy'. P.A.s meant the climber could stand comfortably secure with just the toes on a sharp hold.

The new gear, the new techniques for protection and, most important of all, the spreading fame of the new climbers – all combined to make the 1950s the most prolific decade in the history of the sport so far. At the end of 1949 there were twenty-six climbs in the Lake District that are still graded Very Severe (Hard). In the next ten years fifty climbs were created of that standard or higher; fifteen of them were promoted to the Extremely Severe level when that category was officially recognised by the guide books in 1967. New crags were opened up, among the eastern fells, in Borrowdale, Langdale and Eskdale. With the exception of Scafell, the time-hallowed climbing grounds – Pillar Rock, Great Gable, Dow Crag, the cliffs of Buttermere – were largely ignored. The new men went for crags that were more readily accessible from the valleys; that were lower-lying and dried out more quickly; and where the rock faces had not been comprehensively explored already.

Among the new recruits were many who were to make, in one way or another, significant contributions.

George Fisher of Keswick, later to open his climbing shop on the corner site where the Abrahams' photography shop had been, was making new routes in Borrowdale by 1950. Within two years he was joined by Des Oliver, now a National Park Ranger, who claims to have been the first man in the valley to wear Vibrams, what they called 'Commando soles'. When the others first saw them, he remembers, they laughed. But before long they were all wearing them. He also remembers coming across a diminutive Keswick schoolboy who was scrambling about on Little Round How on Haystacks. He and another leading Keswick climber of the day, Jim Barber, were on their way to Pillar Rock but they stopped to instruct the boy and his companion in the rudiments of the game, how to tie the knots and belay themselves. Next day they all went to Kern Knotts to have a go at the Buttonhook Route which had not been repeated for many years. They did it and the boy enjoyed it so much he wanted to do it again immediately, with him leading. They refused to let him try. But one week later, when Oliver and Barber were passing that way again, they looked up to see the lad cheerfully leading his friend up the Buttonhook. 'The problem', Oliver says, 'was containing him.' It is a problem that many other people have had to face subsequently. The boy was called Paul Ross. He was only sixteen but soon he would be making his own ferocious routes in his own, very determined way.

In the mid-1950s a young librarian from Yorkshire, Tony Greenbank, got a job in Kendal and took to climbing with a group from the K Shoes factory. Soon bored with his work in the public library, he moved to the Outward Bound School in Eskdale: 'It changed my life', he says. 'It was like going to university for me. I did lots of climbing – and it was there I started writing.' Today he lives in Ambleside and still divides his life between climbing and writing, doing both with equal ebullience. Other recruits from Yorkshire included Doug Verity, son of the great Yorkshire and England spin bowler, and Brian Evans, an art student in Leeds who later became a printer and publisher. Evans was a part-time tutor for the Mountaineering Association and one of his pupils was a small, round-faced young man from Bradford called Allan Austin. Austin took to climbing immediately. Before long he was spending all his spare time on the crags, usually with Evans. In 1956 he made his first Lakeland route, Stickle Grooves on Pavey Ark. In the next twenty-one years he was to create seventy-five climbs in the District, the majority of them in the Langdale area, many of them 'Extremes'. But it was not his climbing so much as his strength of character that was to make him a powerful influence in the 1960s, when he emerged as leader of the Langdale 'purists' in their fight against the piton-wielding 'iron men' of Keswick, led by Paul Ross.

There was a strong contingent from the Carlisle area. It included Mike Thompson, anthropologist and wit and the first British soldier to discover that you can escape from the army by running, however hopelessly, for Parliament; Dennis English, one of the best and neatest climbers of the time, who now runs a climbing shop in Carlisle; and the enduring and redoubtable Ray McHaffie, once described by Thompson as 'the original Jaws of Borrowdale'.

McHaffie is certainly articulate. His enthusiasm for climbing has not waned with the years. And his story, how he came to climb and what it did for him, might be taken as the definitive text for all who believe in the character-forming – or character-reforming – influence of the sport.

He grew up in a broken home and was brought up, by his grand-mother, on Raffles, one of the toughest housing estates in the North of England. At school he was good at games – Carlisle United gave him a trial as goal-keeper – but not interested in the lessons. At fourteen he left school to work briefly with a painter and decorator, then for many years in a timberyard. Soon he was the leader of a gang of 'Teddy Boys' and, in a gang fight, lost the use of his left eye.

He seems to have felt no resentment about this and it saved him from having to do National Service. Then, one day, a neighbour asked if he would like to go to the mountains on the fell walkers' bus which left Carlisle at 9 am on Sunday and returned from Seatoller at 8 pm. He tried it and enjoyed himself so much he was soon walking 25 miles in the fells every Sunday:

> One Saturday, though, messing about in the River Eden, I split the bottom of my foot open on a broken bottle and had to have eight or nine stitches. So I went on the bus next day with a hob-nailed boot on the good foot and a slipper on the other. I couldn't do a long walk so I wandered up to Sty Head and came across Kern Knotts. I knew nothing about it but I climbed up the Crack, hand-jamming, and down the Chimney. Those were my first routes. I did them solo and had no great difficulty. I didn't know I'd done a rock climb till on the way home I saw a photo of the Crack in Abrahams' shop window. My mates didn't believe I'd done it so I went back the next Sunday and showed them. After that I went and soloed Napes Needle. I got to the shoulder all right but couldn't do the last bit, the mantelshelf move. I was sitting there when two monks came along with their gowns tucked up into the rope round their waists. The first one nipped up easily. But the second couldn't do it. So I tied on and, with the confidence of a top rope, managed it. Reaching the top I said 'That was fucking 'ard', and the monk said 'It's time you went down, boy'.

By the mid-'50s McHaffie was climbing regularly and hard, in summer and winter, doing second ascents of many of Peascod's routes in Buttermere. It was the saving of him. Gradually, he gave up the 'Teddy Boy' life of gang fights. In 1965 he left his job in the timberyard and moved to Keswick. He lives there today with his wife and three children. He has a job with the National Trust, building footpaths up the fell sides to protect them from erosion. And he enjoys his climbing as much as he ever did:

> It's the adventure of it, the excitement. I just seemed to enjoy it as soon as I started. No one taught me. I must have seemed reckless. Some older Carlisle climbers said they'd give me three months to live. But I've never pushed myself to the limit. I often wonder, if we'd had the modern gear when I was younger, what standard I would have reached. Because when I started, you were told you should never fall off. Though I did, of course ...
>
> I've done 200 new routes and never one of them to impress anyone. It doesn't have to be hard, as long as it's a nice route. I've never been competitive. I climb for enjoyment. And I still get as much enjoyment out of doing a Diff. as out of doing a new route or an Extreme – that's why I'm still climbing after all these years.

There were hundreds more, many young men and some young women, who joined the sport in the 1950s. Among the more notable were Mick Burke from Wigan; Geoff Oliver (no relation to Des Oliver) who came from Newcastle and had been inspired to climb by Bill Murray's book

Undiscovered Scotland; Jack Soper, studying geology at Sheffield University; and Les Brown who had a physics degree and a job at the Windscale (now Sellafield) nuclear plant.

The decade that began with Arthur Dolphin's climbs and gathered pace with those of Greenwood and Harold Drasdo, Joe Brown and Don Whillans, ended in a ferment of activity. Allan Austin was busy at the southern end of the District, creating Cascade on Pavey Ark in 1957; several good routes, including Golden Slipper, on the same crag the next year; and, in 1959, Inertia on Gimmer and Troll's Corner on Pavey Ark. To the north, meanwhile, Paul Ross was bringing his gymnastic skills and his piton hammer to bear on previously untouched expanses of very exposed rock – on Lower Falcon and Black Crag in Borrowdale, Castle Rock in Thirlmere. In April 1959, with Bill Aughton in support, he climbed a ferocious route on Castle Rock which he then described, with characteristic *élan* and complete shamelessness about his use of artificial aids, in the pages of the Fell and Rock *Journal*:

> ... Swinging onto the right-hand edge, I reached a spike for a sling, and by standing in this a few more feet were gained. Progress seemed impossible now as far as free climbing was concerned.
>
> Up to the left I noticed another slight projection, but it was not until after much strenuous swinging and chipping that this became suitable for a single line sling. Transferring myself to this sling – my perch for the next hour – was no mean feat as it needed very little encouragement to roll off. Eventually I managed to jam a piton into a wide crack to steady myself and started to hammer at a knife edge up to the right, trying to find a weakness to make some sort of spike on which to hang yet another sling ... We named the climb Rigor Mortis, as we thought it a rather stiff problem.

In 1958 the brilliant Scots climber Robin Smith, a student at Edinburgh, paid a flying visit south and on one day, 3 May, created two impressive routes on the East Buttress of Scafell – Chartreuse and Leaverage.

The summer of 1959 was unusually fine and dry, and brought a spate of new climbs. In Langdale Mick Burke climbed Warlock and Schizen on the eastern Raven Crags. Les Brown used his long reach and phenomenal finger strength to create Inertia on Gimmer; Moonday on Scafell East Buttress; and Caesar, which lies alongside Cleopatra, on Buckstone How. Geoff Oliver, seconded by Norman Brown from Darlington, climbed Agony, a fierce wall climb on Castle Rock, scraping loads of moss off the lower slab with his hands as he ascended.

It was Oliver and his group who brought Pillar Rock back into the action. For eighteen years no new route had been made on the crag which had been so central in the period, a century earlier, when rock scrambling was evolving towards rock climbing. But Oliver had spotted some unclimbed lines on the west face. On 13 June he arrived at the foot of the face with four friends. He led two of them up Vandal, a steep but well-protected climb, and the other two climbed the curving groove of Goth. Both routes are graded Very Severe (Hard).

The sport was booming, even more spectacularly in North Wales than in the Lake District. The '50s had been an explosive decade. The '60s were to be more contentious.

9

The Aid Controversy
1959–1973

ALLAN AUSTIN was another of those outstanding climbers who signally failed to look the part. He was, as he still is, of less than medium height, with a pale round face, and broadly built – his nickname was 'Tubby'. His voice is quiet, flat almost, but he talks with firm assurance and a leavening of wry, understated, Yorkshire humour. He works, as he always has, in the small business he took over from his father – buying waste wool from the mills around Bradford, cleaning and grading and then re-selling it. He has no illusions: 'It's a sort of living but my lads aren't coming into it. Wool will be gone in ten years' time.'

In the late 1970s he badly twisted his right arm and damaged a ligament and that put an effective end to his climbing. He misses it:

> I used to go climbing every week-end, usually to Langdale. On Monday evenings I'd go to some local gritstone outcrop, soloing. On Wednesday evenings I'd go out with the lads, do a few routes, then go to the pub. We didn't drink heavily – I only got drunk at the odd club dinner – but we used to have a right good time. When you've been climbing for 30 years its hard to envisage life without going to the crags. I still keep active, go walking and sailing and bird-watching. But it's not the same. The adrenalin doesn't run. I miss a lot of things – especially those Wednesday nights.

The most striking aspect of Austin's personality is his dedication to truth. He gives the impression of being totally honest himself and expecting the same rigorous standards from others. It was this that made him the key figure in the controversy that raged about the Lake District crags during the 1960s and into the '70s over the use and abuse of artificial aids – pitons, slings, étriers – as a means of getting up steep and difficult rock.

He was not particularly athletic at school and he was a late-comer to climbing. But when he did discover the crags, at the age of twenty, he took to them immediately. At first he wore nailed boots, clinkers, but he

174

soon switched to 'rubbers', then Vibrams when they came in, then P.A.s. Brian Evans was his usual companion. By 1956 they were creating their own routes on the gritstone and limestone crags near home in the evenings, in and around the Langdale valley at weekends. Brian Evans says:

> Austin was more powerfully built than me, much the same height but broader and a lot stronger. He liked overhanging cracks, which he could hand jam. But he was very good too on the delicate, airy stuff. And he was very bold, pushy. He was competitive. If he had his eye on a new line, he'd keep very quiet about it – he didn't want anyone beating him to it. He had secret crags. But he was tolerant, too. He didn't have intense rivalries. He did no weight training or work-outs in the gymnasium. But he never smoked and he wasn't a big drinker.

In May 1960 Austin made one of the best of his many routes, Astra on the east wall of Pavey Ark. Today it is graded Extremely Severe and gets the full three stars for quality. Its creation grew out of his admiration for Dolphin. He got hold of the climbing diaries Dolphin had kept and repeated all his routes, then set about developing lines that Dolphin had spotted but not climbed. Astra follows the route of Hobson's Choice for nearly 100 feet, the first two pitches. But at the point where Dolphin paused and then moved leftwards, opting for the easier alternative, Austin pushed on to the right. In the guide book he described the next 70-foot pitch in these words:

> Across the foot of the impending right wall of the corner runs a narrow, easy-angled slab. Cross the slab to the far side. The wall round the corner is steep and severely undercut but the next objective, a prominent flake, is only a few feet away. Climb across to the flake (strenuous) and then work up and back left until the angle eases and a resting place is reached. Above on the right is a crack in a very steep wall. Insert a piton and use it to step round the edge on the right on to a slab.

That is the crux and, just above it, there is a stance. Austin belayed himself there and his second, Eric Metcalf, climbed up and led on through.

Metcalf was nicknamed 'Matey' in sarcastic recognition of his very taciturn manner. He was a good climber, slightly built and wiry, and he took a more purist line about artificial aids than Austin:

> I remember once Matey was about 30 feet above me on Scafell and I shouted up 'I'll throw you up a threader – you can get one in there.' But he said, 'I can't do that. I couldn't do it on the Mer de Glace face of the Grépon, you know.' And he wouldn't have a threader. Now that's ethics carried to a super degree.

There were others – Ken Wood and John Syrett among them – who refused to use any kind of artificial assistance on a climb. If they could not do it, using only the holds that the rock itself offered, they preferred to leave it undone. Austin has great admiration for such fixity of principle, but when he was making very exposed new routes he carried a few pitons and a hammer and, very sparingly, used them.

He became the leading spokesman for the 'clean hands' group, originating mostly in Yorkshire and operating mostly in Langdale, not because he was the purest of the purists – by his own admission, he was nothing of the sort – but because he was asked, in the mid-1960s, to update the Langdale guide book and because, in doing so, he took a firm view of what constituted a proper first ascent and what did not. Where serious principles were at stake, he did not shrink from confrontation. Twenty years later, in the Fell and Rock *Journal*, Pete Whillance wrote:

> There is little doubt that Austin's attitudes and approach to climbing had a strong influence on his companions, and the fact that only two of the 25 climbs he established in Langdale during the sixties employed a peg for aid (one each on Astra and Rainmaker) stands in stark contrast to the developments in Borrowdale during the same period.

A talented group, centred on Keswick, had been active in Borrowdale throughout the 1950s. They included the Fisher brothers (George and Dick), Mike Nixon, Des Oliver, Jim Barber, Ian Smeaton and others, and they got on well with climbing visitors from Carlisle and the North-east. By the end of the decade, the leading spirit was Paul Ross.

He was twenty-two years old in 1960 but still small and very boyish in appearance. Light and wiry, he enjoyed a highly favourable strength-to-weight ratio. He was also supple and gymnastic. But more important than that, he had tremendous drive. Those who saw him leading climbs were impressed by his speed and agility and determination. 'He was dynamic', Chris Bacon says. 'He kept the momentum going. He would spring for holds. If he saw a good hold ten feet above him, somehow or other he'd manage to get to it.' He did a lot of solo climbing. Ian Smeaton saw him descend Kern Knotts Crack, solo, and says he did it in a sort of controlled slip, very fast. He loved exploring new ground: 'I get a big thrill', he said, 'out of not knowing what's coming next. I'd rather make a new route, even an easy one, than climb something that people have done before.' When he was making a very hard new route, Rigor Mortis for example, Ross was prepared to spend a lot of time, putting in pitons and fixing slings, both for protection and as points of aid. And when he had made a new climb he wrote it up in the climbers' books and kept a detailed note in his diary. He wanted the credit as well as the climb.

Most of his routes were in the northern part of the Lake District, in Borrowdale and on Castle Rock, Thirlmere. One of his regular partners was Peter Lockey who came from Newcastle and is now joint owner of the L. D. Mountain Centre there. But in 1960 Ross, accompanied by Ralph Blain, chief instructor at the Ullswater Outward Bound School, made a raid south and put up a new route in the heart of Austin territory, in a manner calculated to give maximum offence.

The line, close to Kipling Groove, was one that Arthur Dolphin had spotted and even named. He called it, enigmatically, If. It is only 130 feet but it took Ross four and a half hours to lead it. Most of the time he spent banging in pitons. He explained: 'We did If as a totally provocative route, up an incredible piece of rock ... Greenwood provoked me into it. I got Geoff Oliver interested in turn and he tried it twice before I did it. He was a little bit that way, trying to provoke people, but he never pulled it off, he was a nice guy.' The implications are clear. Ross did pull it off. He was not a nice guy. And he did not give a damn.

When Austin's guide book came out in 1967 he included If and described it as 'Artificial and very severe'. In his list of first ascents he added the comment: 'Many pitons were used. R. James making the second ascent a few months later halved the number, and today five or six seem sufficient.' A new game was emerging – climbing very hard routes with fewer aid pitons than your predecessors.

On one occasion Austin and Ross climbed together. It was in the spring of 1956 on the day when Austin and Brian Evans had made their variation start to the Central Climb on Kern Knotts. By chance, they met Ross and roped up and climbed the Buttonhook Route. Austin was impressed: 'Ross was a very good climber and a brilliant technician. He seemed to find things very easy. It never seemed that easy to me.' There was no personal animosity between them but their contrasting attitudes made a clash inevitable. Allan Austin took climbing seriously: 'I thought a lot about the sport. I really thought it was great. I cared about it and I cared about what other people were doing to it. There's no point whatever in caring if you don't say so.' Ross, on the other hand, was in it purely for fun, for thrills and laughter. Recalling the earliest days of his climbing, he said:

> Those were the best. There don't seem to be so many laughs nowadays. We used to have some frightening times now and again, but when we'd got down again we used to have a good laugh and forget about them. Nowadays, there's not always the same enjoyment. Too much competition, for one thing. Climbing's a thing to be enjoyed, not endured.

So he banged in his pitons and chipped at the rock to make spikes and stood in slings to take a rest and swung about on them like a monkey across the dizzy drops in cheerful disregard of all environmental or ethical considerations. He liked to stir things up. He was mischievous and irreverent and no respecter of established reputations. In 1958 he had been in the Alps with Don Whillans on the epic ascent of the Southwest Pillar of the Dru – when Whillans first encountered the young Chris Bonington, and when Hamish McInnes had his head fractured by a falling rock halfway up the route. Bonington recalled the time when their two parties came together:

> Whillans and Ross were not getting on. They were hardly speaking. When Hamish
> got his head smashed, we changed partners. Don hauled Hamish up and I climbed
> with Paul, taking the pitons out. Don called Paul 'the spoilt brat of Keswick'. It
> had all started when Paul stood up to Don. Don wasn't used to that. But nobody
> got Paul down – he was very much his own man, a brilliant character.

Ross had left school at sixteen. He worked for a while for the Forestry
Commission, delighted to find he was being paid for strengthening his
hands and arms for climbing. Then he became an instructor at the
Ullswater Outward Bound school, where Ian Smeaton was among his
colleagues. In the summer of 1962 he fell seriously ill with tuberculosis
of the spine. He was out of action for more than a year, in hospital in
Carlisle, then in the sanatorium at Threlkeld. When he emerged, he
acquired a basement café towards the bottom of Lake Road, Keswick.
He called it The Lamplighter and it quickly became a popular haunt
for climbers, a cheerful and lively place with bar billiards and table
football, much folk singing and guitar playing, endless talk and argument
about climbing.

The group that gathered around Ross came to be called 'crag rats'.
It was hardly meant as a compliment but they were not insulted. They
had no pretentions, most of them anyway, to be mountaineers. They
had no love for fell walking and did not go to a mountain summit unless
a rock climb led them there. Their obsessive interest was in getting
themselves up very steep rock. Unlike the Langdale scene – Allan Austin
and Brian Evans both married climbers – the Keswick group was exclusively male. At weekends they would camp or bivouac below Falcon Crag
and when the authorities moved them on they used the caves near the
Bowderstone. They were kept on the move among the Keswick pubs,
too. They went to the weekend dances and some of them got, fairly
regularly, into fights. Sometimes they drank too much and then drove
their motor bikes far too fast up the valley. They could be reckless and
disputatious and competitive but their behaviour was, according to
them, high-spirited and good-hearted.

Their enthusiasm subjected Borrowdale to an exploration even more
intense than that which Bentley Beetham had conducted a generation
earlier.

In the spring of 1962 Ross was at work on the broken cliff of Walla
Crag. In August that year Ray McHaffie and Adrian ('Ado') Liddell, a
carpenter from Carlisle with a long reach and an even longer 'neck',
climbed The Niche on Lower Falcon, using pitons for protection and for
aid at two points and also to prise out a lot of loose blocks. In the same
month Paul Nunn, a big man from Manchester who went on to become
a history lecturer at Sheffield Polytechnic, created Plagiarism on the
same crag. And in September McHaffie and Les Kendall made the first
complete Girdle Traverse of the cliff. All three routes were graded

Extremely Severe. In 1964 Paul Ross, just out of hospital and still encased in plaster, explored some buttresses of rock he had discovered above the road to Watendlath. But the great year for discoveries was 1965.

Many years before, McHaffie had set off up a steep crack on the northern face of Goat Crag, the big, dark, vegetated cliff that looms above the village of Grange on the western side of the valley. Heavy rain had finally driven him down but he mentioned the matter, one day, to Les Brown, the scientist from Windscale. Brown did not forget. Some time in the early summer of 1965 he went to look for himself and was impressed. In the weeks that followed he spent many hours abseiling down the face of the cliff and clearing his proposed line of ascent of all obstructing undergrowth and rubble. He drove other climbers mad by dropping broad and tantalising hints in the pubs. They knew he was on to something new and exciting but no one guessed it was on Goat Crag. By the end of May all was ready and on the 30th Les Brown led the climb in four formidable and varied pitches. He called it Praying Mantis. Then he broke the news and set off a frenzy of route-making on the new crag. By the end of the year there were nine high-quality routes there. Moreover, within a fortnight of Brown's climb, Paul Ross and Paul Nunn had made three impressive routes on Eagle Crag in Langstrath, and Brian Henderson of Consett did another one. And the same month, June 1965, Chris Bonington led the Creep on Quayfoot Buttress.

Bonington, who is probably the best-known climber in Britain, has lived in the Lake District since 1971 and, when he is not away on expeditions or lecture tours, still does a lot of climbing there. But he is not primarily a Lake District climber. He grew up in London and found he had a natural aptitude for the sport on Harrison's Rocks, a sandstone outcrop in Sussex. His drive to excel took him first to Snowdonia, then to the Alps, then the Himalayas. He has few Lakeland routes to his name but they are almost all routes of distinction – White Wizard on Scafell Crag and Holy Ghost on Scafell East Buttress; The Last Laugh on Castle Rock, Thirlmere, which he did with Paul Ross and others in the summer of 1965; and two impressive routes on Raven Crag, Thirlmere, The Medlar which he climbed with Martin Boysen in August 1964 using three points of aid, and Totalitarian, climbed the following month using only one point of aid. They are all in the Extremely Severe category.

Bonington had known Mike Thompson since their army cadet days at Sandhurst and, on his forays to the Lakes in the 1960s, he usually stayed at the Thompsons' cottage. 'Mike was the brains', he says, 'and I was the brawn. He had an eye for lovely lines – like Holy Ghost and Totalitarian. He pointed me at 'em and I led 'em.'

Holy Ghost was, in effect, a misjudgement and it nearly became a disaster. Thompson's plan was to create a new and improved traverse of Scafell East Buttress. They had not inspected the route or cleaned it and they made the attempt on a very cold day in April 1965. Bonington led off from the foot of Gremlin's Groove, then traversed rightwards to a stance at the top of the second pitch of Trinity. When Thompson had joined him there and belayed, Bonington rounded a steep corner on to the nose of the buttress, with an overhanging section above:

> By that time I was about 15 feet from my belay. I set off with a blithe optimism up to this vertical nose where there was a foot hold and then a series of undercuts. At that point I was going into a corner and had no idea what was on the other side. The holds were all rounded and I remember going up them in a blind sweat.

One of Bonington's characteristics that has made him so successful as a communicator is his frankness. When he started writing and lecturing about his adventures, the prevailing tradition in Britain was still that of the old-style, stiff-upper-lip understatement. But Bonington described exactly what he had been feeling at the time:

> I was dead frightened when I realised I couldn't retreat. I got round the corner but there was no easy ledge to go for, and nothing to hang on to. So it was a blind alley and I'd had it, and the only thing I could have done was to jump off.

Many lesser climbers know the feeling well and most of those who would never dream of climbing can readily imagine it. In fact, Bonington was so stuck that he called for someone to get above him and lower a rope. But while he waited his courage returned:

> I managed to get a good nut in at floor level, then I started looking around and saw that going upwards – though it was very steep – there were some small holds, and I thought 'I can climb out of this'. It was hard going for another 20 feet to a decent stance ... We called the climb Holy Ghost because it was next door to Whillan's Trinity, and we were so bloody frightened.

The route was graded Extremely Severe. But it was not the girdle traverse they had intended. This was completed four years later by two young climbers, Colin Read and John Adams, starting with the first part of Holy Ghost and going on to complete a superb and consistently demanding traverse, 1,130 feet in length. They called it Lord of the Rings. It was six years before it was climbed again.

The pace of events in Borrowdale had rendered Bentley Beetham's 1953 guide hopelessly out-of-date but the Fell and Rock Club were taking no steps to replace it. So, in the summer of 1966, Paul Ross and Mike Thompson produced and published their own, *Borrowdale: A Climber's Guide.* It took them six weeks to write and it sold in the shops for 15/- (75p). It was revolutionary in a number of ways. For the first time, asterisks were used to denote recommended routes, and the letter 'A' to indicate routes which required artificial aid. There was no apology about aid climbing. In his introductory notes, Thompson wrote:

> Falcon Crag Buttress uses four pegs for aid, Vertigo has seven and the overhang on Wack six. This caused raised eyebrows in Langdale and elsewhere, but the

trend has continued and now several of the best and most popular routes involve mixed free and artificial climbing. More recently some remarkable pure peg climbs have been done, notably The Technician (Long Band Crag), Joke (Lower Falcon) and The Great Buttress (Goat Crag). Arguments which have raged over the ethics of these routes are really irrelevant since the routes are already there and no amount of protest can remove them. More than the stated number of pegs should not be used and efforts to reduce the number are to be encouraged. The man who transforms The Great Buttress from a peg route to a free route is sure of his niche in climbing history.

They deliberately omitted many of the poorer climbs – 'Let us hope they are never re-discovered' – but gave details of how aid should be used on the new, hard routes. Describing the second pitch of Rigor Mortis, for example – the book had a four-page Thirlmere supplement – they said:

> The last ten feet to the piton, which is in place at the top of the white cone, are climbed resting in slings on two flakes. Using an étrier on the piton, tension out across the left wall until a sling can be placed on a minute flake. Use this as a foot hold to reach a shallow groove . . .

There was one more influential innovation. Until this time, Lake District guide books had used only one designation – Very Severe – for the hardest climbs. This was no longer adequate. Standards had risen very fast. So Ross and Thompson split the top-most category into four: Very Severe (Easy), Very Severe, Very Severe (Hard) and Extremely Severe. Their book included 12 'Extremes', among them Praying Mantis, The Niche, The Medlar, Rigor Mortis and The Last Laugh.

The appearance of this unofficial guide book came as an unpleasant shock to the Fell and Rock Club which had always, previously, held the monopoly in the Lake District. Reviewing it in the club *Journal* at the end of the year, Jack Soper admitted the need for an updated guide book, approved some of its new ideas, but deplored its overall attitude:

> It is very well for the authors to make trite remarks on the desirability of reducing aid on originally aided climbs, but this guide has merely pushed us further down the slippery slope of 'cheat, not retreat'. What a shambles would have been made of Deer Bield Buttress or, for that matter, Diagonal Route on Dinas Mot, had they been discovered in Borrowdale in the 1960s!

The year after the Ross/Thompson guide appeared, the Fell and Rock began to bring out its own updated series, under a new overall editor, John Wilkinson. The old editor, H. M. Kelly, who had been in charge for more than thirty years, did not go without a struggle. His strong will came up against the equal determination of a much younger man. Allan Austin was the inevitable choice to compile the new Langdale guide; the vast majority of the impressive new routes there were his, including Gandalf's Groove on Bowfell and several fine climbs on Pavey Ark, Arcturus and The Rainmaker among them. Some of these routes, though, were short, only a single pitch in length. Kelly thought they were scarcely more than boulder problems and not worth including. Austin explains: 'He said how could a 90-foot route be a big route? He was thinking of Pillar Rock and Scafell, where everything was 300 feet long or not worth considering. But these new routes were fine climbs and very hard. And you can get killed falling 90 feet. I felt if you could get killed it was serious.'

Other changes were planned for the series. There would be a new, slightly smaller format, enabling the books to slip easily into the back pocket of the climbing breeches. They would have a plastic, more weatherproof cover. Following the Ross/Thompson lead and also the example of the Climbers' Club guides to Snowdonia, more categories were introduced at the top end of the scale: Very Severe (Mild), Very Severe, Very Severe (Hard) and Extremely Severe. In the end, after some fiery scenes, the new order won the day. Wilkinson assumed the editorship and Austin's book came out.

It included the routes that had only been done with the help of artificial devices, making clear where and how they had been employed. But Austin's dislike of aided climbing was clear. He dismissed Trilogy, a short, articifial route on Raven Crag, in four curt lines. He mentioned Ross's profligate use of pitons on If. He was not dismissive of all aid but he deplored its excessive use and the dishonesty which sometimes resulted:

> What I objected to most of all was people not telling the truth. I don't really care what people do on the crag providing they say so. What I objected to was this business of putting in a piton, standing in a sling, making the move – then leaning back down and taking it out and not letting on to anyone. Or a bit of tension on a traverse that you don't bother to record. I really do object to that. It's dangerous. It misleads those who come after. They believe what you've said. It's not on.

Over the next few years the Fell and Rock issued eight updated guide books, on the same lines and principles as the Langdale guide. There was much catching up to do. As well as the intense activity there had been in Borrowdale and Langdale, some of the old traditional crags had been attracting fresh attention. For instance, in 1960, Geoff Oliver went to Scafell East Buttress and climbed Ichabod, an 'Extreme', using a piton for aid 'without any pang of conscience'. Then a group of West Cumbrians began to find new lines on Pillar Rock. Geoff Cram and Bill Young climbed Scylla in 1963 and Charybdis the year after and more routes followed. In 1966 they went to Gable Crag, virtually unvisited for many years, and added The Tomb to the growing catalogue of 'extremes'.

Les Brown was also ranging widely from his home base at Windscale, cloaking his plans in the usual cloud of secrecy and confusion. Instructors at the Outward Bound School in Eskdale had opened up Heron Crag in their valley during the 1950s and Brown crowned their efforts, in

March 1960, with Gormenghast, a 300-foot route that goes boldly up the central pillar. He had a *penchant* for fantastic literature which was reflected in the names he chose. In June 1960 he led The Centaur on Scafell East Buttress. Later came Psycho on High Crag, Buttermere; then Praying Mantis to launch a flurry of activity on Goat Crag, Borrowdale; then Balrog on Dow Crag; then, in July 1966, The Nazgul on Scafell Crag, which takes a direct line up the steep wall of the Central Buttress – between Botterill's Slab and the Great Flake. He used two pitons for aid at the start of the second pitch. Although the line is plainly visible from below and this was well-known and time-hallowed ground, Brown contrived – as he had done with Praying Mantis – to keep his intentions secret. He successfully misled rival climbers, who knew he was once again up to something very interesting, by telling them he was exploring 'Far East Buzzard Crag', a cliff that existed only in his mind.

Despite the level of activity, there is no doubt that the Snowdonia men of this period were climbing at a generally higher standard than those of the Lake District. Some of them made marauding forays to press the point home. In June 1962 Pete Crew and 'Baz' Ingle, leading figures in the new wave of development on Clogwyn du'r Arddu, went to Dove Crag and climbed a new route on the big blank wall between Dovedale Groove and Extol. To make the lesson unmistakable, they called it by the Welsh name for homesickness, Hiraeth – 'because we were longing to get back home again to Wales'. But Crew was still in the Lake District a week later, to snatch another 'plum'. He heard that Allan Austin, 'Matey' Metcalf and Jack Soper were planning an attempt on the Central Pillar of Esk Buttress the following Sunday. So he got up early that day, made a dawn start and was established on the climb when the Langdale trio turned up. They had to content themselves with making two other shorter routes and, to mark their disappointment, calling one of them Black Sunday. Towards the end of the decade another raiding party from Wales, Richard McHardy and Paul ('Tut') Braithwaite, created The Viking on the Tophet Wall of Great Gable.

The Viking was the first route made in the Lake District that was later to be graded E3, Extremely Severe 3. It is a measure of the speed at which standards were rising that not long after the 'Extreme' category was introduced, it was necessary to add higher grades. The Climbers' Club, in their guide books to North Wales, experimented with a category they called 'Exceptionally Severe'. But it was soon evident that the English language's supply of superlatives was not going to be enough to cope, so a system was devised of combining the adjective 'Extreme' with numbers to indicate exactly how extreme. Under this, Jim Birkett's Harlot Face (1949) and Whillans's Dovedale Groove (1953) are now graded E1; Dolphin's Deer Bield Buttress (1951) and Austin's Astra on Pavey Ark (1960) are E2.

The improvement in standards was accompanied and encouraged by improvements in equipment and techniques. Above all else, the 1960s were significant because they saw the arrival of the metal nut (or chock) as the chief means by which the lead climber's progress could be protected.

In the 1950s Joe Brown and Don Whillans and others had shown how to make a long run-out safer by inserting pebbles into cracks and threading a sling round them to make a running belay. Sometimes they would tie a thick knot in the sling and wedge that into a crack. By the beginning of the 1960s climbers with access to workshops or factories were beginning to use specially-adapted metal nuts instead of pebbles. They would get nuts of various sizes, drill the thread out of the middle, and feed nylon line or tape through the hold to make a sling. The leader, when he set off on a climb, would carry five or six of these – each with a karabiner attached – around his neck. On the whole, it was easier to slip a nut into a crack and pull it firm than to hammer in a piton. and it made no permanent mark on the rock. The slings would be removed by the last man.

For some time to come, though, the leader on routes of serious difficulty would continue to carry pitons and a hammer. This was because the early, home-made nuts were too big to slot into very thin cracks. The piton was still the answer if the only available crack was a narrow one. By the end of the 1960s, however, specially manufactured climbers' nuts were beginning to be available, made of light-weight but strong alloys, in various shapes and a widening range of sizes. The smallest ones would be threaded not with nylon but with steel wire slings.

The nuts were quickly in general use. Environmentally preferable to pitons and less exhausting to fix, they gave solid protection and their own particular pleasure – the craftsman's delight in a job well done when the nut slots securely home. In practice, of course, there are often problems. There may be no suitable crack available. Or the reach to it may be awkward, unbalancing. The climber has to take one hand off the rock to unclip his nut from his waist and insert it in the crack and, if he is on tenuous foot holds and a long way above his colleague or his last runner, he may be tempted to push on and hope he does not fall off before he reaches easier ground. Nevertheless, nuts have made a tremendous difference to climbing. A route like Innominate Crack on Kern Knotts, for example, can be protected all the way – a very different prospect from what it was when George Bower and Bentley Beetham first climbed it in 1921. Borrowdale volcanic, the rock of which most Lake District crags are composed, is generous with cracks. By the mid-1960s nut runners were so widely used that the drag on the rope, passing through many karabiners, became a problem and leaders adopted the policy of having two active ropes, clipping one into the runners on the right-hand side, the other into those on the left.

At the end of the decade another important development was emerging. The pioneer climbers had simply tied the end of the climbing rope round their waists, usually with a bowline knot. It meant that a fall of more than a few feet would certainly be painful and possibly injurious, and if the climber could not relieve the pressure on his diaphragm within fifteen minutes or so the results could be fatal. Prospects were improved a little by the introduction of the nylon rope which was more elastic than hemp, and also by the adoption of a wider, separate belt to which the active rope could be tied. But it was the ingenious mind of Don Whillans that came up with a lasting solution. He devised a 'sit harness', with a wide belt of stitched webbing to go round the waist and webbing loops to fit round the upper legs. He invented it for the greater comfort of high-altitude mountaineers who spend a lot of time carrying heavy loads up the fixed ropes. A sit harness, attached to the fixed rope by a metal clamp, would enable the climber to sit back and take a rest. It was found useful on Bonington's Annapurna South Face expedition in the spring of 1970 – when Whillans and Dougal Haston reached the summit – and soon afterwards climbers began to appreciate its advantages in wider circumstances. In a fall the initial impact would be taken by the thighs as well as the waist. If the climber was left dangling for some time, he could do so in comparative safety. And there was another side-benefit – extra webbing loops at the back where the nut slings could be carried.

The 1960s also saw considerable advances in the field of information. John Barford's *Climbing in Britain*, published soon after the Second World War, had been overtaken by events. In 1965 it was superseded by another Penguin book, Alan Blackshaw's *Mountaineering*. Like Barford's book, it was produced under the aegis of the British Mountaineering Council and dealt with its subject in a clear, thorough and conscientious way. In the third edition, dated 1970, Blackshaw had this to say about nut runners;

> It is now universal practice among good British climbers to thread nuts of various sizes onto slings for use as jammed-nut belays, probably the greatest single new contribution to rock climbing safety in recent years. A wide variety of specially designed nuts is now available for all widths of the thinner cracks, and it is advisable to carry a good assortment so as to use all opportunities of anchoring. Most nuts take nylon rope or tape, but probably the most useful of all, at least in the smaller sizes, are those on short swaged wire slings since the rigidity of the wire enables them to be inserted and withdrawn relatively easily.

But the sport was growing too quickly, in too many different ways, for the informational needs of its enthusiasts to be met by the appearance every twenty years or so of a book. The result, as wartime paper rationing receded and living standards began to rise again, was the appearance of a number of magazines specifically aimed at mountain walkers and climbers. They were of variable quality and some did not last long but, by the early 1960s, there were three such publications: *Mountaineering*, the official organ of the British Mountaineering Council which came out twice a year; *Mountain Craft*, which began as a newsletter for Jerry Wright's Mountaineering Association, then evolved into a quarterly, then a monthly magazine; and *The Climber*, another monthly. None of them was particularly distinguished but from them better things emerged.

Mountain Craft became *Mountain*, which, under the driving editorship of Ken Wilson, was transformed into a brilliant bi-monthly, aimed at people in all parts of the world who took a serious interest in moun-taineering achievement at the outer limits of the sport. Well-designed and well-printed, with superb photographs, it was always on the look-out for lively writing and quickly established itself as the sport's leading journal of record. There have been two editors since Wilson left in the late 1970s but the tradition has been maintained. It has a circulation of more than 15,000 and still rising. More than half of the copies are sold in the United Kingdom; one-third in North America; the rest, all over the world.

The Climber became *Climber and Rambler*, not so glossy as *Mountain* and not so international either, targeted instead at the domestic market of all those who liked to walk and scramble in the hills as well as climbers of all levels of ability. By the late 1970s, under Walt Unsworth's editor-ship, it had a circulation of 24,000 copies each month.

The emergence of the magazines reflected and, to some extent, encour-aged a new spirit. Previously, the only regular sources of information had been the annual club journals and they were, naturally enough, primarily concerned with stimulating *esprit de club*. They did not always shy away from controversial issues but their general tone was controlled and gentlemanly and, sometimes, self-congratulatory. Magazines are run for very different motives. They need the readership which will attract the advertisers. To that end they have to be stimulating and argumentative. It was not long before the climbing magazines were giving free rein, especially in their correspondence columns, to the expression of strong views in very strong, sometimes vituperative terms. The issues were the perennial ones – the impact of climbers on the environment; how to devise a sensible and comprehensive grading system; the increasing use of the sport as an educational tool; most popular of all, endless and multifarious variations on the old theme of artificial aids, where and when they could legitimately be used, whether or not certain climbers on certain new routes had done certain things and been less than honest about it when they came to write their accounts.

They were important matters and it was good that they should be disputed openly but the tone in which they were debated was all too often abusive and puerile. Things finally reached such a pitch that Chris Brasher, editor of *Mountain Life*, published an editorial in which he soundly rebuked his own gossip-columnist as well as many letter-writers:

> There is a streak of viciousness amongst some climbers and we very much regret that it has broken out like a nasty childish disease on some pages of *Mountain Life* ... In future please confine such verbal fisticuffs to the school playground ... There is space for controversy but in future there will be no space whatever for personal attacks.

Today, when climbers look back on their young climbing days they remember them as high-spirited and competitive but free from personal or regional rancour. The Langdale men and the Keswick 'crag rats' often climbed together, in each other's areas or elsewhere and in cheerful companionship. For most of them, no doubt, it always was like that. But there is also no doubt that some of them let their local loyalties lead them to behaviour that would have been more at home on the football terraces.

Allan Austin, for example, recalls – still with some bitterness – the day when he and Ian ('Sherpa') Roper went to Castle Rock, Thirlmere, to climb The Last Laugh. They had mentioned their plans in the local pub the night before and when they arrived at the foot of the crag on Sunday morning, it was to find Ross and 'the Keswick lads' already there, with no intentions of climbing. All the way up the route, Austin and Roper were subjected to a barrage of abusive barracking. It was intense enough to unnerve Roper. It could have been dangerous. But it made Austin all the more determined to climb the route, which he did.

Paul Ross left the Lake District in 1969 to seek his fortune in the United States, setting up a climbers' shop in New Hampshire, then a climbing school, then becoming an expert in breeding Jack Russell terriers.

Allan Austin stayed and carried on climbing. In 1970 he created Brackenclock, an E2 on Pavey Ark, using one piton and a sling for aid. More new routes followed in the next few years, most of them in the 'Extreme' grades, and his last – The Overhanging Pitch on Dow Crag – was climbed in 1975.

Austin also continued to attract controversy. In 1973 he was asked by the Fell and Rock Club to update the Langdale guide book. He did so, taking a characteristically firm editorial line. The fierce arguments that followed centred on a route on Pavey Ark called Cruel Sister, a 230-foot climb which is graded E3 and was first ascended in April 1972 by Rob Matheson of Barrow-in-Furness. Matheson used two points of aid. The first time he tried to lead it he was unable to make the move on to the steep rib so he climbed down again, went to the top of the route, abseiled down and – at the crux point – hammered in a piton with a long sling dangling from it. He then returned to the foot of the crag and climbed the route, making full use of the sling. When Austin's guide book came out it made no mention of the route. Matheson wrote angrily to *Mountain* magazine accusing Austin and his co-writer Rod Valentine of 'selfish and bigoted beliefs'. He pointed out that Austin had previously attempted the line and failed to climb it 'and he appears to be condemning my efforts because he himself failed in the past'.

Austin had made no secret of the fact that he had failed on the line – his ascent of Arcturus in 1963 had been the result of that failure. But he stood by his editorial decision:

> Cruel Sister was omitted from the guide because I did not believe it had been climbed. I cannot see how a party can claim to have been successful when, having failed on the crux, they have simply gone round to the top of the cliff, hung a sling down over it, then swarmed up from below. Surely, rock climbing is a challenge, and superb lines like this rib throw down their challenge to succeeding generations of climbers, until eventually along comes someone who can do the climb. I do not see crags as an impressive back-cloth where ruthless men can construct their climbs.

Austin's faith in the next generation, backed by his knowledge of climbing history, was vindicated more quickly than even he might have expected. Cruel Sister was climbed free – without any artificial aids – in 1975 by two Carlisle men, Jeff Lamb and Pete Botterill (no relation of his pioneer namesake). The day of 'the jackals' had dawned – those who made a point of re-climbing established and aided routes and eliminating the points of aid until they could be done completely free. Cruel Sister, cleared of her pre-placed sling, was admitted to the 1980 Langdale guide book.

— 10 —

The Story so Far

1973-1988

A MILE out of Keswick, in the village of Portinscale, lives a small, wiry, weather-hardened man who is seventy years old and who embodies, perhaps as completely as anybody, the old idea of the all-round adventurer. He was in the navy in the Second World War and commanded one of the rocket assault ships that heralded the liberation of western Europe, on the morning of 6 June 1944, by bombarding the German strongpoints on the Normandy coast. In 1955 he got a year's leave from his job as a teacher of English to work in the Antarctic on the South Georgia Survey. Some ten years after that he and a friend were put down by plane at a remote spot in Canada's North-Western Territories to spend the next five weeks canoeing themselves back to civilisation. More recently, he was President of the British Mountaineering Council for three years. His name is Tom Price.

He still spends as much time as he can out of doors, guiding visitors up the mountains, camping and trekking, skiing, sailing, canoeing, fell walking, scrambling and climbing. Most years he manages a trip to bigger mountain ranges, the Alps, the Andes, the Himalayas. When bad weather or darkness force him indoors, he draws or paints, writes the occasional article for a climbing journal and reads, usually true stories of exploration and adventure. His heroes include the mountaineers Eric Shipton and Bill Tilman, Joshua Slocum the round-the-world lone voyager, and – topmost of all – Ernest Shackleton and Frank Worsley, who sailed their little open whaler across 800 miles of icy water to South Georgia in 1916.

Like so many in this story, he was a Yorkshireman in origin, born near Wharncliffe Crags. But it was in the Lake District that he discovered rock climbing, quite by chance, at New Year 1937. He met a man who had a rope and no companion, so Tom Price agreed to go with him to Pavey Ark. He went, he remembers, 'with great trepidation'. They wore

189

nailed boots and had no slings or runners. But as soon as he got on the rock he was hooked. It was much easier than he had expected. It was exciting. And it was visually stimulating: 'What struck me most was how totally the scene changes when you've got a very steep foreground – it enhances the whole scene.' After that, he climbed whenever he could, in North Wales and the Lake District. He was greatly encouraged by Graham Macphee and climbed once or twice with Bill Tilman on White Ghyll.

When he qualified as a teacher he got a job in Workington to be close to the crags. Gradually he drifted into outdoor education. For seven years in the 1960s he ran the Outward Bound School at Eskdale. In the great debate over climbing as part of the education process, he takes a balanced view:

> I'm dead against the notion that it should be compulsory, that all children should be made to try rock climbing. But if they show an interest, they can get a tremendous lot out of it. And it's sometimes those who are most trouble in the classroom who are best on the fells. They learn to be resourceful and sensible. They gain self-esteem.
>
> The trouble with outdoor pursuits education is that it's often badly done. Terrified kids are pressured into doing it and they're put off for life. And a lot of teachers talk too much. They should stand back and let the kids learn some things for themselves. It's quicker and easier for the instructor to demonstrate everything and make it all foolproof and entirely safe. It's got to be safe, of course, but it doesn't always have to *feel* safe. There's no need to be over-cautious. You can let the children have a little adventure. That way some of them will pick up the spirit of the thing.

In 1973 Tom Price was appointed Dean of Students at Bingley College, Yorkshire. He had a testing but auspicious start there. One of the students – they never found out who – had fixed a Christmas tree to the top of the dome. As his first official duty as the new Dean, Price was asked to get it down:

> It was pretty alarming and a sizable audience gathered to watch. Some of the holds were slimy. I only managed to get on to the dome by prizing away a lightning conductor to get a fingerhold behind. But I got the tree down, and it certainly didn't do me any harm with the students.

Among the students at that time, by coincidence, were several who were destined to be climbing stars in the near future – Jill Lawrence, Gill Price and Bonny Masson, Peter Gomersall and Andy Jones. Among the teachers – 'and an excellent teacher too', according to Tom Price – was Peter Livesey.

It was Livesey who was to make the next 'great leap forward' in Lake District climbing, comparable to that of Joe Brown and Don Whillans twenty years before. Like Whillans, he was a remarkable character as well as a remarkable climber. Jill Lawrence, who climbed a lot with him at one time, says: 'Pete's an achiever. He likes to succeed at things, to the extent that he wouldn't bother to start something if he felt he wasn't going to be a success at it – not just a mediocre success but at a high level.' Another regular climbing partner, John Sheard, points out that, although Livesey gives the impression of being careless and disorganised, he is in fact – in those things that really concern him – extremely calculating and methodical. His American rival and one-time *bête noire*, Henry Barber, described the young Livesey as a 'wild-looking, egocentric combatant'.

Chris Bonington got Livesey to lead him up his most famous route, Footless Crow, for the series of films he made for Channel Four in 1985:

> I had considerable reservations about trying to follow Livesey up this climb since, at a standard of E5, it was a couple of grades harder than anything I had ever managed to climb. I was forewarned of Livesey's genius for gamesmanship by an article in the magazine *Crags* in which John Sheard described his running commentary during a climbing film they were taking part in: 'He likes the rope tight, so I'll give the bugger a load of slack'.

Bonington prepared for the ordeal by camera by getting Pete Whillance to lead him up the route a few days earlier. Whillance gave all possible help and a reassuringly tight rope and Bonington managed it. With the camera rolling, though, and Livesey in charge of the top rope, things were very different. As Bonington struggled to master the crux move, Livesey taunted him with the words: 'Come on, Chris. You'd get up fast enough if I dangled a fiver over the edge':

> Every time I screamed 'Tight', the rope would give a couple of inches and at the same time, for the benefit of the microphone at his throat, Livesey would croon, 'I'm pulling as hard as I can. Do you want me to call for a winch?'
> Eventually I ran out of strength and spun out into space. It was just as well I had brought a couple of jumar clamps with me and was able to climb up the rope.

In spite of this treatment, Bonington describes Livesey as 'abrasive, sharp, a brilliant lifeman, a lovely bloke'.

Pete Livesey is some six feet tall and very lean, with long legs and arms and – in the climber's sense – a 'long neck' too, prepared to take risks. He has intense physical energy – and mental energy as well; he writes a regular and lively column for one of the magazines. He is, by his own admission, a complete philistine, only really interested – apart from his work and his family – in his sporting life. The extra thing he brought to Lake District climbing, the quality that made him the outstanding man of the 1970s, was his degree of dedication.

He was born in Huddersfield in 1943. His father was a builder's merchant, his mother a teacher. At the local grammar school he made his mark as a cross-country runner of international standard. When he turned to pot-holing, the story was the same. Later he became a white-water canoeist of the highest class. Today, in his mid-forties, he says:

I like to commit myself. I compete – I want to be the best. I like to get better and better at the thing I'm doing. I know you can't be the best for ever but what you can do as you get older is learn new skills, improve yourself tactically, find new sports. When I stopped competitive climbing, I tried fell running. Now I'm into orienteering, the veteran class, and I'm still getting better at that.

He left school to become a Bachelor of Education, specialising in physical education. Then he studied for a post-graduate diploma in sports science. From that, he went on to take an MA in psychology at Leeds University with a dissertation on motor performance in dangerous environments, especially as it related to climbing. Now, a married man with a young daughter, he teaches 'leisure studies' to post-graduate students at Ilkley College and specialises in 'the psychology of motor behaviour and outdoor education theory'.

Many decades before, Haskett Smith said of Owen Glynne Jones: 'He had studied his own physical powers as a chauffeur studies his car and for that reason he talked a good deal about himself.' Jones kept himself in climbing trim when he was far away from the crags by climbing public buildings and swinging Indian clubs. But if he can justly be called 'the first climbing fanatic', which he was by the standards of his time, he registers very low on the fanaticism-scale when compared with Livesey and some of his climbing successors. Jones was derided as a 'rock gymnast' and took it as a compliment. When Livesey exploded on to the scene, the words used were 'rock athlete' to suggest the competitive intensity that was brought to bear, and 'activist', implying all the ruthlessness of a political zealot.

Although for many years Livesey concentrated chiefly on his other sports – running, caving, canoeing – he started climbing at the age of fifteen, soloing up and down the quarry walls near his home. Soon, in such spare time as he could find, he moved on to the limestone and gritstone crags. He was still, for the most part, climbing alone: 'When I started climbing, I soloed everything. I didn't put in any protection at all. Virtually everything I climbed I was prepared to go solo.' He believes that this gave him his extraordinary self-confidence. He evolved a very precise appreciation of his own powers, what moves he could make and what was beyond him, and his judgement was not influenced in any way by how high he was on the crag or how reliable his protection might be: 'That's what I could do and most climbers can't. Their perception of difficulty changes with the height. They look at a pitch high up and say 'I can't climb that', when in fact they *can* climb it or rather, they could climb it if it were only five feet from the ground.'

It was in the mid-1960s that Livesey decided to concentrate on rock climbing. Steeled to the task, both physically and psychologically, he brought an intensely 'professional' approach to the business of making new routes. When bad weather kept him off the crags he used local climbing walls, already being constructed at sports centres, to improve his stamina. When he set his sights on a new line, he would abseil down the cliff – new equipment made this easy and comfortable – to clean it thoroughly, using a wire brush, and inspect the crux areas. But when he went to do the climb, he took a firmly 'ethical' attitude: 'I hardly ever put pitons in. When I used them, they would be pegs I found already in place, left from previous aided ascents. And I only used them as protection, not for aid. If people don't like bold routes, they should stick to crack lines where they can get plenty of nut runners in.'

Unfortunately, the routes he was soon climbing free were so formidable that his fellow-climbers found it hard to believe he was doing them without aid. This, and some confusion of evidence, led to trouble with Allan Austin. Livesey tells the story:

> In 1968 we'd been putting up some new routes on Austin's Langcliffe Quarry near Settle. Austin was doing the new guide book to Yorkshire limestone so he wrote and asked for my route descriptions and I sent him them.
>
> Three years later we did some routes on Gordale so I sent him accounts of those as well. Then, just before publication, there was an article in the *Yorkshire Evening Post* that said our routes were being left out because the authorities didn't believe they'd been done free. There was some witness who'd seen us pulling up on slings on the Face Route. We later found out that this was Eric ('Spider') Penman and what he'd seen was John Sheard, who was seconding me, hanging down from a sling to retrieve some gear that he hadn't been able to pull out when he was climbing past. But I'd already done the lead and done it free. Because of this, Austin doubted everything we claimed. I was a bit cross at the time and wrote to the magazines.

There were similar clashes at the same period in the Lake District – over Matheson's Cruel Sister and another 'Extreme' on Pavey Ark, Sally Free and Easy, which Livesey climbed using one point of aid. In his revised edition of the Langdale guide, Austin made no mention of either climb.

The confrontation of two strong-willed Yorkshiremen, Austin and Livesey, is perhaps as close as human relationships can approach to the old scientific teaser of what happens when an irresistible force comes up against an immovable object. It was not a matter of personal animosity. Today Livesey says, with amusement, that Austin and he never had a harsh word, that it was one of those public squabbles which neither of the respondents plays much part in. On both sides, it was a question of principle.

Austin saw himself as the increasingly-embattled protector of the honourable Lake District tradition of free climbing:

> The only routes I didn't put in the guide were the ones where they'd put slings in from above. Now they cannot be climbs, can they? Anyone can climb anything if they're prepared to spend enough time on an abseil rope, banging in pegs and

dangling slings from them. When the routes were done free, I put them in the book.

In this respect Austin was struggling against the tide of history. Perhaps he was emboldened to it by the news from South America where the Italian mountaineer Cesare Maestri was conquering the vast blank walls of Cerro Torre with the aid of a petrol-driven compressed air drill and steel bolts. Whatever the reason, Austin's cause was doomed. Virtually all the obvious lines on the Lake District cliffs had been climbed by this time, and young men with ambitions to make their own routes were having to seek them on big, bulging, almost holdless walls. When the holds seemed to disappear altogether, it was natural and sensible to hammer in a piton, fix a sling and pull up on it to make the whole route possible. Austin's argument – that if they could not do it without such aid they should leave it until someone who could do it came along – was asking too much in the way of self-denial.

Furthermore, his rule – that aided routes should be omitted from the guide books – was over-intransigent. Most active climbers welcome news of new hard routes. They do not mind if they involve two or three aided moves, so long as they are justifiable and not too frequent. In a sense, points of aid used on a first ascent made it all the more interesting because it threw down a challenge to the 'jackals' to repeat the climb and, dispensing with the aids, 'free' the route. Climbers bought guide books because they wanted the facts – what routes had been done, where they were, how hard they were, exactly how they had been done. To omit climbs that had been done, simply on the grounds that the editors disapproved of the methods used, was a kind of rewriting of history. For a while the Fell and Rock Club followed the Austin line in their guide books, but now they include routes on which artificial aid was used, describing them in the most aid-free style in which they are known to have been climbed.

The other key issue was that of honesty. It was undeniably important, as Austin argued, that the truth should be known about where and how artificial aids were used. Sadly, he was also right to suspect that there were people who used aid and did not admit it. Wherever competition is keen, there will be cheating. On the whole though, in rock climbing, liars and cheats are quickly rumbled. Most crags are visible from afar. A climber may think he is unobserved when he pulls up on a sling or stands in one or removes a piton, but – certainly if he persists in such practices – he is sure to be spotted before long and the word spreads rapidly. It was unfortunate that, as a result of the wrong eye-witness information he was given, Austin initially suspected Livesey of being – in the modern euphemism – 'economical with the truth'. He was soon made to realise his mistake.

In 1972 Livesey put up several very impressive routes on Yorkshire limestone and, using only one point of aid, made an E3 route on Raven Crag, Langdale, which he named Fine Time. Next year he spent long weeks in the Yosemite Valley in California, polishing his skills and stamina on the big sun-soaked granite walls.

From the point of view of Lake District history, 1974 was his great year. On Gimmer Crag he free-climbed If, the route which Paul Ross had so provocatively over-aided for the fun of upsetting the Langdale men. Livesey renamed it Eastern Hammer and it was graded E3. And he did four breakthrough routes in Borrowdale – Bitter Oasis on Goat Crag, another E3; Dry Gasp on Upper Falcon and Nagasaki Grooves on Greatend Crag, both of them E4; and Footless Crow on Goat Crag, the District's first E5. In their survey of Lakeland climbing in the 1986 Fell and Rock Club Journal, Ron Kenyon and Al Murray say these climbs 'represented a quantum leap in difficulty'.

According to Livesey, the idea for Footless Crow came from some chance remarks made by Ray McHaffie in a Keswick pub in 1972:

> Mac was sending up John Adams and Colin Read, telling them there were lots of routes – like Nagasaki Grooves on Greatend Crag – which they thought they'd done but they hadn't done free. 'Why don't you go and do it properly?' he said. 'And while you're at it, you should sort out the Central Buttress on Goat Crag as well.' He was serious about Nagasaki Grooves but I don't think he really meant it about Central Buttress – he didn't think that was on for free climbing. But that's what gave me the impulse.

The northern buttress of Goat Crag is impressive but not for its beauty. It gets very little sun. It is big and steep, overhanging in places, and vegetated and very complex. It was here, in 1965, that Les Brown climbed Praying Mantis and inaugurated a frenzy of activity by the Keswick climbers. The same year 'Ado' Liddell and Paul Ross put up a route about forty feet to the right, using eight points of aid including pitons, expansion bolts and one 'Fifi hook' which was hung over the rim of a small hold to enable the first bulge to be surmounted. They called the route Central Buttress and the Ross/Thompson guide book said it was 'perhaps the most serious piece of artificial work in the valley'. Towards the top, the climb joined the line followed by Praying Mantis. It was six years before the second ascent was made, by Colin Downer and Guy Lee, and they dispensed with some of the aid. Then, in December 1971, Bill Freeland and George Sims arrived on the scene and climbed the line which is now known as Footless Crow, using twelve pitons, four bolts and one sky-hook.

This was the prospect that confronted Livesey. Soon after hearing McHaffie's challenge, he went to look at the buttress. The next year, 1973, he went to take a closer look. He abseiled down, following the line of bolts and pitons, studying the problems at close quarters, cleaning as he went. It looked, he says, very hard, but he thought it would go free.

It was on this reconnaissance that the idea for the name, Footless Crow, came to him. Many interpretations have been offered. The most common is that there is no ledge big enough, on the main pitch, for a crow to find a perching place. Bill Birkett says 'The name was given because, being so overhanging and with no place to rest, the climber must keep moving – hopping from one minute hold to the next, never daring to stop.' Others have discerned subtle allusions to phrases of Dylan Thomas – or T. S. Eliot – but Livesey does not know which poems he is supposed to have got his inspiration from. David Craig, another poet as well as a keen climber, feels that the name 'has the surreal folk wit of phrases like "clockwork orange" mixed with the implication (or so I read it) that a crag so steep is fitter for some maimed or hybrid bird than for us normal mortals'. It must be a good name if it can strike so many appropriate resonances but Livesey came by it, he says, by happy chance:

> On my way to have a proper look at the route I passed a band of Dutch hippies camping in the valley and they had a van with a big crow painted on one side, with its feet chopped off. Then I inspected the route – no resting place, you've got to keep flying – and it just came to me that Footless Crow would be a good idea. I named the route long before I climbed it.

In 1973 he tried to climb it, with John Hammond seconding, but failed – 'through inability and fright', he says – just below the crux.

The following spring found him working as an outdoor pursuits instructor in the Lake District and he determined to have another go. The day was 19 April 1974:

> I'd no one to climb with but there was a sailor working at the centre, Robin Witham, and I persuaded him to come along and hold the rope. We'd done a day's work and went out in the evening. It was nice weather and the rock was reasonably dry. And I just did it. I can't remember much about it. Later, when I did it for Bonington's film, I found the crux moves hard but the rest of it easy. The first time, though, it all seemed much the same standard. The crux was clean and very obvious – there were very few holds so there was no choice, you had to use them all. The rest of the route was more subtle and technical. Of course, it's been cleaned up a lot since then, so it's easier now, and the gear's better now and you can get a lot more protection in. All I had were a few nut runners – there were no micro-nuts in those days – and the rusty old bolts and pegs the others had left in place. I wore E.B.s and a Whillans harness.

Livesey took an intellectual pleasure in fixing his running belays:

> You have to be careful to clip the rope into the runner so it doesn't drag or catch over the rock. The important thing in ropework is having the strength not just to climb the route but to hang around long enough to select and place your belays, and then have the strength to go on climbing afterwards. It's like a game of chess – being two or three moves in advance the whole time – and there's considerable skill involved putting the runners in place.

The main pitch is almost 170 feet, with the crux about halfway up. It is relentlessly difficult all the way, with no ledges to rest on or comforting jug-handle hand holds and very few cracks to take nut runners. Once above the crux, Livesey ran into another problem:

> Soon I was getting a lot of drag on the rope. The sailor lad, Robin Witham, was perched as high up as he could get, on a little ledge about 20 feet above the ground. I ran out of rope when I still had some 30-odd feet to go. There was nowhere to belay – no protection points at all. The rock was dirty and dusty – I hadn't bothered to clean up the top part because it looked easier than lower down, though it was still about Hard V.S. standard. There was only one thing for it. I told Witham to untie himself and then I soloed to the top, dragging 160 feet of rope through the runners behind me.

The climb – bold, strenuous, sustained – was fiercer than anything done in Britain at that time, a couple of grades harder than anything in the Lake District. When he heard his route had been done free, Bill Freeland gave up climbing – for a while. Perhaps still reluctant to believe such things possible, the Fell and Rock *Journal* did not mention it – nor any of Livesey's other routes of that creative year.

Six weeks later, with John Sheard in support, Livesey made another fierce climb just to the right of Footless Crow. He called it Bitter Oasis and explained his reason in these words:

> Virtually led on sight, I climbed the very steep groove, all the time making for what I thought was a gently-sloping ledge. But when I got there the 'oasis' I'd hoped for turned out to be an overlapping, vertical wall, and the climbing went on being very hard, with nowhere to rest. I had to push on for another 30 feet before I found a belay ledge.

On the afternoon of 22 June Livesey went to Greatend Crag in Borrowdale to look at Nagasaki Grooves. The route had been climbed three years before by that prolific team, Colin Read and John Adams, using five pitons for aid. Livesey, solo, climbed it free. His only form of protection was a back rope – a climbing rope firmly belayed to the bottom of the crag and clipped, in six-foot loops, to the back of his harness. As he gained height, he would release a loop at a time, fixing running belays wherever possible. It made for hard work – the crag is steep and he must have been reluctant, more than once, to take one hand from the rock to release another length of rope – but it was worth the effort. At the foot of the groove, just below the crux of the climb, he came off. The rope caught him. He got back on the crag and finished the route.

He then walked down the valley to Upper Falcon Crag where he had his eye on a new line. He climbed it, solo. There has been confusion ever since about its name, Dry Grasp or Dry Gasp. The latest guide book uses the former, other accounts give the latter. Both are, in their different ways, appropriate and Livesey cannot now remember what his original choice was. What he does remember is that it was a very hot, dry afternoon and both crags were dusty. Almost at the top of Upper Falcon, he had some trying moments as he struggled to release a further loop of his back rope and then fought against the rope drag as he reached for the final holds.

Perhaps there was a comfortingly dry hold to grasp at the top. Perhaps he uttered a dehydrated sigh of relief. Ron Fawcett, yet another Yorkshireman, and the next rock climber to display skills comparable to those of Livesey, was of the Dry Gasp school because he described the route in these words: 'A gritstone-like wall that doesn't relent for 80 feet, all without a rest, and, as its name suggests, a real throat-wrencher. Protection is poor low down and only fair higher up; a real wall of horrors.' In the same year Livesey went to North Wales and astonished the regulars there by climbing the Right Wall of Dinas Cromlech, an E5.

In the Lake District the other major event of 1974 was the first ascent of The Cumbrian on Esk Buttress. This 270-foot climb had been regarded, for some time, as 'the last great problem' on the crag. It was conquered in May 1974 by Pal ('Tut') Braithwaite and Rod Valentine. In his account in *Extreme Rock*, Al Phizacklea says:

> Rod reached the groove after using two nuts for aid, and found that his only remaining small nut, a round, home-made one, wouldn't fit – with the resultant 70-foot fall he became the first of many suitors to be spat from that repelling cleft. The following day, Tut completed the route after using an additional peg to gain the groove, which he had to clean as he climbed.

When he heard about this, Livesey weighed in with a will. Rod Valentine had been Austin's chief supporter in the fight to exclude aided routes from the guide books. Now he had used aid on a new route. Livesey wrote in *Mountain* magazine:

> Braithwaite and Valentine pulled the lowest trick in years. It was Valentine and his Fell and Rock Club cronies who had a lot to say about leaving routes with aid out of the guide books. 'Avoid the rush to get into print,' they said. 'If you can't do it without aid then leave it for someone better.' The various factions operating in the Lakes couldn't help but agree with these strictures, so we all had a look at this Esk Buttress line and left it to someone better. The new guide was about to go in print and who rushed in to get it but Valentine and Tut.

Not long after that, Livesey went up and reduced the aid to one point. In 1977 the Yorkshire brothers, Martin and Bob Berzins, climbed it free and it was graded E5.

There was yet one more significant event in that highly significant year, 1974. A twenty-five-year-old from Manchester, who already had many hard routes on Pennine gritstone to his credit, came to the Lake District and went to Bill Peascod's crag in Buttermere, Buckstone How, and climbed a route which he called Brutus because it runs immediately alongside Caesar. It is short, only thirty-five feet, but hard. Modestly, he graded it Mild Extreme (though it was put into the E3 category later, after Jeff Lamb had fallen from it and badly injured his leg). The young man's name was Pete Whillance. Over the next ten years he was to average 30–40 new routes every year, establishing himself as the most consistently prolific of Livesey's successors.

But Livesey was not yet finished with the Lake District. In 1975 he soloed Bowfell Buttress Eliminate, an E1, and – partnered by Jill Lawrence – created the bold E3 route, Rough and Tumble on Dow Crag. He also, to general astonishment, soloed the 1,200-foot girdle of Scafell East Buttress, Lord of the Rings. This route had first been climbed by Read and Adams in 1969. It was not repeated until six years later when Ed Cleasby and Bill Birkett did it, with no artificial aids. Then Livesey did it solo, overtaking two roped parties *en route*. The Climbers' Book at the Packhorse Hotel in Keswick contains these entries about it: 'Captain Fantastic was climbing on his own – in his own way! On the descents from Holy Ghost and the top of Phoenix Direct he seemed to float down the rock. I saw it. Steve Clegg. This is how it appeared to us as well. P. Whillance. P. Botterill.'

The next three years saw more Livesey creations in the Lake District, most of them in the E4 category. He concluded with a characteristic bang. With Pete Gomersall, his former pupil, seconding, he climbed Das Kapital on Raven Crag, Thirlmere, which is now graded E6.

It took the Lake District some time to recover from the impact of Livesey's 1974 assault. But before the end of the decade there was much activity. A powerful wave of young climbers were finding new and ever-harder lines on traditional cliffs and unearthing, often literally, new crags. They were helped by further advances in equipment.

More and more climbing walls were being designed and built – they appeared in Carlisle, Cockermouth and Ambleside as well as at sports centres in bigger cities and the universities – and these enabled climbers to practise moves and build up their strength and stamina at times when bad weather made the crags themselves uninviting. Before long there were many who preferred indoor walls – warm and windless, with familiar holds and an admiring audience – to the real thing.

Protection of lead climbers was greatly enhanced by the invention of the 'friend' – a metal cam device on a spring. The climber pulls a trigger to make it narrow enough to slip into a crack; when the trigger is released, the cams expand to grip the sides of the crack firmly. They are reliable and, on the whole, quicker and easier to fix than nut runners. Equipment manufacturers also produced micro nuts, threaded with fine, high-tensile wire, for use in very thin cracks.

In the mid-1970s a new idea was imported from Yosemite. Climbers there, often working in great heat, had taken to using chalk, magnesium carbonate or gymnastic chalk, to absorb the sweat from their fingers and keep them dry. They carried it in a bag fixed to the back of the harness. More and more British climbers were visiting California – Livesey, Fawcett, Whillance and many others – and some of them began to use chalk on British crags.

There was initial resistance, chiefly on environmental grounds. Although some climbers continue to deny it, chalk does mark the rock. Given time, no doubt, the notorious downpours of the Lake District would wash it all away, but – on the more popular 'chalk' routes – it is being applied far faster than the rains can remove it. This creates a further, climbing objection, for on these climbs every hand hold is now clearly indicated by splashes of white. And this effectively eliminates the element of route-finding, working out for yourself the exact set of holds and moves required to solve the immediate problem, that gave so much mental exercise and pleasure to previous generations.

Despite these considerations, chalk was soon in general use among the leading climbers of the Lake District and it remains so to this day. It is habit-forming. Climbers carry chalk on days when their fingers are more likely to freeze than sweat. You can see them, below a hard section, studying the rock and dipping first one hand, then the other, into the chalk bag as a sort of nervous tic.

By the early 1980s there were two more developments in equipment, both of them popular. The makers of climbing boots came up with a new synthetic rubber that was tacky and gave greater adhesion to rock. 'Sticky boots', worn very tight on the foot, became the thing. And the problem of holding the rope when a companion falls was much eased by the introduction of the sticht plate, a small metal device, tied to the front of the harness, through which the active rope is fed as it is paid out or hauled in. It enables the rope to be locked as soon as anyone falls. Before this, the climber managing the rope often had his hands badly burned by the friction of the rope running through them before he could stop it.

Increasing interest in the harder routes brought about a further refinement in the grading system. The idea of numbering the 'Extremes' was generally approved and accepted. But this grading referred to the whole of the route – the technical difficulty of its moves, the variety of its problems, its steepness and the quality of its protection, how far the leader might fall if he came off. Now climbers wanted a more exact indication of the physical difficulty of the hardest moves on each pitch of the climb. A new system called 'Technical grades' was devised for routes in the Very Severe and Extreme categories. In ascending order of difficulty, the grades are 4a, 4b, 4c, 5a, 5b, 5c, 6a, 6b and 6c. Thus, on Jim Birkett's Overhanging Bastion, for example, the second and third pitches (comparatively easy) are 4b and 4a, but the fourth pitch, involving the crux move from the top of the pinnacle on to the gangway, is 5a. The long top pitch on Footless Crow is 6b.

Among the new arrivals of the mid-1970s, Ron Fawcett was probably the finest climber – tall, lean, powerful and bold. He followed the Livesey example and trained very hard, traversing climbing walls, doing press-ups and pull-ups, weight-training and running. But he was too fond of sunshine and warm rock to make much impact on the Lake District story. He did, however, push the technical grades up one notch further when he free-climbed Hell's Wall on Bowderstone Crag in Borrowdale in 1979. It is graded E6 6c.

Before the end of the decade Jim Birkett's son, Bill, was beginning to produce the first of many new routes, mostly in the Eastern Fells. Jim had stuck to his rule of doing nothing to influence his boys towards climbing. Bill discovered the sport for himself, with a friend, at the age of fourteen:

> It was only then that I found out my Dad had been a climber. He'd taken us walking in the fells but never mentioned climbing. But I was talking about it one day and Mum said, 'I think your Dad's done some rock climbing.' So I went to a climbing shop and looked in the guide books and found page after page of mentions of R. J. Birkett. Amazing!

Bill has none of his father's famous reticence. Although he studied civil engineering, he now makes his living out of climbing – writing books and articles about it, occasionally lecturing, testing equipment. Among his fellow-students at Teeside Polytechnic was Richard ('Rick') Graham – now a partner, with Andy Hyslop, in the Rock and Run shops in Ambleside and Sheffield – and it was Birkett and Graham who opened up the North Buttress of Dove Crag. In May 1980 they climbed Broken Arrow, E5 6a, alternating the lead and using two points of aid. Next month they created the superb Fear and Fascination, close by and much the same standard. Birkett says: 'Rick and I alternated but he completed it with a fantastic pitch, one of the best I've ever done, continuously overhanging, sustained, for about 150 feet. It's only had one other ascent, I think – it's certainly had a lot of failures.'

In May 1981 Birkett and Graham climbed another route on the North Buttress, Asolo, which is graded E3 and gets three stars in the latest guide book but whose chief claim to fame is that it was the Lake District's first sponsored climb. Sponsorship had been a vital factor in expedition mountaineering for more than half a century. The first Everest expeditions in the early 1920s had been partly financed by money from national newspapers and film-makers. After the Second World War, Chris Bonington exercised his talents as a wheeler-dealer to induce banks and business houses and industrial companies, as well as publishers and newspapers and movie-makers and equipment manufacturers, to put up the large sums of money that made his expeditions possible. By 1980 many other sports were unashamedly tapping sources of finance from all directions. Bill Birkett thought it was time rock climbing felt some of the benefits:

> I engineered it to cause controversy. I went to a firm that made rock boots and told them that if they gave us the gear, we would give their trade name to the route. There was nothing controversial about the climb itself – it's a good route and we did it free. But the name caused a lot of discussion. It was an attempt, really, to shake up the manufacturers and get them to pump more money into the sport. And it worked. There's lots of sponsoring now.

In 1982, still on the same buttress, Birkett and Graham climbed Fast and Furious, E5 6a.

Increasingly, climbers were being forced to seek their new routes in places that their predecessors had considered too forbidding. But all possible lines on some of the traditional crags had not yet been claimed. There was a surprising flurry of activity, in the mid-1970s, on one of the most thoroughly explored cliffs of them all, Scafell Crag. In 1976 Pete Botterill and Steve Clegg climbed the wall to the left of (Fred) Botterill's Slab and called the route Shadowfax. They had already, the year before, made the first free ascent of Les Brown's Nazgul to the left of the Great Flake. Now, just to the right of the Great Flake, John Eastham and Ed Cleasby tackled the very steep wall which had long been contemplated. They found it magnificently airy but easier than it looked. They called it Saxon E2.

There was action, too, on Scafell East Buttress. Pete Livesey and Jill Lawrence climbed Lost Horizons in the dry late summer of 1976, though they were criticised for abseiling down beforehand, not only to clean and inspect the route but also to get some protection in place and a point of aid. In May 1977 Ed Cleasby and Rob Matheson worked for two days to force an adjoining line which they called Shere Khan. Freed of all aid by Ron Fawcett, it is now graded E5 6a.

It seems incredible but the Lake District, so tiny in comparison with other mountain regions, was still yielding new climbing grounds after more than 100 years of steadily mounting exploration. Some of them were small and most were heavily vegetated and slimy – it was these qualities that had protected them from attention. Borrowdale was particularly generously endowed with such places and its opportunities were seized by a Keswick-based group who shared Paul Ross's swashbuckling approach to the sport and who were prepared to outdo Bentley Beetham in the matter of determined gardening. The hard-core members were Colin Downer, Dave Nicol and Chris Bacon. They were joined, from time to time, by Andy Hall, Dave Hellier, Ray McHaffie, Bob Wilson, Ian Conway and a very talented and 'necky' climber from Tyneside called Dave Macdonald. Their central driving figure was Downer, a gymnastic climber, a ruthless gardener of crags and a flamboyant extro-vert personality.

In the winter of 1974–5 they spent long hours swinging about on abseil ropes, wielding saws and axes and crowbars, hammers and chisels, yard brushes and wire brushes, to make ready the central area of Greatend crag. The 1968 guide book had described it discouragingly:

> This crag, though large, is little frequented on account of the dense vegetation and general dankness which accompanies it. There still remain dead trees and ashen soil from the great fire ... Many of the grass ledges and trees are remarkably unstable, while the rock is shattered in some places ...

Removing all these hazards was bound to be noisy and threatening to the security of the operation. One day, it is said, they were busy on the crag when one of them spotted a fellow-climber, known to them but not included in the current enterprise, who was walking towards the foot of the cliff, hand in hand with a girlfriend. 'Look out,' was the cry. 'That's Chas McQuarrie. Pretend to be hanging vegetation.'

On another occasion, according to Downer, he had asked Chris Bacon to remove a small tree that was shading part of an intended route. The trunk was nearly sawn through when the Lake District Warden, Roy Harding, was sighted down below. A warning was immediately sounded. Bacon struggled gallantly, for many long seconds, to hold the tree in place and prevent it from toppling noisily down. But in the end he had to let it go. They knew they were in trouble. It so happened, however, that Dave Nicol arrived at the top of the crag a few moments later and it was he, unaware of what was going on, who was sitting on the base of the recent tree, holding the incriminating saw in his hands, when Harding exploded on to the scene. Nicol took the brunt of the abuse. Then he had to help the others clean up the area as best they could.

Stiff wire brushes and a soft hand brush were used for the final touches and the rock was finally deemed ready towards the end of April 1975. Several good routes, more than 200 feet long and in the Very Severe (Hard) grade, resulted: among them, Greatend Grooves, Earthstrip and Greatend Corner. Two years later Dave Nicol added Banzai Pipeline to the bag.

In the winter of 1983–4 the same group made another discovery. Downer claimed to have found it. On his way to Black Crag, he said, he hopped over a fence, very close to the main road up Borrowdale, to see what lay behind a blanketing screen of trees. To his great delight, he found solid Borrowdale volcanic rock, about 100 feet high and nearly vertical. There was no sign that anyone had ever climbed there. He told his gang and swore them to secrecy, with lurid descriptions of what would happen to them if they talked. If anything, their approach this time was even more ruthless than it had been on Greatend. Downer used a car jack to lever one particularly resistant boulder out and it detonated into a thousand fragments when it hit the ground. On the summit plateau they diverted water courses to give their routes a chance to dry out. Vegetation was hacked and sawn and scraped away.

In the hope of remaining undetected, they started their depredations as far away from the valley road as possible. They never parked their cars near the crag. On at least one occasion, suspecting they were being followed, they switched cars. They got much pleasure from tormenting others in the pubs by talking, conspiratorially, about 'Crag X'.

In fact, this range of low crags, Grange Crags, was not entirely unknown. Ray McHaffie, still ubiquitously exploring, had been there in the 1960s and done one or two climbs. He had a shrewd idea what they were up to and this was confirmed for him when he got a Mafia-type 'Keep off or else' message. He sent the reply: 'I was climbing there when your Mam was changing your nappies.' As a result, he was formally invited to join them.

There was an additional complication. Although the crags themselves and the summit area belong to the National Trust and are free, consequently, to all comers, the ground-level approach to some of the climbs is through private property. The 'crag-baggers' did not let this deter them. One day, Downer was halfway up the crag, prospecting a route, and Tony Watts, an old friend on a flying visit from Canada, was at the foot of the cliff, managing the rope. Suddenly, Watts became aware of a figure at his shoulder. 'Do you realise', the stranger said, 'that you are trespassing?' 'I think', Watts replied, 'that you are confusing me with someone who would give a damn about a thing like that.'

Early in 1984 a number of short but demanding new routes were made. Among them were Driving Ambition E1, Desmond Decker E2 and Fender Bender E3, all led by Downer; and McHaffie's Mercedes V.S. and Traffic Warden E1.

When the climbs had been done and the big secret was out at last, the facts were recorded in the Climbers' Book at the Packhorse, Keswick. The entry included the words: 'Anyone repeating these routes on Nagg's Buttress may be challenged for trespassing. However, the owner lives in Leeds!!! And is a banker!!' Beneath that, in another hand, comes the comment: 'The above entry is unethical as is climbing here.' For a short while there were solicitors' letters and threats of legal action. Then the dispute subsided. By this time Downer and company had moved further up the valley to open up Bleak How in Langstrath.

Many new climbing grounds have been brought into service in the last two decades. Their height was not the important thing. H. M. Kelly would have dismissed some of them as mere boulders, unworthy of attention. But what the modern climbers wanted was that they should be previously untouched and very steep.

Top-quality limestone climbing was made possible in the Lake District – though not during the nesting season – when Chapel Head Scar near Newby Bridge was discovered in the early 1970s. It enjoys a sheltered position and soaks up most of the available sunshine, and the rock is good. Al Phizacklea, a draughtsman at Vickers and an expert climbing photographer, is a great fan: 'It's a beautiful place,' he says. 'It's closer to the heart of the Lakes than Tremadoc is to Snowdonia, yet climbers don't see it as a wet weather retreat. The fact is Chapel Head has the greatest concentration of hard routes of any crag in the District.' Among them is his own Wargames E5 6b.

In 1976 Bill Birkett launched the development of Raven Crag, Threshthwaite, on the eastern slopes of Hartsop Dodd. Within ten years there were sixteen routes there, all 'Extremes' and all, for some reason, with names related to the motor car. Internal Combustion, climbed in 1986 by R. Smith and J. W. Earl, is E6 6c.

In 1978 Jeff Lamb made a major contribution when he climbed three 'Extremes' on Reecastle in the Watendlath valley. Reecastle, averaging 100 feet in height, supplies a high proportion of the hardest climbs in the 1986 Borrowdale guide. There has been much work, too, on the smaller crags of Caffell Side, across the valley.

Not to be outdone, Pete Whillance presided over the re-opening of Iron Crag in the Shoulthwaite valley, just south of Keswick. Virtually nothing had been done there since the New Year of 1899 when O. G. Jones and the Abraham brothers and their father made an epic ascent of the loose and slimy Chimney in atrocious weather. More than eighty years later, on 12 June 1981, Whillance and Jim Loxham, the National Park Warden in Ennerdale, went to the Left-hand Buttress and made two routes, both E1. A month later Whillance returned with Dave Armstrong and, in the course of one week, they put up four more climbs, two of them – Marble Staircase and Black Gold – in the E4 grade.

And there were finds further east a few years later – Iving Crag, Kentmere; Black Crag at the head of the Rydal valley; and Erne Crag, a mile to the south. Many climbers were involved – Bill Birkett, Tony Greenbank and Colin Downer among them – but the fiercest route was the work of Tom Wallington and A. Mitchell. It is on Iving Crag and little more than fifty feet in length but it is graded E6 6b and it was not done until after careful preparation. They inspected it thoroughly, put in pitons for protection, and fixed slings for aid and practised the moves. They called it Shaken not Stirred.

Pete Whillance went to live in Carlisle in 1974. He worked, on and off, as a scaffolder which helped to keep him fit and mentally attuned to heights. He smoked too much, twenty cigarettes a day, but otherwise did everything he could to maintain maximum climbing fitness:

The best training for climbing is climbing. I was out all day every Saturday and Sunday and often a couple of days during the week as well. Today's top-level climbers train as an athlete does – they climb a lot and when they can't do that they're on the climbing walls, or weight-lifting or circuit training or jogging. In any sport, you're striving towards perfection, trying to perform to the very best of your ability. With climbing, though, there's an extra ingredient, the danger. That enhances it that much more for me. I've had one or two big falls, screamers. I've fallen 120 feet. But it's not too serious so long as the rope catches you before you hit the deck and you don't bump into anything on the way down. Luckily, most of today's climbing is on very steep rock. and the gear's so good now that you usually don't fall far. One way or another, in nearly 20 years climbing, I never had a serious injury. Maybe I've just been lucky.

It was not just luck. Whillance is a careful, thoughtful climber. He will spend a long time and take a lot of trouble to make sure the running belays are secure. He uses the best possible equipment. And when he tackles steep or overhanging rock his movements are sure and smooth and graceful, cat-like almost, with an elegance that conceals the necessary strength.

He was another natural. As a boy he was a keen collector of birds' eggs and this made him an expert tree climber. On his first day's climbing, in Derbyshire, when he was seventeen, he soloed two Very Severes and did not find them difficult.

Soon after he arrived in Carlisle he teamed up with Dave Armstrong, a local lad who worked as an architectural technician and who had been encouraged to take up climbing by Dennis English. They made a good partnership, usually alternating the lead, both of them calm, thorough and skilful. In the evenings they would go to Armathwaite on the River Eden and traverse across the crag to improve their strength and stamina, then try out boulder moves to increase their suppleness and determine the limits of their abilities. Soon they were making new routes.

They took a strong ethical line. Planning a new route, they would abseil down to clean it up and look at the problems. Occasionally, they might try a move, just to make sure they could reach the hold. But they never top-roped a climb before attempting it free. They did not pre-place pitons or other kinds of protection. Once embarked on the climb they used every possible device to protect their progress but would only use the rock to climb on. They discussed very seriously before deciding that 'yo-yoing' – falling off and immediately trying again and going on until you succeed – was fair. Whillance says: 'Today's top climbers in the Lake District will not do a climb if it requires any form of assistance, any point of aid. It's frowned upon. Artificial climbing is rarely done nowadays. There was a period in the 1960s when it was done, but now it's all about free climbing.'

Between 1976 when they joined forces and 1984 when Whillance left to do a four-year course in outdoor education at Liverpool Polytechnic, he and Dave Armstrong made scores of routes in the Lake District, most of them of the highest quality. The list includes two E5 routes on Eagle Crag, Borrowdale – Coroner's Crack and Dead on Arrival; another E5, Stagefright, on Hodge Close Quarry; and two climbs on Deer Bield Buttress, Desperado E4 in 1977 and Take it to the Limit E5 the year after.

Whillance is a quiet-spoken man, thoughtful and articulate. He dresses as immaculately as he climbs. His manner is controlled and affable. 'Captain Cool' was the nickname some used. But beneath the calm façade there is a sense of tension, which finds some outlet in the names he chooses: Edge of Extinction, Malice in Wonderland, Risk Business are examples, and there are many more. 'A lot of the climbs I put up', he says, 'are very, very serious. Serious to the extent that you may kill yourself if you fall off.'

When he was planning his *Lakeland Rock* series for Channel Four television in 1984, Chris Bonington chose Whillance and Armstrong to be the double-act stars of his final film. And they chose to try, with the cameras on them, to climb a new route on Tophet Wall of Great Gable which they had been considering for more than a year and which had twice repulsed them. On two occasions in 1983 they had failed to do it because the weather was too cold and their fingers would not get working properly.

One summer evening in 1984 they abseiled down the wall, cleaned up the route with wire brushes, and decided it could be made to go – on one condition. The crux was more than 200 feet up, a thin crack line up a sixty-foot slab which overhung severely. A fall from there would be very dangerous indeed. It would be possible to get nut runners in during the climb but it did not look as if any of them would be really secure, 'stoppers'. The solution was obvious enough – to hammer a piton in place beforehand and make the protection rock solid. This had been widely done in the Lake District for years but it had never been done by this partnership. They had doubts about its morality. They discussed the matter and finally decided that, in this instance, the end justified the means. A piton was pre-placed.

The most exciting moments of the resulting film showed Armstrong's struggles to reach the piton, clip a karabiner to it, and get the climbing rope through the karabiner. He is the taller of the two and has a long reach but it took him several trips before he managed to lean far enough across to do it. When he descended to their belay ledge, Whillance said, 'What took you so long?' Then he roped up and floated up the wall, deriving confidence from his piton protection but not using it for aid. He climbed fluently, making it look – as the masters do – quite straightforward. They called the climb Incantations. It is graded E6 6b.

More than anything else in these years, it was the example set by Whillance and Armstrong that helped to keep intact the Lake District tradition of free climbing.

— 11 —

CONCLUSIONS

ON THE last weekend of June 1986 the Fell and Rock Climbing Club celebrated the centenary of the first ascent of Napes Needle. They staged an exhibition in the barn of the hotel at Wasdale Head, telling the story of Lake District climbing. Scores of climbers went to see the show and many of them took the chance to climb the Needle in honour of the man who started it all, Walter Parry Haskett Smith. Later, a special historical edition of the club *Journal* was published.

Many climbers take an interest in the history of their sport. They know that in climbing, perhaps more than in other sports, each generation stands on the shoulders of its immediate predecessors; the leading figures of each new generation start from the point reached by the top climbers of the previous generation.

The often-used statement – 'It's all in the mind' – is an exageration, but it is a meaningful one. The psychological factor is all-important. Physical balance, suppleness and strength are needed but, without confidence, their combined efforts will get one nowhere. Better clothing and equipment and protection techniques have all helped to raise standards of performance, but in the last resort, in each succeeding generation, the progress has been made by the men who dared to push back the limits of what was thought humanly possible: Haskett Smith and O. G. Jones in the last century; Fred Botterill and Siegfried Herford at the beginning of this; H. M. Kelly and Maurice Linnell after the First World War; then the working-class locals, Jim Birkett and Bill Peascod; then, from the end of the Second World War to the present time, Arthur Dolphin and Allan Austin, Don Whillans and Peter Livesey.

The sport has seen great changes, particularly in the last forty years. The most obvious one is the way in which its popularity has increased. Until the 1950s a couple of climbers, going out for the day, might confidently expect to have the crag to themselves and, if they found other

209

parties there, they would almost certainly know them and be friends. Today, if the weather is fine, you will probably have to queue up to get on to the popular routes on the crags of Borrowdale and Langdale. Ropes get crossed and tangled, the ledges get overcrowded; the hills are alive with the sounds of climbers trying to sort out the confusion. Those who seek solitude, communion with nature, have to do an hour or two's fell walking first to find some secluded and unfashionable cliff.

The actual climbing is slower than it used to be and more methodical, with frequent pauses for the placement of running belays. As a result, it is much safer too. In an article in the Fell and Rock *Journal* of 1981, John Wilkinson reported that between 1906 and 1944, when the club membership averaged about 500, twelve members were killed climbing; from 1945 to 1980, when the membership averaged 900 and a great deal more climbing was being done at a higher general standard, only three members were killed. 'I can only attribute this', he wrote, 'to the vastly improved protection available during this later period.' Between them, karabiners, metal nuts, slings, 'friends', pitons, specialised climbing boots, nylon ropes and all the other items of gear which climbers now carry as a matter of routine, have saved countless lives. So have the mountain rescue teams.

There are some who believe that the improvement in protection, especially of the leader, has transformed the character of the sport. Allan Austin says:

> The giants of the past were genuinely very hard men, mentally very tough, who seldom if ever flapped and had this terrific drive. What made them great was that unflappability, and it's not needed to anything like the same extent today. The demands are quite different now – patience, strength, gymnastic ability, stamina, efficiency with the equipment, they're all needed, but not the ability to stay cool and to push on regardless of the dangers and difficulties. If Joe Brown or Don Whillans were lads today and just starting, they probably wouldn't take up climbing. They'd choose something else, cave diving perhaps.

The pioneer climbers were explorers in the geographical sense, moving on to unknown ground in a way that is no longer possible in the Lake District. The big rock faces have all been thoroughly investigated. They are drawn and described in detail in the guide books. And if, as will surely happen, more little crags are discovered and developed in the years to come, they will inevitably be inspected with the safety of a top rope and cleaned and studied and prepared before they are climbed. They are not explorers now and many of the leading climbers today are not, strictly speaking, mountaineers either – they take no pleasure in fell walking: they do not visit the summits; they would not dream of going out in foul weather; they have no interest in the changing landscape, the history of the region, its natural history, or even in the nature and origins of the rock they are climbing; they do not climb down their routes. Geoff

Oliver puts it this way: 'For many of them today the crag is just a gymnasium. They learn on a climbing wall and the crag's an extension of that. They miss a lot of pleasure.'

As the sport has expanded quickly in terms of the numbers of practitioners and standards of achievement, it has also narrowed and become more specialised. And it has become more intensely competitive.

One of the leading partnerships of the mid-1980s has been that of Paul Cornforth of Ambleside and Paul Ingham of Penrith. They only bother with very hard routes on rock, E5 or E6. In the Lake District they climb on Reecastle in the Watendlath valley or on some of the steeper crags of Borrowdale or on the limestone at Chapel Head Scar. They go to Yorkshire a lot, usually to Malham. They spend as much time climbing as the weather allows. Ingham says:

> The new routes nowadays are all short, just one pitch, but very steep. We always inspect them closely first, abseil down with a wire brush and clean the lichen off. When necessary, we rehearse moves, making sure we can reach the next holds – otherwise, you're wasting your time. And we pre-place pitons. The modern routes are so hard that you have to abseil down and bang the pitons in – it wouldn't be possible to hang on and put them in from below. But we don't use bolts in the Lake District, only on limestone. And when we come to do the climb, we don't use the pitons for aid, only for protection. If I needed a point of aid, I wouldn't do the climb, I'd come down and train harder until I could do it.

They take their training very seriously. Ingham is a vegetarian. He does not smoke and hardly drinks. He is of medium height and lightly built and never puts on weight:

> During the winter we climb on the Ambleside wall four times a week, two nights and on Saturdays and Sundays. There's a circuit round the overhanging wall and you go round and round, stamina training, until you fall off from exhaustion. We do problems too, finding the hardest moves we can make. We do weight training to strengthen the upper body and the arms and fingers. I do pull-ups on to the bar with up to 30 kilograms tied to my harness.

Ingham is not attracted by any other sports. He does not ski and he dislikes ice climbing – 'It's too cold', he says. His only interest is in the conquest of extremely severe sections of dry rock, but it is a possessing interest, virtually an obsession. Asked what his motives are, he replies:

> It's got to be the challenge – it sounds corny but that's what it is. With new routes, you have to think of ways of doing them. Sometimes it's very complicated. There was a route two years ago and it took two days just looking at it to figure out how it could be done. Then it took another couple of days to do it. I can spend 24 hours working on one move.
>
> When we've got a new route all ready, one of us does it while the other protects him. Then the leader abseils down, taking all the gear out. Then the other one does it.
>
> We don't allow any resting on pre-placed pitons – that's aid. We don't rest on nut runners either. It's cheating. You can rest on them when you're practising but when you come to do the climb, you've to do it all in one go, without resting.

That is the sport, at its outer limits, in the late 1980s – a world away from the occasional, convivial holiday pastime that it was a century ago. Some older climbers, who remember what it was like in the Lake District in the 1930s and 1940s – the danger, the exploration, the *camaraderie* – believe the sport has been changed irrevocably and very much for the worse. Don Whillans spoke for them when he said:

> These fanatical competitive nutters aren't mountaineers – they don't love the mountains. They're competitive people who drift into climbing and for a while they're at the top of the tree, writing articles and all that – then they're gone! They wouldn't dream of climbing remote mountains in the Himalayas or China. They want their climbs to be in the magazines in a month's time – some little bit of rock they've climbed. They've never bivouacked in a storm, or climbed a rock that's covered in ice!

The remark is strangely reminiscent of the sort of things the Victorian Alpine mountaineers said about the Wasdale Head pioneers, a century ago. 'Rock gymnasts' and 'chimney sweeps' were the terms of abuse then. Walter Larden wrote in his *Recollections of an Old Mountaineer* (1910):

> Taking the Lake mountains as an example one may state broadly that the British climber could not have learned how to climb, nor trained his judgement and nerve at all, unless he had intentionally attacked every mountain on the 'wrong side'. Thus, from the first, he had to *invent* difficulties ... It is the more reckless crag-climbers who are responsible for the accusations of levity and foolhardiness so often brought against climbers ... There are those among them who climb for the excitement only; who would far sooner spend their day climbing in a gully that affords exciting 'pitches', but makes no demand on endurance or mountaineering knowledge, than in gaining the sublime heights of Monte Rosa or in traversing the magnificent Col d'Argentière. Let such recognise frankly that they don't care for the mountains, and that they are incapable of understanding that which has been the lifelong passion of men who stood head and shoulders above most of us.

There is a natural tendency among older men to believe that the only proper way to do things is the way they did them when they were in their prime. But most Lakeland climbers, certainly most of those I have talked to, take the tolerant view. If the sport were not developing, they say, it would be dying. It is right for young men to want to break new ground. There have always been pushy and ambitious newcomers and they have invariably upset some of the veterans. 'Climbing is a continuously changing sport', Chris Bonington says, 'but I can go on pursuing the sport in the way I enjoy so much and I think I can be tolerant of what the new generation is doing.'

For anyone, however, who cares about climbing and about the Lake District, there must be limits to *laissez-faire*. In two important respects, there is some cause for apprehension.

The first of these is environmental. This is an issue that relates not just to climbers but to all who use the Lake District. It is a small area, dangerously vulnerable, and the pressures on it continue to mount. Many campaigns have been waged over the past hundred years. At first, it was the developers and exploiters who won the big battles – the valleys of Thirlmere and Mardale were transformed to supply Manchester with water; in Ennerdale and on Whinlatter Pass vast tracts of fell side were planted with symmetrical lines of drab, life-denying conifers. More recently, the environmentalists have won most of the battles, though not all of them – in the 1970s the fast and obtrusive A66 road was forced through, across the northern part of the National Park, despite all opposition.

But the most serious environmental threat by far is that of 'people pollution' – the sheer weight of numbers of those who want, for assorted reasons, to holiday in the Lake District. At present, more than 11,000,000 people visit the District each year and the numbers are growing. Their cars and caravans and tents fill the valleys. The passage of their boots erodes the slopes, disturbs the wildlife and destroys rare plants. Their motorbikes and power-boats shatter the silences. They leave tons of litter in their wake. Climbers form a very small percentage of this invasion and the great majority of them respect the character of the region and behave accordingly. As always, though, there is an active minority who do not – who leave tin cans and plastic containers at the foot of the cliffs, who 'garden' too ruthlessly and climb too close to nesting birds.

A conference was held at the National Park Centre at Brockhole in 1984 called 'Adventure and Environmental Awareness'. It concluded by recommending, among other things, that outdoor education centres should be encouraged to adopt nearby crags and look after them; that a code of practice be drawn up for climbers and scramblers; and that a booking system be instituted for regular users of the more popular training crags to present overcrowding. Such a system is already operated at Lindale Crag near Grange-over-Sands.

The danger is this: if numbers continue to increase at the present rate and if a sufficiently large minority of climbers continues to flout the generally accepted rules of conduct, then the time may come when the National Park authorities feel they have to apply controls. It could mean a permit system, allowing access to certain areas or crags at certain times, possibly for a fee. Climbers might be required to show certificates of competence or 'good character' before they could get a permit. The friendly National Park warden would become more like a warder or policeman. It would be the end of the freedom of the fells; the end, too, of the open, free-and-easy, unregulated tradition of Lakeland climbing.

The other, and probably more immediate, threat springs from within the sport – from the intensified competitiveness which is being created partly by the pressures of publicity, partly by what they call 'the professional approach', but chiefly by money.

Many of today's top climbers are 'professionals' in the sense that they earn their livings through climbing. They act as guides. They work as instructors at outdoor pursuits centres. They publish magazines, write books and articles, take photographs, make films and give lectures. They design or manufacture or sell equipment. There is nothing reprehensible in this. The danger comes when money-making takes over as the prime motive. As recent history shows, the sporting world is particularly prone to mercenary corruption. The 'professional foul' became common practice in soccer when salaries and transfer fees began to soar; big-value prizes have driven athletes and others to take drugs to improve their performances; team captains and umpires shout angrily at each other on the cricket field; on the once decorous and cheerful courts of Wimbledon there is now hardly a smile to be seen.

Climbing has been happily free of such excesses but it may not be so for much longer. Competition has increased in the recent past, is increasing, and seems certain to increase even faster in the near future. The European countries are showing the way. On the continental mainland, on both sides of the 'Iron Curtain', competition climbing has established itself as a popular spectator sport and a career opportunity for good climbers. A few of Britain's best young rock athletes cross the Channel to take part.

Competition climbing is totally safe. The contestants are protected by a top rope throughout. Sometimes it is conducted out-of-doors, on real rock; sometimes indoors on a climbing wall. Initially, a few years ago, it took the form of a race, speed climbing. The contestants were taken, one by one, to the foot of a difficult climb that was unknown to them, then timed as they climbed it. If they fell off, they were disqualifed. The one who did it fastest won first prize. More recently a new form has been favoured. A route is created which gets progressively harder and finally approaches the impossible. On climbing walls this can easily be arranged; on outdoor crags it may mean some doctoring of the rock to create or eliminate holds. The winner is the one who gets highest before he falls off.

The great majority of Lake District climbers say they will play no part in this kind of contest. It calls for neither courage nor route-finding skill. There are no points for style. The only quality that is being tested is the ability to make very awkward and difficult movements of the body in the vertical plane. They have no desire to display their expertise, or otherwise, in front of a large audience.

But there are some, among the young, who are very interested and the question is whether they should be able to play at competition climbing in Britain as well as in Europe? It is the most widely and fiercely disputed issue at present. In a way, the discussion is pointless because it is inevitable that it will spread to these shores. It is most unlikely that it will ever be seen on the crags of Lakeland, partly because of the storm of protest that would be raised and – more pertinently – because of the notorious unpredictability of the weather. A competition would be rendered hopelessly unfair by a downpour, or even a shower, halfway through. But before very much longer someone will stage competition climbing in some auditorium somewhere in England and British climbers will compete and many people, perhaps the television cameras as well, will go to watch. And it is hard to see any good and sufficient reason why it should not be allowed. It may be a bizarre mutation and far removed from the original springs of the sport but it is still recognisably related to climbing. Disapproval should not lead to prohibition.

More directly relevant to the Lake District is the question of 'bolting', the pre-placing of metal bolts to make very difficult routes possible. The practice is widespread on Yorkshire limestone and has become common at Chapel Head Scar and Hodge Close Quarry. There is an almost unanimous consensus among Lakeland climbers that it should not be allowed to go on to colonise the traditional crags.

Rock climbing has come a very long way in just over one hundred years. When Haskett Smith began, he thought the 'Alpine rope' was 'illegitimate'. Sir Jack Longland recalls a day in 1936, when the sport was roughly half its present age, when he was walking in the Dungeon Ghyll area and carrying a sling with a karabiner attached. He had just started to use them. A stern-looking man of military bearing approached, saw the offending objects, stopped, glared at him and said: 'It's people like you who commit vandalism in the mountains.'

Today, no climber – unless he is planning to solo something well within his ability – goes out without a rope and several nut runners and slings, each with its karabiner. The great majority of today's climbers, in the Lake District at any rate, respect the basic rules of free climbing and use their equipment only to protect themselves. And they climb, for the most part, for the original motives – for adventure and exercise, the company and the comradeship, for 'fresh air and fun': As Bobby Files wrote to me recently, 'I think that I am probably representative of many climbers of my antiquity – my sole reason for climbing was pure enjoyment, enjoyment of the climbing itself and also of the environment.' Above all, they retain the vital element of uncertainty as to the outcome. They give the rock a chance and like to climb near the limits of their ability. It is this that makes it exciting. If they fail, there is always another day. If they succeed, the euphoria will last well beyond the first long pint of the evening.

As to the future, only two things can be predicted with absolute confidence. The first is that rock climbing in the Lake District will continue – and continue to give delight. The other is that standards will go on rising.

For all their talk of the 'professional approach', rock climbers still do not train as single-mindedly as Olympic athletes. When they do, new grades will be created. Already, on Clogwyn du'r Arddu in Snowdonia, a young, full-time rock athlete called Johnny Dawes has climbed a 150-foot route which he called Indian Face and which has been reckoned so serious as to require a new grade, Extremely Severe 9. There is nothing of that grade in the Lake District at the moment. But there are many who are assiduously working on the problem.

Where will it all end? Bill Peascod used to say that the ultimate would be reached when a climber could move, like a fly or spider, across a completely smooth and holdless ceiling. So there is still some progress to be made . . .

→ SOURCES AND BIBLIOGRAPHY ←

This book is the result of information gathered from a variety of sources:
1) Recent interviews with climbers, whose names are listed in the Acknowledgements.
2) Past interviews with climbers now dead: Lord Chorley; Sir Claude Elliott; Dr Raymond Greene; Colonel 'Rusty' Westmorland; Bill Peascod; Dave Macdonald; and Don Whillans.
3) The journals of many British climbing clubs but particularly those of the Fell and Rock Climbing Club of the English Lake District, especially its 'historical' editions of 1936 and 1986.
4) The various editions of the Fell and Rock Club's guide books for climbers.
5) Climbers' books from pubs and huts, most particularly the Climbers' Book that was kept at the Wastwater Hotel from 1890 to 1919, now in the Archives of the Fell and Rock.
6) Several climbing diaries including those of J. W. Robinson, H. V. Reade and H. M. Kelly.
7) The climbing magazines, especially Ken Smith's articles about Lakeland climbers of the 1920s and 1930s which appeared in *The Climber and Rambler*.
8) Many printed books, foremost among them:

Abraham, George *The Complete Mountaineer* (Methuen, 1907)
  Mountain Adventures at Home and Abroad (Methuen, 1910)
  On Alpine Heights and British Crags (Methuen, 1919)
  Modern Mountaineering (Methuen, 1933)
Bailey, Adrian *Lakeland Rock* (Weidenfeld and Nicolson, 1985)
Barford, J. E. Q. *Climbing in Britain* (Penguin, 1946)

Benson, Claude E.   *British Mountaineering* (Routledge, 1909)
Birkett, Bill   *Lakeland's Greatest Pioneers* (Robert Hale, 1983)
           Classic Rock Climbs in Gt. Britain (Oxford Illustrated Press,
           1986)
Birkett, Bill with Geoff Cram, Chris Eilbeck and Ian Roper   *Rock
   Climbing in the Lake District (Constable, 1987 edition)
Blackshaw, Alan   *Mountaineering* (Penguin, 1965)
Bonington, Chris   *I Chose to Climb* (Gollancz, 1966)
              The Everest Years (Hodder and Stoughton, 1986)
Brown, Joe   *The Hard Years* (Gollancz, 1972)
Chorley, Katharine   *Manchester Made Them* (Faber and Faber, 1950)
Clark, Ronald   *The Victorian Mountaineers* (Batsford, 1953)
Clark, Ronald and Pyatt, E. C.   *Mountaineering in Britain* (Phoenix
   House, 1957)
Cooper, W. Heaton   *Mountain Painter* (Frank Peter, Kendal, 1894)
Craig, David   *Native Stones* (Secker and Warburg, 1987)
Crowley, Aleister   *Confessions* (Jonathan Cape edition, 1970)
Gray, Dennis   *Rope Boy* (Gollancz, 1979)
Greene, Raymond   *Moments of Being* (Heinemann, 1974)
Griffin, A. H.   *In Mountain Lakeland* (Guardian Press, Preston, 1963)
Jackson, Herbert and Mary   *Lakeland Pioneer Climbers* (Dalesman,
   1980)
Jones, O. G.   *Rock Climbing in the English Lake District* (Longmans, 1987)
Kirkus, Colin   *Let's Go Climbing* (Thomas Nelson paperback edition,
   1960)
Moffat, Gwen   *Space below my Feet* (Hodder and Stoughton, 1961)
Oppenheimer, L. J.   *The Heart of Lakeland* (Sherratt and Hughes, 1908)
Peascod, Bill   *Journey after Dawn* (Cicerone Press, 1985)
Perrin, Jim   *Menlove: the Life of J. M. Edwards* (Gollancz, 1985)
Pyatt, E. C. and Noyce, W.   *British Crags and Climbers* (Dennis Dobson,
   1952)
Robertson, D. G.   *Mallory* (Faber and Faber, 1969)
Ross, Paul and Thompson, Michael   *Borrowdale: A Climber's Guide* (Ross/
   Thompson, 1966)
Sansom, George S.   *Climbing at Wasdale before the First World War* (Castle
   Cary Press, 1982)
Scott, Doug   *Big Wall Climbing* (Kaye and Ward, 1974)
Seatree, George   *Lakeland Memories* (Observer Office, Penrith, 1923)
Smith, Haskett, W. P.   *Climbing in the British Isles* (Longmans, 1894)
Sutton, G. and Noyce, W.   *Sansom: the Life and Writing, of Menlove
   Edwards* (privately printed, 1960)
Unsworth, Walt   *Because it is There* (Gollancz, 1968)
            Encyclopaedia of Mountaineering (Robert Hale, 1975)
Whillans, Don and Ormerod, A.   *Don Whillans* (Heinemann, 1971)

Wilson, Ken   *Hard Rock* (Hart-Davis, 1975)
                     Classic Rock (Granada, 1978)
Wilson, Ken and Newman, Bernard   *Extreme Rock* (Diadem Books, 1987)
Wright, J. E. B.   *The Technique of Mountaineering* (Nicholas Kaye, 1955)
Young, Geoffrey Winthrop   *Mountain Craft* (Methuen, 1920)
                     Mountains with a Difference (Eyre and Spottiswoode, 1951)
Young, Geoffrey Winthrop and Sutton, G. and Noyce, W.   *Snowdon Biography* (J. M. Dent, 1957)

·INDEX·